falling
INTO
LANGUAGE

chris
WALLACE-CRABBE

falling
INTO
LANGUAGE

OXFORD
UNIVERSITY PRESS

Melbourne
Oxford   Auckland   New York

OXFORD UNIVERSITY PRESS AUSTRALIA
Oxford   New York   Toronto
Delhi   Bombay   Calcutta   Madras   Karachi
Petaling Jaya   Singapore   Hong Kong   Tokyo
Nairobi   Dar es Salaam   Cape Town
Melbourne   Auckland
and associated companies in
Berlin   Ibadan

OXFORD is a trade mark of Oxford University Press

National Library of Australia
Cataloguing-in-Publication data:

Wallace-Crabbe, Chris, 1934–
   Falling into language.

   ISBN 0 19 553140 X.

   1. English literature — History and criticism. I. Title.

820.9

Edited by Mary Sharp
Cover design by David Rosemeyer
Cover photograph by Diana Petruccelli
Typeset by Best-Set Typesetters Ltd, Hong Kong
Printed by Impact Printing, Melbourne
Published by Oxford University Press,
253 Normanby Road, South Melbourne, Australia

Contents

Acknowledgements

A number of the chapters here had their origin in the form of articles published in the following journals: *The Age Monthly Review*, *Meanjin*, *Overland*, *The Journal of Popular Culture*, *Southerly* and *Scripsi*. 'Beginning' was published in *Autobiographical and Biographical Writing in the Commonwealth*, Universidad de Barcelona, edited by Doireann MacDermott; 'The Loud Posters of Kamala Das' in *Kamala Das*, C.R.N.L.E., Adelaide, edited by S.C. Harrex and Vincent O'Sullivan; 'The Quaker Graveyard in Carlton' in *The American Experience*, Hale and Iremonger, edited by Joan Kirkby; and 'Squatter Pastoral' in *A Tribute to David Campbell*, edited by Harry Heseltine, University of New South Wales Press. 'Struggling with an Imperial Language' was first offered as my public lecture from the Chair of Visiting Professor of Australian Studies at Harvard University, in December, 1987.

I owe a considerable debt of gratitude to Harvard, to Mather House, to Linacre College, Oxford, and to the Department of Foreign Affairs in Canberra. A grant from the Arts Faculty at the University of Melbourne helped with the final preparation of the manuscript.

Many of the ideas which have been developed in this book arose in the first instance from discussions with colleagues and students. A particularly fertile forcing ground has been the Honours seminar, Studies in Autobiography, which I have conducted for a number of years with my eloquent friend, Peter Steele. Unhappily, two people who have played significant roles in the development of my critical map, Vincent Buckley and Alan Davies, have both died recently; and far too early. Other critics and poets whose conversation has meant a lot to me include Graham Burns, Marion Campbell, Kerryn Goldsworthy, Kevin Hart, Seamus Heaney, Alec Hope, Evan Jones, Graham Little, Peter Pierce, Ian Reid, Ron Simpson and Mike Weaver. In the preparation of this manuscript for publication, Lisa Jacobson did a sterling job. Tanya Robinson, Eileen Whittaker and Nancy Williston all played their part. Above all, I should like to thank my wife, Marianne, for the patience and vigorous good humour with which she has put up with it all. Not for nothing does her middle name stand for wisdom.

Introduction

Writing a Self

What can be more compelling than the temptation to catch the author, right there, in or behind the lines of the text? At a time when much highbrow fiction tends to be lacking in narrative thrust, readers may well feel inclined to withdraw, either into these fat supermarket tit-and-gun novels or into the kind of writing which 'really' tells us all about the author. Autobiography turns out to be especially fascinating these days, not least because its territories fan out into the mixed-farming areas of memoir, journal, diary, letters and Mailerian 'faction'.

At the popular end of the market, memoirs and autobiographies encroach on the general fiction paddock. In the arty-modernist upper middle ground, writers find new ways to smudge the borderline between memoir and fiction, or even to deny its existence. And on the high-falutin' slopes of academic research or critical theory autobiography has exerted an increasingly magnetic attraction for the past ten years or so: nothing could be more serious fun than systematically dismantling real lives or anatomizing confessions.

As the critic Michael Tobias has observed: 'The individual is our hitching post, our most interesting subject matter. He instills in us the titillation which is vicarious thrill'. Where do we want to locate authors and what do we want to make of them? Surely we want to perve on their exposed flanks by way of the eloquence of their writings. In the present theoretical climate there is a complicating one–two about this. As soon as an author has been flushed out the front door by a confluence of impersonal discourses, he/she is smuggled in the back door with the groceries. Indeed, I would be inclined to say that the authority of the author has hardly been impaired at all; it may have been quaintly redistributed but it probably stands higher than it did in the heyday of Cambridge-style practical criticism.

A great deal of modern life has moved over into the autobiographical mode. In a way that I particularly welcome, literary
criticism keeps laying claim to the peculiar nature of its historical
authority by incorporating chunks or capsules of autobiographical material into its serious work. Back in 1974 when I did this
myself, including an autobiographical sketch in a book of literary
essays, it was with some faint misgivings. Now I would do it
without batting an eyelid.

Another striking thing is this, that Barthes, Derrida, Lacan,
Kristeva, Spivak and Eagleton have been installed as literary
heroes like the worst sacred monsters of the old, despised,
aesthetic–humanist dispensation. Their texts demystify earlier
'literary' texts only to reassemble an aura around themselves.
Thus Lacan, hardly a critic at all in the literary sense but a sort
of magus-clinician, expands on Freud's writings by replacing
them with lurid flowers of his own rhetoric, such as:

Leads him on so far that he cannot stop until he reaches the grottoes in
which the chthonian Diana in the deep shade, which makes them
appear as the emblematic seat of truth, offers to this thirst, with the
smooth surface of death, the quasi-mystical limit of the most rational
discourse in the world, so that we might recognize the place in which
the symbol is substituted for death in order to take possession of the
first swelling of life.

(1980, 124)

This is commentary as prose poetry. But it is not my concern
here to wrestle with those dazzlingly spangled amphibians. Let
us return to the swing door which has LIFE on the one side and
TEXT on the other. Simple though its promise may seem to be,
this doorway is capable of almost endless problematization,
even for those who fall short of Lacanian pessimism about the
referential power of language. Let us not forget, after all, that
of the critical terms which were popular a generation ago the
one which has been most scornfully and completely discarded is
enactment.

So the critic wants to get rid of the passage back to real life
and to keep it open at the same time: to have her cake and eat
it, too. But to say all this is little more than to say, with a kind
of sage banality, that human nature never changes. Cheering
enough, too. No matter how rigorous the theorist may be, he/
she usually turns out to want that most deeply appealing quality

available to writing, impact. A plangent or shocking sentence sticks in the mind; a dry abstraction fades away.

Again, no matter how theoretical we may want to be with the tops of our heads—the area given to tertiary elaboration—we all know that autobiographies are of interest because they are about people's lives. It is when we try to locate those lives that the plot begins to thicken. Even more than other books, autobiographies and memoirs are layered like filo pastry. At the very least, we can discern five levels of experience being invoked. Firstly, there was an actual life, a life which the author has lived and which is quite inaccessible, although some of its documentation may be lying around. Secondly, there is the author's present memory of that gone life, which is both immeasurably less than the life and also in places more, because it involves later elaborations, screen memories, and the like (I think of Keats's pithy remark that 'the next step is to paint from the memory of gone self storms'). Then we come to the memories which the author actually wants or needs, the ones that make themselves present right now, that throng around the writer, as writer. At a fourth level, there is the autobiographical manuscript which this writing self produces. And fifth, there is the printed book, amended by editors, hedged around with disclaimers, aggrandized by puffs, set in twelve-point Garamond type, and so on. The five strata are related to one another in terms of loss, repression, selection and expansion.

The good autobiographer must persuasively negotiate these layers of self-life, must not only seem to have melded them together but have done so with plenty of narrative seduction. Then the reader comes to the party, keen to find a coherent life process in the book and even happier if it contains photographs, since they seem to inhabit a different order of reality from mere print: they show people really *at it*.

Of course, the writer, manic or cowed in front of the faithful typewriter, may negotiate these strata almost blindly. When I sit down to write a piece of reminiscent prose I simultaneously feel that I am getting down on paper what actually happened to me at some time in the past and that I am trying to make words or sentences do their eloquent tricks; I do not think about getting an array of conceivable selves into some kind of order, at least not until the time comes for looking back over what I have written. Only then can the internal censor begin unpicking the

writer. It is surely the censor who can stand back abruptly in the
course of Edwin Muir's beautiful *Autobiography* and write that:
'There are zones of childhood through which we pass, and we
live in several of them before we reach our school age, at which
a part of our childhood stops for good. I can distinguish several
different kinds of memory during my first seven years'. Certainly he seems radically unlike the Muir who has just written:
'The sun shone, the black field glittered, my father strode on,
his arms slowly swinging, the fan-shaped cast of grain gleamed
as it fell and fell again: the row of meal-colored sacks stood like
squat monuments on the field'.

As readers, it seems that while the writer's fiction holds us we
are licensed to be the fly on the wall. We are both cajoled and
baffled by the fact that this text stands in for a life; we stare
brokenly into the re-run past of Muir or de Beauvoir, Facey or
Oriel Gray. The author invents—however spontaneously—a
narrator who manipulates a character whose acting out of the
suppositious life we are permitted to see.

The narrator commonly harrumphs a good deal, insisting that
a present—and by implication impressive—performer has developed out of that bemused, colourful character, the shape of
whose life we are following through the book. It is the decollet-
age of an autobiography that seduces us into believing that we
are glimpsing slides and stages of a mortal existence: but our
narrator remains close at hand, a wardrobe mistress carefully
adjusting the degree of revelation. A colleague of mine, Peter
Steele, has observed that in this kind of writing there are always
complicated relations between the raw and the cooked: more
even than in poetry we want 'imaginary gardens with real toads
in them', but the gardens must also have verifiable historical
locations. It would be intolerable if the autobiographer allowed
'Wangaratta' to refer to Inverness or Carthage.

The several subjects of autobiographical writing sharing the
one name are related by complicated manoeuvres in time. For
the reader, the heart of the matter is this: the author is probably
dead by now (but may not be), his/her narrator is certainly alive,
and the protagonist was alive. The author has produced all this
narrative in the hope of unifying them, of selling them to us as a
package. Seldom will a writer be quite as sceptical or self-ironic
as Sartre was when he called his text *Les Mots*.

When I try, as I did in *My 1930s* (1974), to write something
about what happened in my childhood, the gestures of rhetoric

in quest of truth are extraordinarily complicated. Turning back to that essay now, the first sentence to catch my eye contains the self-same phrase, 'extraordinarily complicated':

Behind us, down at the bottom of a garden lovingly terraced on summer evenings by my father, is a great big, elaborate block of flats, extraordinarily complicated: Moorish, Californian, Jub-jub, what you will.

In writing this, I was trying to evoke, to recapture, the sheer exoticism of that block of flats in my childish eyes. A single image, the flats, has been combined with a recurrent process, my father's gardening, and with a sense of the steep terrain, 'terraced'. But what about the adjectives? I could not have recognized the appropriateness of 'Moorish' before I was eight or nine, and of 'Californian' before I was fourteen. 'Jub-jub', with its roots in Edward Lear, sounds more plausible in a small boy's awareness, but its application to architecture comes from a lecture I heard Joseph Burke give at the end of the 1950s. In trying to reproduce the powerfully simple clarity of a childhood impression, then, I have had recourse to quite disparate strata of language, quite different ages of the self. Those flats, in which I tended to locate events from fairy tales and the Arabian Nights, turn out to be a very complicated object to build out of language. The present tense which the passage employs is full of false confidence—even though those flats are still standing, in 1990.

Back to that hitching post, the depleted individual or past self. An author hands over the created protagonist as a hostage to God (as Rousseau explicitly did) or to history, certainly to readers and their desires. The story of that character is meant to be somehow illuminating. The self's uniqueness is precisely what is educative, representative about it.

Such writing is constrained by all manner of tacit conventions. Autobiographers and memoirists are quaintly unfree in that they are not allowed to kill off their central characters, having foregrounded those characters as incipiently identical with the writerly self. They might well say, with Wittgenstein, that 'Death is not an event in life. We do not live to experience death'.

Equally, writers do not know much about their birth, apart from the belief that they have been born into a world of sorrows and, perhaps, of sentimental education. But they do scan backwards hard, looking for signs and portents. The memories which appear to come from closest to the birth-gate are especially privileged: we have come to recognize them as numinous. They glow.

At the more lurid end of the scale, autobiographers write very little of interest about sex. Unlike novelists, they have a strong tendency to suppress accounts of sexual experience altogether. At the more modest end, they write hardly anything about headaches, the dentist's, bowel habits or covetousness; and surprisingly little about eating. Nothing that is daily proves amenable to autobiography. The book of the self should pass through significant stages, through epiphanies and climaxes. These stages may even have something in common with the impact of lyric poem: they image a self turning the corner, on the way to somewhere significant. Both lyric and autobiography 'make special claims to intimacy with the reader', as Fay Zwicky puts it in one of the essays from *The Lyre in the Pawnshop*; their implicit claim is that they are directly tapping the deepest strata of personal experience.

As it happens, lyrics are also always like other lyrics. The weight of history moulds the cup which receives the wine of life. In the same way, autobiographies and memoirs are developed out of other similar texts. All memoirists are conservative at heart, but try to offset this by small gestures of formal rebellion. All autobiographies make tacit allusion to a hypothetically normal model of the genre, the plain self-life-story. They are always daringly departing from a norm we shall never find—but many of whose features we can easily recognize. Wendy Capper (1988) has shown how thoroughly A. B. Facey's *A Fortunate Life* is modelled on the patterns of traditional fairy tales; and yet Facey's book seems to epitomize the dinkum or natural telling of a plain man's life story. Great heaps of other texts press down, even on the people who do not read them.

For all this, no autobiographies are quite normal. All have something wrong with them—perhaps it is life that causes the trouble. Scratch an autobiography and, quick as a flash it will turn out to be a memoir, a journal, a diary, letters, reflections, notes, a novel, confessions, or just *advertisements for myself*. But in every case the author is sending out a set of signals, insisting that 'I am the bloke (or sheila). I suffered. I was there'. Author, narrator and character must be taken together: if not as three people in one carriage, then as one person in three carriages. Such is the autobiographical trinity.

Last and dodgiest, autobiographical writing is supposed to

tell the factual truth. So is lyric poetry, but only emotional truth is required there, an expectation Stendhal registered when he wrote that 'Like Shelley, I breathed only in sighs'. The prose memorist is expected to maintain a certain factual fidelity to historical, political and, as I suggested earlier, geographical details. Some autobiographies are deeply enmeshed in this fidelity: Roger Milliss's *Serpent's Tooth*, for instance, which is very much a political history of the mid-century Australian Left, for all that it is subtitled *An Autobiographical Novel*. At the other extreme, writers like Nabokov and Virginia Woolf try to lyricize themselves out of history, locating the self in an album of epiphanies. Even their fictions of self, however, are supposed to be compatible with the facts as we have received them from avowedly objective sources. Woolf is not free to change the date of the Post-Impressionist Exhibition, yet Yeats is free to invent a bizarre clown called George Moore. The terms of the autobiographical contract contain a great deal of small print.

Two of my own poems raise questions about the relation between the poet who writes and the self whom he depicts or dramatizes. They point us quickly to a major formal difference between most poems and prose autobiographies: poems are short; and hence so much more in a poem depends on closure. Closure and omissions generate a lot of the punch in a poem; they can also leave it clouded in obscurity because too little information has been put on display. Of the two poems below, 'Scotland as Conversation' smells more like autobiography, but may at the same time be the more cryptic. Readers may well need to be told that one winter I went up to Dundee to give a reading with two Edinburgh women poets, and that afterwards we talked long into the night about growing older and *rites de passage*. How much information of that kind does the poem need?

SCOTLAND AS CONVERSATION

Trains and snow, rails and snow,
but slippery marmalade Dundee
is chiefly built of conversation,
that and a stagey lighted dinner
to plunk some mediaeval tune
out of elaborate darkness.
All the real chat came later on:
— I can't remember why I got
    married.

— What was getting engaged all
   about?
— It used to be about shower teas.
— Why did I ever change my name?
— We never actually thought about
   things then.
— All of it seems so long ago.
— How nice it is, not to be young.
— I simply reply, 'I don't knit'.

There was that, and reading verse
for almost next to nobody
in a town as crude as a country
        dunny,
but chiefly talk, natter and talk,
sole basis of reality
yet fueled by trains and snow.

You know, as one gets rather older
(not us, of course, but one)
resources get diverted into
software of conversation,
the traps, the tropes, the epigrams
replacing jute and marmalade.

And then, of course, you get snow.

The other poem is also offering my self as subject, but the self
here is dramatized as operating in psychic rather than in social
space. It also—while seeming a simple expression of my successive moods—turned out to have acquired a formal scaffolding
through the chromatically related images of lemon juice, terra
cotta, wheat, yellow light, banksia heads, cereal, butter and
new-baked bread. Not until I had almost completed the poem
did I notice that this chain of images had got up and taken over,
transforming an expression of some personal feelings into what
might be called Formal Arrangement in Golden Tones. The
history of painting as well as of poetry was leaning heavily on
my biro as I got these stanzas down on paper. And somewhere
amid all that flurry of intertexuality *Dry Goods* lays claim to
being about a bit of my life.

DRY GOODS

It is surely winter;
the sun spills like lemon juice;
I danced last night
having sung under claret the night before

but all this arvo
as a clean wind goes combing wattle blossom
I seem to be a piece
of chipped terra-cotta
that an archaeologist has found
in a tumbledown tomb.

Don't worry, serious scholar,
it may be that I contain
two dozen ears of wheat
to grow
                then ripen again
three thousand years late.

Not yellow light but some faint smell
under the north wind's fingernails
whips up
one of my oldest follies,
the firm illusion
that I will live for ever.

Having said even this much
I begin to feel triumphant,
as hairy and assertive
as big banksia heads displayed in a vase,
and could make a cardboard model of paradise
from some old cereal packet,
glowingly in possession of
the gaze, the voice, the nothing.
Don't worry,
it is surely the case
that we shall be reborn
golden as butter on a chunk of new-baked bread . . .
but where? in what form? . . .
and how can we know that we are?

But poetry goes further than this; withdraws further than this, deeper into that terse bright country without explanations which we regard as most poetic. I am talking of that mode of intense, spontaneous-seeming utterance which Stephen Dedalus defined as the lyrical mode, the pure cry of epiphanic concentration. Lyrics are, in one sense, purely autobiographical utterances, yet they are so truncated that the *bios* is given short shrift, self becoming merely that which gives voice to a hyped-up moment. The atomic question which lyrics raise is whether we are most ourselves in moments of peculiar intensity. And what they ought to do is provide the reader with enough resistance to make the moment stick or grip. 'The Fish Enchantment' springs from a remarkable sight which I glimpsed one summer afternoon while surfing. Moreover, it is the paradoxical word, 'unrepeatable', in the second-last line (what could be more repeatable than the seas?) which provides the crossing or resistance which this glassy little poem holds up to the reader, wedging itself into a niche in time.

THE FISH ENCHANTMENT

Transcendent though
this jadegreen surf can always be
I was shaken or swayed
fronting a little below one wave's high lip
chartreuse translucently
still for a moment, brimmed with sun,
and in its wall of glass
a row of little fish in profile posing
no higher than my head.
But all things pass,
visions included, and its going led
to doubt and back to rumpled miles
of unrepeatable sea
running like lace away, a long ago.

Let me just add that when I look back on this poem it seems in large measure to have been written by that high green wave and that row of tiny fish. It is as though the event literally impinged on my life and I had to do nothing but transcribe it. As in an autobiography, the text has now become the piece of life.

This book is concerned with the many ways in which self falls into language: with how the autobiographical text replaces the gone life, with the gestures which announce its claims to liveliness, with the ambiguous personality of lyric poetry and with the self, or selves, which I am bringing into my own critical acts and arguments. It is a book about the vivacious impurity of all literary works, their lingering smell of humanity. Instead of marginalizing autobiography as criticism in the past has often done, I want to present it as a normative genre, a central fiction.

1

Beginning

*Our being is a rapid sketch, an immediate gesture, a cry of aston-
ishment that mounts to our lips*

Poulet

The opening, the first phrases, gesture or movement, of a text
has a peculiar power over us. Nor are writers loath to make the
most of this peculiar force, this head start over the still bemused
reader. Title, blank endpapers, title page are behind; flap notes
and an introduction may or may not have been read; the text
proper stands revealed, and this is the eye-catching threshold.
Think of 'Call me Ishmael', or 'Unemployed at last', or '—They
order, said I, this matter better in France—', or 'In the beginning God created the heaven and the earth'. The books have
begun, the march has been stolen, the white paper is marked
with the first prints of a narrative. Dear reader, you are hooked.

But if beginnings are always arresting—or the very opposite
of arresting, that is to say chivvying on, since traction is what is
at issue here, not resistance—how much more power they can
claim when the text is not merely a novel or history but an autobiography. For, if an autobiography lays claim to a life and replaces it with language, then the beginning of the text lays claim
to generation or birth. It announces how, from these dumb endpapers and taciturn title pages, the life which the book recounts
suddenly came to be.

Ways in which this beginning of the self-tale is carried out are
remarkably various. I see them as tending to fall into three
broad types or categories but, before spreading them out, let us
look at an absolutely classic beginning, appropriately enough
the beginning to one of the earlier English memoirs, something
from well before the Age of Autobiography. *The Diary of John
Evelyn* begins like this:

I was born about 20 minutes past two in the morning (on Tuesday)
being the xxxi and last of October Anno 1620, after my Father had

been married about 7 yeares, and that my Mother had borne him 3
Children viz. Two Daughters and one Sonn, about the 33rd Yeare of
his age, and the 23rd of my Mothers.

(1983)

This is duller than Lemuel Gulliver: what an intolerably sober
Halloween is here recorded. Nevertheless, it is central enough
to what we all tend to expect of the beginning of autobiography
or memoir. The person is born; we find out to whom and
precisely when. Within five paragraphs we shall find out precisely where. The book testifies promptly to a world of facts,
facts which in turn support it.

We shall find the comic application of this kind of dinkum
factuality in the first two sentences of Clive James' *Unreliable
Memoirs*: 'I was born in 1939. The other big event of that year
was the outbreak of the Second World war, but for the moment
that did not affect me'.

We want our authors to surprise us, which is exactly what
they want to do, for the most part. Few autobiographical works
over the last couple of centuries have set out quite so bluntly
from the Meccano pieces of rude fact as did Evelyn's *Diary*. But
most autobiographers have something like this in the backs
of their minds as the bare minimum opening, upon which they
will set out to play their more persuasive, or arresting, variations. Their openings can be clustered, I suggest, under three
headings: the way of Samuel, the way of Romulus and the way
of Hercules.

Some writers are too crafty to be catalogued in this way at all.
Thus the cunningly, immensely self-conscious Roland Barthes
opens his book, *Roland Barthes*, with a fine flurry of playful
aporia:

To begin with, some images: they are the author's treat to himself, for
finishing this book. His pleasure is a matter of fascination (and therefore quite selfish). I have kept only the images which enthrall me.

But this is reflexiveness taken to an unusual extreme, even for
the autobiographical act. It is the studied gesture of a *faux-naif*
impromptu actor, designed to be set down carefully in print,
opposite a handsome photograph of an old street and steeples
in Bayonne. It is a post-modern attempt to keep familiar genres
at bay akin to Sartre calling his book *Les Mots*, or to Mailer
offering a whole series of quasi-beginnings to *Advertisements*

for Myself, to wit, A Note to the Reader; First Table of Contents; Second Table of Contents; First Advertisement for Myself; Beginnings.

In general, though, I see texts of self still commonly beginning by way of the three modes named above. Let me amplify them.

The way of Samuel approaches the existence of the personage/author/narrator by way of ancestry. Its initial ordering is like that of Auden's early lyric which begins,

Before this loved one
Was that one and that one
A family
And history
And ghost's adversity

or, more seriously, like that of the infant Samuel in the first book of that name; Samuel is introduced and hence partly determined by his genealogy.

Thus, that most timid of Australian autobiographies, W.K. Hancock's *Country and Calling*, begins with a Prologue entitled, 'My Father as a Young Man' and follows this with a first chapter which again starts with Hancock's father: in this case with an account of his one hundred per cent British lineage and long, active life among his parishioners. The sense here, very much borne out in the book's equanimity and reticence, is of an author–protagonist who is all too unwilling to project himself onto the scene—or page. This sorts well with his delicate obliqueness later when it comes to introducing his Australian fiancée into the narrative; she sidles in as *la donna mittagongesca* or, more succinctly as D.M. All this contributes to the modest personage Hancock depicts in his book, the frugal, sensible young man who made it to All Souls'. His is what Adrian Stokes once called 'an unswerving mildness'.

Such correlation of the way of Samuel with reticence in display of the autobiographical personage is also to be found in Henry Handel Richardson's *Myself When Young*, where it is introduced by a shy-seeming disclaimer in the speaking tones of one giving a talk to a small discussion group:

It has never been my way to say much about my private life. Rightly or wrongly, I believed this only concerned myself. And I trusted my husband to supply, on my death, any further information that might be asked for. Now that he is gone, however, there is no one to take his place, and so I propose to jot down a few facts about myself, and memories of my childhood, which may possibly be of interest to some who read my books.

First to touch, very briefly, on my parents. My father, Walter Lindesay Richardson, was a native of Dublin, the descendant of two Irish families, the Lindesays and the Richardsons, who had intermarried in the eighteenth century. He was the youngest child of my grand-father's second marriage . . .
(1948)

What HHR has in common with Hancock, as well as gingerly introducing herself by way of her ancestors, is a weak sense of autobiography as art; both might be said to write their lives artlessly; their main imaginative pulse is to be found elsewhere. Beginning has for them no mystery, even though HHR blandly offers us the alluring sentence on page 7, 'It is said that I was able to hum tunes before I could speak'.

Maie Casey, a more sophisticated memoirist, is alert to the dynamic possibilities to be found in dislocations of chronology, possibilities of odd juxtaposition and dissonant echo. Thus, on page 37 of *An Australian Story, 1837–1907*—note the tactical reticence of her title—she proceeds rapidly from placing her mother in the parade of ancestors through an image of their walking together in Brunswick, and one brief reflective para-graph, over a gap and change of typeface into what Bachelard has called 'the land of motionless childhood'. We may note how confidently she declares her stage-management of the past:

But, to return to the tram where my mother is seated wearing her simplest clothes for the walk from the terminus to Stony Park.

In our walks we spoke little, each thinking our own different thoughts as we passed the small weatherboard houses, trimmed with iron lace, in the treeless streets that led to the side gate of the park, in Glenlyon Road. The preoccupations of older persons seem boring and incom-prehensible to children who cannot understand them or their urgency. How should they, with all the long lush years ahead, each year full of the leisurely beauty of the months, which seem never to end! The time of growing seems so slow.

I have promised to keep myself out of this story as much as I can—and how difficult that is—but I feel that I should give you one look at me at the age of seven or eight. This is a good moment to do so, because I saw myself consciously for the first time in a little mirror set in the inside lining of a four wheeler cab that sometimes drove us from the terminus of the tram to Stony Park. I remember the occasion because it gave me a shock.

    My face looked fat and potato-like . . .

(1962, 37)

Although this is not the beginning of Casey's text, we may see her tactics as a blending of the way of Samuel with the way of Hercules, of which more later.

Freud has made the observation that there is nothing in the id that corresponds to our ideas of time, and Maie Casey certainly feels empowered to make use of the freedom this insight bestows on the maker of narratives. A dozen pages after the passage I have cited she proceeds, by way of an account of her grandmother, Sarah Sumner, to a fixed old memory, crystallized years before the mirror episode: one of those magical retrieved moments in which smell, taste and sight are free to mingle outside time. This is the held glimpse of Grannie Sumner peeling a peach for the little girl on the Orient Steamship *Cuzco*, beginning its journey to England. Like Mailer, though altogether less ironically, Casey enjoys making use of a number of possible starting points, cards that she shuffles freely in a book which refuses to allow itself to be narrowly bound by that tyrant, chronology.

The shifting chronotypes of *An Australian Story* bring to mind the question Edward Said has asked about biographical sequence:

One is the problem of biography as embodied in genealogical sequence: to what extent is this sequence adequate for reflecting the ascertainable discontinuities in a man's life? where in this sequence does one locate the beginning if, for instance, psychological knowledge is not based solely on the fact of birth, but upon transpersonal, natural and 'prehistoric' forces like the unconscious or the will?

(1975, 158)

Of the beginnings of autobiographies—books which are products of genealogy, the unconscious, the will and the genres—we may also ask where is the start located: in family time, in a nurturing location or in marvellous memories (screen memories, they may well be) fixed glowing in mental space? Patrick White, like Casey an admirer of modern painting and friend of painters, has like her chosen a modernist plurality of perspective, displacing time into small, angular *tesserae* much as the cubist painters chose to reorder space. In the first three pages of

White's *Flaws in the Glass* we find four short blocks of text separated by wide blank spaces. The first panel recalls the fourteen-year-old White in the glassy Long Room of a neo-Gothic house in Sussex; the second in a broadly concurrent evocation of the thronged streets of London; the third recalls a very little boy, tired, hot, walking with his great-aunt through the streets of Sydney; the fourth turns back to Felpham, in Sussex, and the narrative begins to flow. Restless, deracinated (if we may read back from personage to author), White combines his evocations of contrasted locations with those held moments of recall that mark the way of Hercules. Less sophisticated than Casey's memoir, White's nevertheless displays a similar generic instability.

An obviously stable, and often conventional beginning is by the way of Romulus, a beginning which defines the central character by early physical surroundings. Miles Franklin in *Childhood at Brindabella* roots her childhood from the start in the atmosphere of Bobilla homestead, asserting that 'No other place has ever replaced the hold on my affections or imagination of my birthplace'. Henry Lawson begins *A Fragment of Autobiography* with a careful description of the tent, or hut, at Pipeclay where he was born and makes a great thing of the family's move to 'a two-roomed slab and bark hut' about four years later. Donald Horne pins down *The Education of Young Donald* with an opening chapter which depicts both the manners of the Hunter Valley and feelings associated with regular train journeys into Sydney. As the identity of Romulus interacted with that of Rome, so Horne offers himself as shaped by the Hunter Valley at the same time as he creates it for us: Lawson was formed by the old Pipeclay goldfield, a desolately eloquent landscape which his writings have made over into an image of the typical Australia.

A rather more ambivalent example of the birthplace-as-shaping spirit is to be found on the first page of Martin Boyd's *Day of My Delight*. The opening paragraph is drawn from his grandmother's diary, and it records his birth in Switzerland, with the family in transit, in 1893. It is very much to the point of Boyd's autobiography—and of his fiction, if it comes to that—to see him born neither in Australia nor in Britain, but somewhere which is Continental in its culture, yet at the same time only a staging post. Although the book proceeds quickly to a largely Arcadian childhood spent living around Melbourne, any certainty or rootedness has already been gently subverted; indeed, his first memory, an apparently trivial one, is interpreted by the narrator as an instance of 'irreparable loss', for which both God and parents were held to blame.

Indeed, what we find in Boyd's tactic of beginning is writ large in his whole literary *oeuvre*. Samuel, Romulus and Hercules war in him. Whether in the personal writing of *A Single Flame* and *Day of My Delight*, in the Langton tetralogy, or in a couple of other novels, we can see his imagination having been compelled not only by the process of self-making, but also by his highly visible ancestors, and by an awareness of not quite being an Australian or an Englishman but that ambiguous thing, a European, shuffling to and fro in between.

We may add that like Maie Casey Boyd displays chronological restlessness. His narratives reveal their misgivings about progress tacitly as well as explicitly. He finds some consolation in epigrams.

What I have called the way of Hercules in precisely what we most seek, expect and love in autobiographies: not a literal strangling of serpents by a prodigious babe—although Miles Franklin has an infant encounter with a black snake at the opening of her autobiographical novel, *My Brilliant Career*— but something marvellous, a handful of marvels, rather, drawn from the jewelbox of earliest childhood memories. Rarely, very rarely, they may be events of great public impact, like the hurricane that shatters the island of Levuka on the first page of K.S. Prichard's *Child of the Hurricane* (not a memory, but concurrent with her birth and manifestly much impressed upon her); but as a rule they are intimate events, or screen-memories, which psychic time has burnished to a wonderful glowingness: Proustian or Wordsworthian moments fixed in the amber of undeliberate consciousness.

We feel, too, that they are seeds, growing points, the beginnings of processes which will go on and fill out a lifetime. As Poulet writes,

What is memory, for example, except starting from a taste, from a scent, from a clamour of bells identical to those perceived in the depths of the years, a grand movement of reminiscence, which, like a sky-rocket, opens itself up and reveals a fan of new memories.

(1977, 304)

Again and again, autobiographies are constructed so as to under-
write such a belief in a germinal process. One of the boldest and
it may be simplest cases is that on the first page of Randolph
Bedford's rambunctious *Naught to Thirty-three*, of which title
we may note in passing that thirty-three is, impudently, the
Christological year:

My first memories were of colour, and I managed somehow ever since
to get colour and surprise into my life. At the side of our garden was a
chain of pools—green—banked, sheltered from dust, and altogether
beautiful; although the lower pools were used as basins for the swimming of dogs beloved, and the very distant ones for the drowning of
dogs superfluous. Grey geese led yellow goslings across green grass to
pale blue water.
    This was my first conscious impression in colour. More than thirty
years later I recognized that early colour scheme in the work of Luca
Della Robbia, in the village church at Santa Fiora, Tuscany.

                                                                    (1976)

This is at once typical and parodic. Typical of the autobiographical seeds of memory is the aura of that colourful sentence.
'Grey geese led yellow goslings across green grass to pale blue
water'. But Bedford's sense of causation is quite brisk and external when compared with the delicate unfoldings of self which
we find in more artistic autobiographies. Will is doing some
of the work of imagination; or, to put it another way, we do
not quite believe in the probity of Bedford, the boisterous
narrator.

    Few Australian autobiographies open with a deeply stirring
crystallization of 'a taste, a scent, a clamour of bells'. Such a
beginning, at once eloquent and artful, is more common in
autobiographical novels, where art is, as it were, licensed to
strut and evoke. The first sentences of Elizabeth Riley's *All that
False Instruction* strike out at once for that freedom novel
writing can bestow:

The first thing I remember, I was running in the long summer grass
above my grandmother's house with a red dog. The red dog was much
bigger than I was; he leaped over me, rolled me, licked my face.

                                                                    (1975)

And from these established motifs, the kiss and the facial surface, the narrator can cut at once to her father, his face, his
freckled skin, his custard-making. Similar eloquence, in straight

autobiography however, attends the narrator's first memory of her father in *Childhood at Brindabella*, although in that case it is the memory of a remembering that is recorded.

Perhaps we may correlate the general lack of aura, the general lack of Herculean openings, with the fact that a large majority of Australian autobiographies are workaday affairs, a little benumbed by facts, unwilling to dare greatly in artistic shaping. It may be, as Richard Coe has argued, that most of them have also been benumbed by the authors' doubts as to whether they can feel any sustaining culture around them. Whatever the truth of the matter, it is certainly the case that one of the finest and subtlest of our autobiographies can also boast one of the most challenging and subtle beginnings.

I refer to Hal Porter's *The Watcher on the Cast-iron Balcony* which begins with a traumatic memory that is not, oddly, from early in the narrator's life, then cutting back on the next page to stages from beyond the memory threshold, only to slide rapidly into the age of six and that Bellair Street, Kensington, house, the reconstruction of which is one of the greatest achievements of the book, bearing witness not only to knowledge of culture, furniture, architecture, but also to the vital, restless appetites of the young boy who is dramatized within it, the prematurely perceptive Watcher:

They spend money on rubbish, toys for their toy. They cannot know that they themselves are clouds only, symbolic blurs meaning certainty and warmth and happiness, slaves without faces in a small universe where everything else is exquisitely clear.

The detail!

The colour!

Except in dreams, neither detail nor colour has ever since been so detailed or coloured; the fine edge of seeing for the first time too early wears blunt. But the first seeing is so sure that nothing smudges it. Take Bellair Street. Bellair Street, built about 1870, is a withdrawn street overhung by great plane-trees and is on the way to nowhere else. It is only several blocks long and, so far as the houses are concerned, one-sided. This is because it is the last street, three-quarters of the way down, of several streets lying horizontally along the eastern slope of a ridge crowned with Norfolk Island pines, non-conformist churches of brick the colour of cannas or gravy-beef, and a state school of brick the colour of brick. The slope makes it necessary to ascend from the front gate of 36 along a path of encaustic tiles, next by eight wooden steps to a front veranda . . .

(1963, 11)

Narrator or personage? Memories or screen memories? Elements of general and particular, learned and retained, the visual and the haptic, are so artfully entwined here that we could never unpack the passage into its component truths. The relations between narrator and personage are expressive in their dramatic fluidity.

It is especially interesting to notice that, like the young personage in Sartre's *Les Mots*, the young Porter is depicted as having found human beings less solid than things (in Sartre's case, than books), and the dynamism of autobiographical time leads us to ask whether this is a point about the kind of child who will become an autobiographer or about the way in which an autobiographer reconstructs the child. This ambiguity is allayed or harmonized by the lyrical *verismo* of such early recollections. They conquer scepticism just as they conquer the fluid past:

I remember the face of Father's gold pocket-watch, and the hair-line crack across its enamel, but not his; I remember exactly the pearls and rubies in Mother's crescent brooch but not her eyes. Except for Mother's singing, I cannot hear them . . .

(10)

The self-tale must needs be extremely sophisticated to persuade us thus of both the rememberings and the forgettings which accompany its transactions with the world of historical facts.

The opening of *The Watcher on the Cast-iron Balcony* prompts me to one further reflection—one of many that are possible with so rich a book. The cases of Boyd and Casey and White might have tempted us to assume that complex or sophisticated openings are only likely to be found in the work of authors cushioned by a childhood in the *rentier* classes, those whose self was underwritten by a good deal of tangible property. Let it be said then that Porter's background, along with the details he so memorably recreates, was unimpeachably lower middle class.

2

Forgetting

It is the deeper strata of the person, in which emotion and striving are rooted, that mark out certain life patterns with a mnemic accent while others remain neglected.

W. Stern

If a great deal of the seductiveness of books and poems springs from their seeming to be focused on acts of remembering, it is partly because these acts show up bright against a far larger darkness, that of all the forgotten life. Behind the luminous days of Wordsworth's daffodils, or of his 'Stepping Westward' there lurk or slant away all the unnoticed days; the dramatic visitations in Hardy's *Veteris vestigia flammae* poems are all the more poignant or shocking because they stand against the days —ah no, the years—during which he had forgotten or suppressed his long past with Emma. As in historical or mythological paintings, a seized moment of text bears witness to a large duration of invisible sub-text. The speech echoes against the silence from which it springs.

All works of literature are to an extent acts of retrieval. Life escapes, it is lost, and the writer erects, creates this verbal substitute on paper, a complex of gestures adding up to a larger, formal gesture which is time regained. Not for nothing do writers keep journals and notebooks: these are the half-way house between life and letters, or perhaps three-quarter way.

This confrontation of recall and loss is generally a true condition of writing, but it is vastly more so in the couple of centuries since the rise of Romanticism, centuries in which autobiographical retrieval—retrieval of almost anything at all: witness Daniel Spoerri's *An Anecdoted Topography of Chance*, a catalogue of the objects lying on his kitchen table in Paris one morning in October 1961—has acquired a status as a process of almost inexhaustible interest. Such interest, such capacity to fascinate, is amoral or transmoral; the findings are not of events emblematic of human vices and virtues. Uniqueness, personal particularity, these are the guarantees of the most piercing reality, however generically familiar the fictive mode in which they are embedded or enamelled. These or those glowing events were not merely written *by* the author: they actually, or 'really', happened *to* him or her, so we are encouraged to believe. They are enforced by our awareness that they are oncers, as individuated as this morning's egg stain on my trouser knee. Their *gestus* is not a moral posture, unless there be such oxymoronic entities as existential moral postures.

In the modern contract, then, the author affects to forego ethical fables of the common good; he shows his hand, which means showing the ink-stains on his fingers, dirt under the nails, callouses, scar-tissue, even the slashed wrists. As Philippe Lejeune has observed in *Le Pacte autobiographique*,

l'autobiographie est le genre littéraire qui, par son contenu même, marque le mieux la confusion de l'auteur et de la personne, confusion sur laquelle est fondée toute la pratique et la problematique de la littérature occidentale depuis la fin du XVIIIe siècle.

(1975, 13)

If author is person, if particulars are in, if oncers resound, why not record all the particulars, all the oncers, hundreds upon hundreds of pages of details all in some measure numinous to the progress of one life? It is precisely this question which is raised by the two greatest novels of our century, *Ulysses*, which affects to recall everything about Joyce's Dublin of 16 June 1904, and *A la recherche du temps perdu*, which immensely amplifies the acts and materials of remembering which Proust had recorded, and attributed to himself (or to someone not yet severed from the author's self despite this character's coexistence already with a family of Guermantes and with a French village called Combray) in the manuscript of *Contre Sainte-Beuve*. Both these long novels, utterly different though their demeanours are, raise the question of where to fence the field, what if anything to leave out.

But in this dilemma nature has come to the rescue, as she so often does. If the literature of the last two centuries is permeated with remembering, it is also, and not surprisingly, shot through with forgetting. They lean together like ignorance and knowledge, sin and virtue, each meaningless without the other. For remembering to be of any dramatic significance the thought-voice must have shown itself to be capable of forgetting. This is what activates Beckett in his famous distinction between passively automatic remembering and active curiosity in his little book on Proust:

> Proust had a bad memory—as he had an inefficient habit, because he had an inefficient habit. The man with a good memory does not remember anything because he does not forget anything. His memory is uniform, a creature of routine, at once a condition and function of his impeccable habit, an instrument of reference instead of an instrument of discovery. The paean of his memory: 'I remember as well as I remember yesterday . . .' is also its epitaph, and gives the precise expression of its value. He cannot *remember* yesterday any more than he can remember to-morrow. He can contemplate yesterday hung out to dry with the wettest August bank holiday on record a little further down the clothes-line. Because his memory is a clothes-line and the images of his past dirty linen redeemed and the infallibly complacent servants of his reminiscential needs. Memory is obviously conditioned by perception. Curiosity is a non-conditioned reflex, in its most primitive manifestations a reaction before a danger-stimulus, and seldom exempt, even in its superior and apparently most disinterested form, from utilitarian considerations. Curiosity is the hair of our habit tending to stand on end.

> (1931, 17–18)

The remembering which literature practises may take the opposite form, claiming not the Proustian retrieval but the 'Time Passes' we find in Virginia Woolf's intermezzo passage of *To the Lighthouse*, yet the effect remains one of claiming to hold blocks of the escaping flux: as words, as sentences, as paragraphs, as a shapely interlude through the wastes of which the Great War has inexorably poured. Like this passage, books obtain their *frisson* by recording flux and passage, but themselves sit immobile on library shelves, squared out with print, blocks of substantial paper. A library or 'resource centre' claims to be what remains, a community's ganglia of memory, source become resource. Life has confronted paper and left behind books; the books statically claim to hold the quirks of gone life.

A perfect, complete memory would be indistinguishable from idiocy, a point Borges has turned into an occasion for ironical if sad narrative in 'Funes the Memorious': the mind of Funes is strictly idiotic, it is a primitive process in which ego, super-ego and subconscious are as yet undifferentiated; only in a backward village would he have survived so far, and in order to lead us back into the human world his author must have him die. To be a moral creature, one has to be capable of forgetting. Some things must matter more than others. Without this, no art, no meaning, the return of chaos. Or to put it spatially, a cartographer cannot define the shape and limits of the land without indicating the sea. A parallel, though factual case to that of Funes is explored by A. R. Luria in *The Mind of a Mnemonist.*

But Beckett has gone further, asserting that Proust went in search of lost time so successfully because he 'had a bad memory'. The *mémoire involontaire* of which Proust was so brilliant, so memorable an exemplar, may have peculiar elasticity and force in a consciousness which has difficulties with memory. As Benjamin puts it, 'Inattention is the dream bird that hatches the egg of experience.' And if Beckett is right we might say that Proust was first picked out as a potential artist by his capacity for inattention and then made of it a creative tool, a tool which he used or rather fell into again and again as part of that *reculer pour mieux sauter* process which, on Koestler's argument, springboards so many acts of creative activity.

Whatever the biographical truth of this, many modern works locate their numinous moments, their secular epiphanies, in perceptions which affect one as having swum up randomly in a distracted or inattentive consciousness. Take as an example Connie Bensley's poem, 'Short Story':

As I knocked the cup from the shelf
My mind flashed up reprises:

That glass you dropped, the dark hotel room,
My letter in the rack, your car driving away.

A masterpiece of precis.
The cup hit the floor. I turned to pick up the pieces.
    (*Times Literary Supplement*, 25 December, 1981)

This gives us the familiar mode concisely and knowingly, one miniaturist's form masquerading as another, short story and lyric both being kinds which display their sheer serendipity, their *haecceitas*, their capacity for recording surprises. And the diminutive size of this lyric is part of its point, its dramatic 'precis': a once continuous relationship is now forgotten; it has left four vignettes to point the story, and even these, the poetic fiction claims, are only activated by an accident which cunningly proves to be a metaphor for 'break-up'. The trigger fires off the event, recollection, as unpredictably as five bells over Sydney

Harbour recall Joe Lynch to Slessor's reverie or as the moon dropping below the roof-tree brings a premonition of death in Wordsworth's superbly-named 'Strange Fits of Passion'. Again and again strange fits of passion thrust themselves out of the general darkness of inattention, amnesia or repression.

As J. H. van den Berg has shown in his *Metabletica, or The Changing Nature of Man* (1975), there have been at least a few real changes in the psyche within historical time. One of these is the discovery of childhood as a distinct state, its illuminated testimony yielded up to us in vignettes, whether of genuine memories or screen memories—which are, though complicated in origin, no less genuine. Why do we now thus value our 'childish things'?

Where mediaeval literature presupposed an orderly universe and a rational or morally coherent narrative voice as literary guide, virtually all modern fictions presuppose the universe to be dark, chaotic, entropic, and the narrator bound to play only such rules as he finds in his hand. His subjectivity, comic or saddening, is at the heart of his authenticity; that he has forgotten most things is not his weakness but a proof that he is genuine. Yvor Winters' grievance against what he calls 'romantic irony' represents a natural archaist's anxiety at this amoralized new world. Yet the available moments, the romantic epiphanies, the spots of time, are not offered as *merely* random. They are charged with significance, with a representative glow. Manifestly modern though this tradition is, it has still borrowed some of its habits of symbolic vision from the Hermetic line, from the techniques of Neoplatonic signification. To extrapolate from Wordsworth (here addressing a child),

If thou appear untouched by solemn thought
Thy nature is not therefore less divine

So, even, are the remembered 'meadow, grove and stream'. So, even, are the vivid modulations of consciousness itself.

By the time we arrive at Imagist theory, anything recovered from the flux and capable of being verbalized is divine: 'concentration is the very essence'. There is a divinity which shapes our memories and sharpens our perceptions, our duty in turn being to 'employ always the *exact* word' and 'render particulars exactly'. Decades earlier, almost alone and often clumsily, Hopkins tried to forge an explicit theology for these new currents of perceptionism. One of his syntactical tricks is to render his marvellous perceptions into the plural, so that they will seem to exemplify a general case. So we have

Glory be to God for dappled things—
For skies of couple-colour as a brinded cow;
For rose-moles all in stipple upon trout that swim;
Fresh-firecoal chestnut-falls;

and

As kingfishers catch fire, dragonflies draw flame

It is no accident that Hopkins was also a careful keeper of journals. He hoarded the treasures of his eye, holding them back from oblivion. Not even his strong faith could prevent the lovely contingent from disappearing. Nor, of course, could he pass on into the paganism of Stevens, who was capable of believing that transience or destructibility was itself the great source of value, 'the mother of beauty.'

Whether in Hopkins or in Pound and the Imagists there is a limiting factor about the expressiveness of these marvellous trouvailles, these brilliant, snatched flowers of perception, and this is that they tend to be static. They can allude to but seldom render sustained or complicated movement in time. An epiphany is, but it does not *trace*; this is at the very root of Pound's difficulty in finding any kind of structure and sinew for *The Cantos*. Hardy, being a great rememberer and a great forgetter, had a strategy for dealing with this problem in his lyrics, which was to allow the syntax considerable complication. Thus we get

Saying that now you are not as you were
When you had changed from the one who was all to me,
But as at first, when our day was fair.
                                          ('The Voice')

and also

Where the bark chars is where, one year,
    It was pruned and bled—
Then overgrew the wound. But now, at last,
    Its growings all have stagnated.
                                          ('Logs on the Hearth')

The interesting tenses of verbs can play out the relation between different parts of the furniture of consciousness, retaining a vital and even a moral dynamism. Such dynamic verb-chains enact for us what Ribot, speaking of memory in general, called 'the unstable compound phenomenon in all its protean phases of growth, degeneration and reproduction.'

The further point to be made about 'The Voice' and 'Logs on the Hearth' is that, despite the dramatics of memory, both leave us with a powerful impression of annihilation, of blankness, of mere wintry wind 'oozing' through thorn-bushes and a once-climbed apple tree burning away to ash. In each poem annulment yields the imaginative thrill. The very text which is trying to hold something against destruction is gaining its power from registering that destruction. The paradox is akin to that of tragedy. The poem says, once I knew such life as this and now all I have to give you are patterned words on the page. Much as the black typeface stands out between the wide white margins of the page, the retrieved blocks of experience stand out against a universal wastage of experience. As Empson says,

Because we have no direct or indirect knowledge of death
It is the trigger of the literary man's biggest gun.

There is, I think a relation between imaginative aura and the potential for deep confusion, or at least nescience. This is what underlies Benjamin's remark about it not being particularly interesting to be able to find your way around a city: what matters is to be able to lose yourself in the city. Then its corners and buildings can acquire aura; then it becomes like a forest. Turning explicitly to memory, he declares a direct relation between definition and obscurity, names and silence:

An experienced event is finite and confined to one sphere of existence, but a remembered event is infinite because it is only the key to everything that happened before and after it.

Within any cognitive framework there is a peculiar charge of mystery about not-knowing; whether it be the preconscious, the unconscious, the forgotten or the arcane sub-text, the area of darkness exerts its fascination over the islands of light. And, as the above quotation suggests, we try to read them as keys to or symbols of all that is inaccessible. The modern mind hungers to turn all sorts of data into instances of personally-charged symbolism; the key is all the more fascinating because the rooms are not illuminated.

There is danger and fuzziness in such habits of response. Take Wordsworth's dealings with the indistinct, where we also find a disingenuousness born of the unwillingness of that egotistical sublime to admit or declare his capacity to forget things; his Hartleian optimism disinclines him to admit that experience gets lost: he offers himself as the very opposite of an amnesiac, a living current of associations. But if he draws a blank on forgetting (except in the dynamics of 'Surprised by Joy'), Wordsworth is peculiarly interesting in his handling of the related conditions of inattention and distraction. In 'Strange Fits of Passion' he gives us the soporific effect of a horse's motion on the rider's mind; in 'Resolution and Independence', both the comic inattention of the speaker to the old leech-gatherer's narrative and that significant declaration of sunny cheerfulness that stifles care, 'My whole life have I lived in pleasant thought,/ As if life's business were a summer mood'. We get the cryptic but related line, 'A slumber did my spirit seal'; and in 'Tintern Abbey' something that edges closer to amnesia, those 'gleams of half-extinguished thought,/ With many recognitions dim and faint'. In Book VI of *The Prelude* we find, in the Simplon Pass lines, a peculiar dramatics of inattention and anticlimax preceding the vision of 'the great Apocalypse'.

In reading Wordsworth with biographical foreknowledge, we also take note of a strand of undeclared repression, or suppression. The love affair with Annette Vallon has been expunged from the 'poet's mind' offered for our inspection in *The Prelude*. It might be said to be declared in costume by 'Vaudracour and Julia', and to be a detectable impulse in the formation of 'The Ruined Cottage', 'Ruth' and the 'Complaint of a Forsaken Indian Woman'. But in all these cases we are obliged to read it in. Perhaps Wordsworth's failure to allow much for forgetfulness has a direct connection with the important piece of his life he is busily repressing. After all, amnesia may be more or less functional.

Furthermore, nobody in literature is wholly consistent about what he or she remembers or forgets, a point which is made quite simply by Randall Jarrell's long poem, *The Lost World*, an oxymoronic work which claims to have lost the world of the speaker's childhood while presenting it to us in vivid, extensive detail.

If a novel may be said to have a consciousness, if its community thinks and feels, then there are a host of analogues for

forgetting or repression in the nineteenth-century novel. There
are the buried childhood of Heathcliff and the shrouded one of
Pansy Osmond; the hidden pasts of Bulstrode and Henchard,
the latter's containing that dark act of wife-selling; the con-
cealed relationships between Frank Churchill and Jane Fairfax,
Grandcourt and Mrs Glasher . . . their names are legion, their
assignations clandestine; there are the overseas disappearances
of Provis and Angel Clare; there is the locked room upstairs in
Mr Rochester's house, the dark and troubling truth it conceals;
there are false names, misleading addresses and Carker's hol-
lowing out of the financial operations of Dombey and Son.
Above all there rises to brilliance among the galaxy of genres
the detective novel, that form in which the obscene, suppressed
and deeply traumatic past is patiently, delicately brought to
light: much the same sort of thing as psychoanalytic practice,
and, like that practice, swaying between science, hermeneutics
and sympathetic magic. Perhaps the sleuth is our truest modern
hero.

There is one modern occasion where a whole novel, and not a
detective thriller either, is structured on many overland acts of
forgetting, lying, deceit and inattention. This is that quin-
tessentially modernist text, *The Great Gatsby*, a narrative in
which all the details are manifestly (or darkly?) questionable, in
which even the cruxes withhold or divert us away from what
might have been information, directing us instead into the per-
verse excitement of loss:

Through all he said, even through his appalling sentimentality, I was
reminded of something—an elusive rhythm, a fragment of lost words,
that I had heard somewhere a long time ago. For a moment a phrase
tried to take shape in my mouth and my lips parted like a dumb man's,
as though there was more struggling on them than a wisp of startled air.
But they made no sound, and what I had almost remembered was
incommunicable forever.

                                                          (Fitzgerald, 1950, 118)

The slipping dance of images here, the barely recovered fragment and the dumb lips, not to mention the way in which a
measure of the authorial experience has been displaced onto
another character, an emanation, has immediate connections
with a quite different, but just as strongly self-displaced, study
of lost time and engulfed experience, Kenneth Slessor's marine
lament, 'Five Bells':

Yet something's there, yet something forms its lips
And hits and cries against the ports of space,
Beating their sides to make its fury heard.

Poetry has a crying need for lips: they are precisely the means
of articulation which it must always lack. They frame the mouth
of the ghost that haunts the text.

'Five Bells' is apposite to our train of concern here for deep-
laid historical reasons. The orthodox literary tool for exploring
relations between retention, retrieval and oblivion is the elegy.
(*The Great Gatsby* is, of course, a fictive prose elegy.) Coming
not to bury but to praise, it is tactically committed both to
recalling past events and to stressing the fact of present annihilation of the past. 'Five Bells' stands squarely in the tradition,
at its modern end; not only is the poem imbued with a doubting,
jittery modern consciousness, but it is also biographically favoured by the stubborn fact that its subject, Joe Lynch, died
by water: died, indeed, in an enclosed or internalized body of
water, Sydney Harbour. The layers of metaphor lie thick on the
declared loss:

Where have you gone? The tide is over you,
The turn of midnight water's over you,
As Time is over you, and mystery,
And memory, the flood that does not flow.

No, but it has tides, we might go on. Available to the poem are
images of the sea with which to exemplify annihilation and flux,
but also to body forth internal darknesses. The five bells of the
title tell not merely time but marine time, not only a temporal
construct but an unfamiliar one; they are imposed on tidal time,
on stellar time and on the private time of the reminiscent consciousness. The vessel whose bells ring out in the darkness
below the speaker's window is a warship. Its aggression blasts a
way through the repressed materials of gone life to vital memories of Joe. In the words of David Rapaport, 'a given situation
appeals to a certain set of strivings which in response deliver the
proper materials into consciousness.'

One recovers so little: that is the hell of it, from one angle of
looking. But as we have already observed, forgetting is also
salvific, leaving us room to move and offering at least a substantial illusion of free will. (Which is in practice the same as *having*
free will.) As Auden wrote in the hurly-burly repartee of *Paid
on Both Sides* (1930), 'By loss of memory we are reborn/ For

memory is death'. Out of amnesiac darkness we gratefully gather the Anglo-French pun, *souvenirs*, and its cousin, *rêverie*.

Romantic and post-Romantic poetry present us with a whole series of tactics set up to cope with forgetting and at the same time to enlist its contrasting force. Again and again in such poetry we feel the immense cathexis attached to a retrieved image or epiphany, testifying to the effort it has cost to drag this experience out of the gulfs of oblivion. Edward Thomas's 'Adlestrop' is a perfect example of such powerfully random recall, being filled with the trope of an express train halting suddenly at an obscure siding, and being so shaped as to pass rapidly to an ending which is no ending but a rhythmic and syntactical driftaway, trailing off across the names of shires. Many such images in modern literature tacitly or declaredly carry the implication that they represent the return of the repressed; at the very least, they come to us charged with phantasy, trailing clouds of subjective glory. From Wordsworthian spots of time to the strict delineations of the Imagists, they are designed to have a status like momentary gods, or like peaks of *Einfall*.

In *Tintern Abbey*, ostensibly spurred by a landscape revisited, Wordsworth offers an interesting mental map of a tripartite system of memories and recoveries. First there are the remembered forms of natural beauty: forms which have been capable of sustaining him 'in lonely rooms, and mid the din/ Of towns and cities'. Second, after a colon and a dash, there is a cluster of more puzzling phenomena, 'feelings . . . of unremembered pleasure', and lest its paradox should not be taken, the adjective is repeated three lines later in 'little, nameless, unremembered acts/ Of kindness and of love'. These buried phenomena are, the syntax declares, also products of natural beauty experienced in the past. A further complication in this passage lies in the suggestion that the unremembered feelings may have *caused* the unremembered acts of benevolence—remarkable speculation! Wordsworth is groping in the dark here, but he seems to know what he is after, and it involves leaving the subconscious undisturbed.

The third and more familiar psychic state avowed in this passage is a visionary one, contingent on access to what Freud was to call the oceanic feeling. It transcends all memory, just as it transcends the body–soul division; it leads to the point where, tamed by harmony and by joy, 'We see into the life of things.'

All three stages are seen to be the results of a process by which natural perceptions were retained by the imagination as 'forms of beauty'. Given the marvellous visual detail of the first paragraph of the poem, it becomes hard to tell whether we should attach any Neoplatonic weight to the word, forms. Probably not, as the poem's logic puts it.

One may be even more psychically daring, driving a poem straight back from the known to the unknown, the visible to the invisible, the available world to the wholly repressed world of early childhood. This is what A. D. Hope does in his poem of Dantesque regression, 'Ascent into Hell' which in its resonant conclusion lays claim to a vision located amid primal chaos: a verbal representation of the birth trauma, re-run backwards, the *fons et origo* reached at last. There is stunning poetic effect to be had from a fib like this; besides, it releases what is arguably the most personal poetry Hope has ever written.

For the modern consciousness there is always a springy zest to be had in standing memory and amnesia on their heads. Taking an entirely different tack from Hope's monodrama, Hardy lyricizes the market dames in 'Former Beauties', only to turn desperately on his verbal heel in the final stanza:

They must forget, forget! they cannot know
　　What once they were
Or memory would transfigure them and show
　　Them always fair.

Hardy is never more charged with deep cunning than when he sounds to be lyrically simple. Here emotion's ardent thrust belongs to the Hardyesque speaker himself but is projected in wan hope towards those flowerless marketwomen. And the final sentence is laden with linked unlikelihoods that unpack very slowly. We are back with Hardy at what he called 'the *other side* of common emotions.' A canny old man and compulsively subversive of fixed knowledge, he wrote of this and other poems in the Preface to his 1909 volume, *Time's Laughing-stocks*, 'As a whole they will, I hope, take the reader forward, even if not far, rather than backward.' What this actually means about consciousness and the plot against the past, Hardy is not around to tell us. But a long creative life like his must be built upon strategic amnesia; it was essential to one who could remember as Hardy could.

Truth is, his great asset was that long life, which enabled him

to orchestrate the most intricate, even devious relations between loss and retrieval, old mortality and old Wessex. In
'During Wind and Rain' he even went so far as to expropriate
the memories of another person, his first wife, Emma. The
poem conceals its provenance. And the epiphanies can be juxtaposed just as the poet chooses.

It is no accident that so many of the texts mentioned here are
ones which close up the gap between author and literature. Just
as concern with memory rises with the spread of autobiographical modes, so does its dark underside, an interest in forgetting. The first great exemplar of this blurring spread of self-
dramatization, Montaigne, begins his essay, 'Of Liars', with this
throwaway sentence:

There is not a man living whom it would so little become to speak from
memory as myself, for I have scarcely any at all, and do not think that
the world has another so marvellously treacherous as mine.

Forgetting and the show of forgetting have become poetically
important for a linked bundle of reasons, then: because such
obscurity accentuates the vividness of retrieved images, letting
the epiphany blaze forth; because it enables that poetic self-
begetting—Harold Bloom insists that the origins of strong
poetry are always to be found in repression; because significance
would be impossible without wholesale forgetting; because the
lost material can cast a shadow of mystery, a ghost of conflict,
across the text; because the real symptoms must always be
repressed, leaving a site of anxiety around which, pearl-like,
the poetry forms; and because it is only human to forget. And
literature is, after all, an account of our being human. If it is
not such an account then it remains worthless, mere scraps of
lettered paper blowing in the breeze of history.

3

Ending

A novelist is free and powerful in ways which an autobiographer cannot possibly hope to share. Above all, the novelist can end a book anywhere, so long as that end point seems artistically right. The novel can run through several generations, or through a crammed week; it can kill off all its characters; and it can certainly include the death of its major character, something which it frequently, memorably does.

But the autobiographer must leave the central character alive, as we have already noticed. Indeed, the life-book ends with a transformation scene in which we are made to realize that the character has become the author, a protagonist finally taking on like a cloak the title-page of his or her book. And to do so our protagonist must have been alive when the last black marks scarred the manuscript paper. Editors and publishers may have packaged this papery life posthumously, but even this packaging cannot gainsay the life-bound condition of autobiographies and memoirs.

It is in vain, then, that I have looked for a memoir that ends with an author's death. The nearest possible approach to such a delicious conclusion occurs in the last entry of Alice James's diary: 'Oh, the wonderful moment when I felt myself floating for the first time into the deep sea of divine *cessation*, and saw the dear old mysteries and miracles vanish into vapour!' But that was merely her third-last sentence, being followed immediately by some fine Jamesian irony as she threw in the saving observation that 'The first experience doesn't repeat itself, fortunately, for it might become a seduction'. It is left for a reader to write in the death itself after this as a dense curtain of final irony.

Of course, readers always read the historical death back into an author's oeuvre, where they can. All interpretations of Keats's poems and letters rub the premature death into the writings, bending them all so that they will funnel down into that supreme final declaration that 'I always made an awkward bow'.

Unlike Keats, the autobiographer is setting out expressly to write a life, or a representative section of it. The book is laying claim to the flow of that life. And at the end he or she must shape the life-book's closing pages so that they do justice both to life and to art: so that they can further the illusion that a life has magically been made over into this book.

More than this, though. Why should the autobiographer die at all? Surely it is the case that he or she has deliberately turned author into character, self into a fiction, in order to circumvent mortality. These surviving pages, with the story of an eponymous persona woven through them, sail on into the future leaving the mortal scribe in dust and ashes. The mortal self becomes a surviving text, a little empire of words which stays there on the map. As Poulet put it in the case of Balzac's novelistic impulse, 'I am a point, a centre, from which I can set out to extend myself everywhere, exist everywhere, and become everything'. It is an open question whether the novelist, the poet or the autobiographer is the greatest narcissist, making the universe over into versions of self.

But in thus guaranteeing a papery immortality, the autobiography has crushed buzzing, blooming liveliness down into a coherent book, obedient to all sorts of generic rules, among them the rule that a book should have an aesthetically satisfactory ending. The close of an autobiography should accordingly show a family resemblance to the endings of earlier memoirs, or novels, or histories, or even poems.

Yes, poems, for the endings of some autobiographies reveal the author's choice to finish with a kind of lyrical suspension, a musical fluidity which can seem to leave so much still open. There are two endings to Joan Colebrook's *A House of Trees*— and we shall come back to double endings shortly—the former of which goes:

I was dimly understanding that the world which had made me what I was was breaking up and changing, that the water around me could not for one moment remain still, that the water bore me away, that the water was history.

Despite the awkward moment of 'was was', this is poetically metamorphic syntax, proceeding by means of anaphora to change the world into water, the water into a life process and

that process into history. Running away into the mobility of a
future life and ending the narrative are the same gesture, much
as they are at the end of *The Getting of Wisdom*.

Patrick White ends his curiously disarticulated *Flaws in the
Glass* with a burst of poetic orchestration: poetic not only because crammed with images, changes of light and snatches of
birdsong, but also in that its syntax is so grandly orchestrated,
running on splendidly through eleven lines and twelve consecu-
tive phrases in apposition, the whole ending on the word 'grace'.
This is not all that White's coda is up to. Ambitious as we would
expect him to be, he has tried to push his memoir as far as it can
be made to go by changing over into the future tense and
seeking to entertain the likely circumstances of his death. But,
since even the future tense will not yield up an actual death, will
not get us to the point we reached with Voss and Stan Parker
and Hurtle Duffield, White can give us in the end only the stage
set with its lights and music. So that grand sentence begins thus:
'If I were to stage the end I would set it on the upper terrace,
not the one moment of any morning, but all that I have ever
lived . . . ' Like any serious writer, he wants both life and art at
the same time, both 'all that I have ever lived' and deliberately
planned theatre. There is the bit where you give it, and the bit
where you take it away.

As we have already seen, though, dying does not have a big
part to play in autobiographies, apart from that little bit of dying
we do every day. In his *Golden Builders* Vincent Buckley included two lyrics with the title, 'Practising Not Dying', and this
is surely a central practice of the self-book. It rehearses a series
of strategems for outwitting the death which waits somewhere
in the wings. It fixes the fluttering life on paper.

Where to end, then? In *Mucking About*, Paul Hasluck sets
out with a very simple prescription: 'All autobiographies ought
to end about the age of thirty-five'. Classical, Christian, correct,
this is the Dantesque point for embarking upon a dark journey
of exploration, *nel mezzo del cammin*. In the circumstances one
cannot easily forget Emerson's epigram on the whole endeavour
of *The Divine Comedy*, 'autobiography in colossal cipher'.

Sir Paul Hasluck goes on, less modestly, to claim that a public
figure falls out of the realm of autobiography when he reaches
maturity, and falls into history. I wonder what that claim seeks
to hide.

Hasluck's autobiography is in large measure a political book, having for its title a larrikinish figure of litotes, hardly typical of the general tone. As for its ending, this takes place at the point in the narrative where Hasluck has been elected as a Liberal M.P. in the 1949 elections. He then unmasks narrator and character, turning back into a seventy-year-old author, a literary man giving us his Horatian boast about the conservative power of art:

That ends the book. I have written from memory. The chief document of memory is a white wall in the golden evening light with the shadows of wind-ruffled leaves trembling on it. If I had not written this book, the record would have disappeared with the going down of the sun.

A protagonist may well be buried alive when we close a particular book, but an author survives, being on the outside as well as on the inside, on the cover as well as among the pages. And once that author is safely dead it is the whole construct, the artefact, which lives on, taking over and replacing his or her gone life. Where presumptions about the life once lent their vital conviction to the autobiography, the book now comes to lend conviction retrospectively to a life which took place back in the increasingly dim past. The transactions involved are by no means simple: a writer is a vivisector who plays at resurrection.

The poetic ending of an autobiography may in itself lend conviction to that recovery of things lost, that desired revitalization. To take one instance, I know of no more exciting flourish than the conclusion of Ruskin's *Praeterita*. Written in 1889 amid the damage and distraction of his sad old age, even hampered by a lengthily fussy footnote, it is a remarkably eloquent, even transcendent piece of recuperative prose:

Fonte Branda I last saw with Charles Norton, under the same arches where Dante saw it. We drank of it together, and walked together, that evening on the hills above, where the fireflies among the scented thickets shone fitfully in the still undarkened air. *How* they shone! moving like fine-broken starlight through the purple leaves. How they shone! through the sunset that faded into thunderous night as I entered Siena three days before, the white edges of the mountainous clouds still lighted from the west, and the openly golden sky calm behind the Gate of Siena's heart, with its still golden words, 'Cor magis tibi Sena pandit,' and the fireflies everywhere in sky and cloud rising and falling, mixed with the lightning, and more intense than the stars.

(1949)

Three things about this passage are especially striking. Firstly, the late-Victorian assumption—an assumption which we still tend to share, almost instinctively—that the cities of Renaissance Italy's floruit are inherently salvific, because beautiful. Secondly, there is the double use of that central English pun-word, *still*, in order both to generate the sense of a wished-for calm and to suggest the fluent continuity between past and present experience: such *stillness* is there to heal an old man's present wounds by knotting the strands of his autobiography into a late harmonious unity. And, thirdly, we can hardly miss the dynamism generated by that final chain of conjunctions. As at the end of *Ulysses* (did Joyce know his Ruskin?), the 'and . . . and . . . and' sequence signals life's urgent insistence upon both action and continuity. The final sentence is surely charged with continuing hope in its very incapacity for closure.

Ah yes, unwillingness to close is a common feature in auto-biographical works. Poetic endings often hang gracefully in participles or drift off gracefully, tangentially in literary quotations (Oriel Gray's from Lewis Carroll, Bernard Smith's from Irish legend). Some books signal their reluctance by means of multiple endings. Some resemble Jean-Paul Sartre in refusing to advance beyond adolescence. And Joan Colebrook goes so far as to freeze the time-frame pictorially, using a jacket photograph of herself which is dated 1937, just half a century before the appearance of her memoirs. Thus she goes full circle, turning the author back into the character with whom she ends her story.

But circularity is not an answer to all the problems of narrative, twisting and weaving away as it must after verisimilitude. Conviction takes many different forms; not all of our responses are in tune with the modern, or largely modern, tradition of open endings. Brian Wicker, for instance, observes in *The Story-Shaped World* that 'There is a place for the open ends of Lawrence's novels, but there is also a place for the strong, harmonious ending which emphasizes that we have been engaging only in make-believe'. For all that, the writers of auto-biographies are seldom keen on playing up the element of make-believe in their books; they much prefer to give the impression that their pages have been cut dripping from the living wood. Such is surely the force of Oriel Gray's penultimate remark: 'well, you can't be right about everything'.

Perhaps there is a simpler sense, too, in which autobiographers are unwilling to say goodbye to themselves. Their books end so often with a diminishing sequence of tropes or of little valedictory gestures as, like Nellie Melba, they go on making definite farewell appearances. Best of all, the writer would like somehow to be preserved, pen in inky hand, writing down in a narrator's suasive voice the continuing adventures of that earlier, eponymous self.

It should be said that Hal Porter's circularity serves a different purpose, however. He does not necessarily want to cling to the 'non-innocence' of youth, much as he loves its bric-à-brac, its fashions, its daily routines. Rather, he must keep rounding back to a mortal darkness, hoping that the pieties might finally prove to be adequate. With 'God is dead', he tries the largest gesture he can possibly find to placate the furies, but even this cannot end the book of his childhood and adolescence.

The Watcher on the Cast-Iron Balcony keeps returning to an ending, unable to leave it alone, somehow obliged to keep revisiting, rewriting, it. The protagonist's mother dies—or has just died—on the first page of the book, and again on page 244, and for the last time on page 253, where she finally 'leaves the littered and dirty shore'. A page-and-a-half later the story comes to an end, but with a sentence which only takes us back to the top of page 245, where son and father cross the road to encounter a coyly flirtatious rector.

In these ways, Porter constructs an artful circularity which endeavours to defy ending. His book has been trained around his mother's mature life and death, boxing the dying in, but also being given shape by it. The refusal to allow itself to be cut off by a traditional ending is recognized by the provocative second-last sentence of the book: 'I do not know that, not only have I not started to die, I have not started to live'. Here the narrator-I holds the character-I in a curious suspension, as though he could be released into life at any minute.

Porter's resistance to closure takes other forms as well, most obviously in the procedure of setting his narrated life in the present tense, a tense which briskly attempts to refuse time and change: a tense which is always performing here and now. The present tense is immortal.

What we find in all these works ia an almost superstitious reluctance to finish up the story, or to cry, Enough. The writers are surprisingly fond of ambiguous endings, present participles, odd truncations, tangential quotations from other texts, any trope or syntactial quirk which will suggest that life flows on vigorously beyond the printed page. In this they recall nothing so much as the 'unfinished' character of Keats's later long poems. 'Hyperion', 'The Fall of Hyperion' and 'The Cap and Bells' are all seemingly incomplete (one is literally dubbed, 'A Fragment'), yet each is brought to a close with phrasing which is at once eloquent and full of present vigorous action. It is a trick in the interests of life, a kind of pre-Lawrentian openness to vitalist impulses.

So 'Hyperion' breaks off abruptly in mid-sentence with

                                    At length
Apollo shrieked —and lo! from all his limbs
Celestial . . .

In 'The Fall of Hyperion' the unclosed closure sounds more like something out of science fiction, or like the film, *2001*:

His flaming robes streamed out beyond his heels,
And gave a roar, as if of earthly fire,
That scared away the meek ethereal Hours,
And made their dove-wings tremble. On he flared . . .

Likewise, 'The Cap and Bells' ends with two lines only of a new stanza, lines which once again plunge us into a new, significant action, which is all the more strongly foregrounded by this lopping-off, this framing device. Something very important is on the brink of taking place—and there we are; held by a mere two lines, lines which are at the same time comically alliterative:

Now Hum, new-fledged with high authority,
Came forth to quell the hubbub in the hall. . . .

For all the impersonality for which he is famous (a fame which goes along with his being one of the most visible, one of the most visibly present, of all English writers), Keats was surely exploring the predicaments of a vulnerable self in these verse narratives, and he showed a deep reluctance to bring their vitality to a close—like an autobiographer.

But Keats was not an autobiographer. Rather, he should be seen as a major liminal figure in the writing of self and the construction of un-selves. There is another sense in which autobiographies end without ending. They all entail their own writing: after events stop, the story has still to be written, life falling into that language we have just read. As that oxymoronic sentence will have suggested, much of the grip of autobiographies springs from the way they are dynamic in time. After but alongside the protagonist there moves the author, pen in hand, replacing life with narrative, sometimes even bursting through the fabric as rudely as the mature Edmund Gosse does when in the course of *Father and Son* he emerges, a mature writer, in the Cascine Gardens, far from Protestant England.

As H. Porter Abbott has suggested, 'the end of an autobiography is everywhere present in the writing of it. It is therefore not precisely an event, but an event in progress'. This adaptation of Elizabeth Bruss's conception of autobiography as performative is at once suggestive and misleading. What it fails to observe is that, although the ending points us back into the writing of a self-life, it also terminates that writing. So that in the end there is the valedictory curtain of an ending. Perpetual motion has not yet been discovered.

At the metaphorical level, we should add one more observation, that all these endings have another function. They are papery rehearsals for death itself; they are the authors' mortal exercises.

4

Struggling with an Imperial Language

I sometimes wonder whether all serious writers are obliged to live in a Third World of the imagination: whether for them the existing cultural structures and assumptions always loom up with something like the minatory status of a colonial power.

More specifically, in post-Romantic works of literature the surrounding or antecedent language commonly seems to be an unresponsive jungle in the midst of which the writer has to hack out a clearing where the private sensibility can live and display itself. Is power always resented in modern literatures? Again and again we applaud the dissentient voice, the bohemian swagger, the regional folk idiom, the minority demand, the assault on privilege, the underdog's ironical bark.

For the Australian writer, as in other post-colonial countries, lands with their own 'new' histories, such questions as these have an immediate visible pertinence. Here the case of the individual writer blurs with that of the new nation attempting to define its difference, its true note, if you like, from the initial colonizing power.

To set the scene, I should like to begin with two quotations from nineteenth-century writers in Australia. The first comes from William Woolls, who left England for New South Wales in 1831 and who wrote this within the following few years:

But, nevertheless, Australia is not uninteresting to the lover of antiquity, for we may truly say that many of its scenes are calculated to awaken the most pleasing recollections. Can the admirer of classic lore survey the numerous flocks, which now are seen sporting over our plains, and be forgetful of those primitive ages when kings and queens tended their flocks, and valued them as their chief possessions? Can he behold the vine and the fig spreading luxuriently over the land, and be unmindful of the beautiful passages in ancient writings which speak of them as the attendants of peace and plenty? And can he traverse the wide-spreading plain, climb the summit of the lofty range, or wander 'by gushing fount, wild wood, and shadowy dell', without calling to mind the inimitable descriptions of the ancient poets? In Australia, indeed, he may ponder with increased interest and delight on the wandering lives of the patriarchs, and the sublime language of the prophets.

(Smith, 1975, 52)

For Woolls, so recently arrived from the Old Country, existing cultural models are securely fixed in such phrases as 'the lover of antiquity' and 'the admirer of classic lore'. His rhetoric remains untroubled even when he goes on to make the claim that 'it is manifest that Australia is by no means deficient in objects of interest to persons of a refined taste'. New experiences do not trouble the received equanimity of this observer's prose.

The second exhibit is a short poem by that remarkable novelist, Joseph Furphy. It comes from a posthumous collection of his poems, but was written in the last decades of the nineteenth century. The combat of idioms in these lines underwrites power and class; for a squatter, or prosperous grazier, held the highest conceivable position on the social scale, while the swagman or tramp, at the other extreme, was landless, nomadic, jobless:

ARE YOU THE COVE?

'Are you the Cove?' He spoke the words
  As freeman only can.
The squatter freezingly inquir'd,
  "What do you mean, my man?"

'Are you the Cove?' His voice was stern,
  His look was firm and keen.
Again the squatter made reply,
  'I don't know what you mean'.

'O dash my rags! let's have some sense —
  You ain't a fool, by Jove!
Gammon, you don't know what I mean —
  I mean, ARE YOU THE COVE?"

'Yes, I'm the Cove', the squatter said.
  The swagman answered, 'Right!
I thought as much. Show me some place
  Where I can doss to-night'.

As in his large experimental novel. *Such is Life*. Furphy is aware of how power relations and cultural differences keep disclosing

themselves in idiolect and accent. Our tropes bespeak our fate.
People may make use of distinctive idioms, but may also be
locked into them as a train is obliged to stay on its rails.

We are accustomed to speaking of the English language as
though it were our glory, our treasure trove, the rich savannah
of our mental habitation. Even while acknowledging it to be
historically changeable, we take it in other ways to be a fixed
domain, our fortunate inheritance from History, under her
benign aspect. But what if this rich and resourceful language
should prove to be not such a happy endowment, but something
of an albatross strung around our necks? What if it closes off
experience, or freezes it into predetermined, even uncongenial
patterns?

As soon as this question has been asked, situations will spring
out of the bush to confront us, in which English, that quaintly or
tellingly named language, could be felt as disabling. Many an
Australian Aboriginal, many a writer in the Caribbean, Poly-
nesia or Anglophone Africa, would surely feel like cursing the
tongue which bespoke the British Empire and its old authority.
Two Indian poets of my acquaintance have recently declared
their intention to turn away from the language in which they
established their reputations, preferring to write from now on
in the native languages of their natal regions.

Larger—or should I say, less geographical—scepticisms raise
their heads here. There is that teeming shoal of questions which
feminist criticism has to ask about the phallocentricity of language, about masculinist assumptions woven deeply into the
very fabric of European languages. The pressing of these gender
questions is one of the few success stories of recent literary
criticism, going as it does far beyond the kind of surface vocabulary pruning which gets caricatured in those weak jokes about
'Personhattan' and 'herstory;' well past the revisionist concern
with pronouns or with words like mankind; it reaches beyond
vocabulary, ramifying out into syntax, genre and methodology.
At this point, however, I give it a nod and pass on. But not
without adding that in the discontents of feminist criticism I can
hear another echo, a faint but distinct cooee: that of previous
decades of Australian writers disenfranchised by the Anglophile
academics of the time. We should not throw up our hands in
surprise at the present close alliances between feminists and
nationalists in Australian critical discourse.

The most sweeping scepticism about language which is being

trundled around nowadays is also the least lucidly convincing. I refer to the post-Freudian logophobia of Jacques Lacan. If the mazy rhetorical thickets of Lacan's never-never can be said to have any centre, it is in a strange re-telling of the myth of Romantic childhood as pure, wordless infancy. Damaged by language, by the un-natural rigours of symbolization, the Lacanian ego is blocked off from its true subject, its earlier potential self. As in A. D. Hope's 'Ascent into Hell', we may hear

The enormous Birth-gate whispering, '*per me*
per me si va tra la perduta gente'

Even Hope was obliged to fall out of English into Italian as he approached the massive despair of his poem's conclusion. According to Lacan's glum reading, humankind is from almost the beginning 'insufficient in his natural reality' (the pronoun is not mine: I quote from Alan Sheridan's translation); insufficient, and so doomed to fall into the symbolic systems of language. Within the baroque extravagances and brassily orchestrated slippages of Lacan there remains a hankering for the state defined in Thomas Hardy's words as 'Before the birth of consciousness/ When all went well'. But I am concerned here with the cultural anxieties of adults, not with the prime naturalness of unbabbling babes.

Language may be servitude; language may be freedom. As an Australian writer, my theme is particularly attentive to the kind of elbow-room our writers find they have to work in. Many of my observations would ring plainly familiar, even old hat, to students of American culture. They have been through the mill, too; they have had to work the oracle, making the gift of the gab their own. But we should be careful. Models always obscure truth. Coarse similarities stamp on particular instances. For instance, Australia may well be roughly the same size as the United States but the late Alan Davies could with some justice define our cultural anxiety under the title, 'Small Country Blues'. And, in his book *The Australian Ugliness*, the architect Robin Boyd compacted his sense of our supine position before America's careless power into the one harsh word, 'Austerica'. From our little continent, the United States is, I am sorry to say, imperial, too. Americo-English begins to harry us as Anglo-English has traditionally done.

The question for a long time has been, how can we clear our

own linguistic room and live in it, neither cringing nor strutting. The poet Les Murray, accordingly, ends one of his poems with the Janus-like line, '*We're country, and Western*, I replied'. Yet another of his poems contains the surely-endorsed slogan, 'ENNI PIEPL WYRTH A CRYMPAT HAEZ A NEITIV LAENGWIX', proposed as a likely message on fictive banners of the national future. And the Soviet writer Andrei Bitov, in speaking of the Australian writer's situation, put the matter thus: 'A literature either tries to be universal and out of date, or to be regional. The regional is always up to date, but it is not enough'.

It may be, too, that we should think of many more possible postures or actions in the teeth of the received English language than the cringe and the strut. Coming from a beachgoing nation, after all, I find myself tempted to propose the following four: the shudder, the paddle, the float and the surf. The first two would represent the condition of those writers for whom dealings between English and the physical fact of Australia remained stiff, awkward, tentative; the float is possible for those writers who have come fully to terms with the medium and its possibilities; and riding the surf would be the lot of those writers who added their own distinctive strength to the medium, making it over into a new form of action: in American terms, I would think of Whitman and Mark Twain as writers who had reached that stage, bending the English language into that New World voice which they needed.

But why kick against English at all? The need is partly psychic. Oedipal, we might want to say, if international relations can be conceived of as family romances. It also has its more objective grounds. History did not forge the English language in those moist little islands for the purpose of dealing with Antipodean reality. No wonder that David Rowbotham complained,

Obliged by tongue still to belong
To the absent kingdom of the tongue.
You linger in a bondage grown
Strange to the ground you stand upon.

There come quickly to mind some of the ways in which this imported, immigrant language does not fit the experiences which it is supposed to signify. Its named festivals are jolted out of their seasonal place, and hence shorn of their chains of association: Christmas introduces the summer holidays and New

Year's Day commonly heralds the main blast of heat; Easter is the chief holiday of the autumn; north winds are hot and a southerly brings a cool change. Squatter is a more honoured designation than mere farmer; parishes exist where there never has been a church; the word, village, means a trendy shopping centre or perhaps a cluster of ski-lodges; inner-urban districts are called 'suburbs'. Some slippages can be discerned because names were first used as rough similes derived from home: the she-oak looks like a weeping conifer, while the white cedar does not resemble a conifer at all; box trees are eucalypts and do not look at all like the European box; the wild cherry bears hard nobbly nuts, makes no show of flowers and has needle-like leafage; the mountain ash is an enormous eucalypt; and the Tasmanian tiger is—or was—a wolflike marsupial.

Such a point about nomenclature was originally and sharply made by Harpur:

Never were God's creatures named—or rather nicknamed—after a more barbarous fashion than were our native birds by the first comers. Take for example the following string of names:—there are Old Soldiers, Bald-headed Friars, Leather Bellies, Native Companions, Laughing Jackasses, Doctor Faustuses, Gorgers, Cocktails, Bobtails, and Governor Fovaus. Of the last name, however, it may be remarked, that no two sounds could more closely resemble the notes of the bird so-called—and it therefore may be allowed to pass; especially as it is likely that this resemblance was first detected during Colonel Fovaux's administration of the Government.

But seriously, these vile names should be dropped as soon as possible—and indeed are being dropped—or rather, they are dying off with the old hands. At present, in some of the remote districts, first penetrated by intelligent Squatters, the birds (and most other things) are allowed to retain their aboriginal names, which are generally very beautiful. This is just as it should be, and is indicative moreover of the prevalence of good taste—a thing always, and in all places, worthy of commendation.

(1986, 120)

I could go on belabouring such terms as these, small enough matters in their way, till the cows come home. What is of concern about them, and with much that is read in English or American books, is their suggestion that the language need have no particularly accurate connection with the phenomena of everyday life. At times it seems to belong within the walls of the schoolroom, whereas real life, the nub and grit of dailiness, the sheen or flicker or dustiness of known objects, is essentially wordless.

So the English language lacks a certain fitness or fittingness for us. I am reminded here of two remarks in Seamus Heaney's prose collection, *Preoccupations*. There, in an essay on Belfast, he observes,

> I suppose the feminine element for me involves the matter of Ireland, and the masculine strain is drawn from the involvement with English literature. I speak and write in English, but do not altogether share the preoccupations and perspectives of an Englishman.
>
> (1980, 34)

and later he writes of Hugh MacDiarmid and his grandly mixed diction.

> There is an uncertainty about language here, peculiar not just to MacDiarmid, but to others who write generally in English, but particularly out of a region where the culture and language are at variance with standard English utterance and attitudes.
>
> (196)

Given what he admits, we might even feel like asking Heaney from what security of standpoint he can declare that what he perceives is an uncertainty about language. The slippery slide of relative positions is lying in wait for us here. What I would say, however, is that a succession of Australian writers, from Furphy and Herbert to Bruce Dawe and Jack Hibberd have made a deliberate virtue of linguistic uncertainty and jaggedly mixed diction. Such writers use a book stylistically as a position paper. And their writings involve a rejection of Anglo-English, a flouting of continuous literary decorum, a disproportionate jangling of idiolects and a playing with the flourishes of Ocker Baroque. They risk not being understood abroad, of course. And they also fall into interesting paradoxes. Furphy's wonderfully aggressive and nativist novel is saturated in echoes from the Bible and Shakespeare. Even he was unable to get away form these rich precursors.

As any post-structuralist will point out at this point, it is an awkward question, how far an individual writer is free to make such policy decisions, and how far bullying discourse systems hedge in any possibility of choosing. Peter Conrad, an expatriate critic, puts the determinist question another way. In a *Times Literary Supplement* article, 'Footholds in the Sunburnt Country', he adapts a question which puzzled Enlightenment naturalists thus:

Since Australia has stood the world on its head, its poetry inherits a scrambled array of disjected images, as incongruous as the cards in the Tarot pack. The puzzle is to determine what those images refer to; to improvise a system which might account for these stranded metaphors and left-over, damaged symbols.

(19 December, 1986)

This is the platypus argument against natural law, reborn as poetics. But it has its point. We inherit a colonial language whose symbolic systems have been scrambled by displacement. But for the writer bent over pen or word-processor the question remains this, in R. A. Simpson's words, 'how much is accident and how much choice?'

The poets, novelists and playwrights whom we take seriously believe that they are free to choose and make. In the best cases, surely, the causal factors that poured into those recalcitrant, rebellious many-faceted texts were so manifold that it would be a massive task of detection to unpick and evaluate them. Did J. L. Lowes prove that Coleridge lacked creative independence? Furphy and Jack Hibberd, Judith Wright and Kenneth Slessor, each created restless, idiosyncratic texts the character of which nobody could possibly have predicted, least of all a critic whose main presumptions were of the Anglo-English dispensation.

There are yet more extreme acts of rebellion, explicitly political rejections of the values, assumptions and hierarchies contained in the English language. These are coming from some writers among Australia's ethnic minorities: most passionately from the younger Aboriginal writers. The poet, Lionel Fogarty, writes for instance in an aggressively improvised argot which mingles slang, pidgin, telegraphese and straight English lines like 'We must understand the many ways/Mr. Shakespeare is a racist'. Fogarty struggles for a position within language to fight the language from. For him, and for some of his fellows, it is indeed a prison-house. Unlike Kath Walker, an older Aboriginal poet, he cannot accept the given language as his tool of critique. But neither can he stand utterly outside it.

As I have already suggested, it is not merely the glen-and-dale problem, not merely a matter of vocabulary, which keeps Australian writers on edge. Values are embodied in language in such a host of different ways. I am especially reminded here of a

remark which Barbara Johnson has made about the logophobia
of Derrida and Lacan. She writes that

The relation between these two attempts to break out of spatial logic
has yet to be articulated, but some measure of the difficulties involved
may be derived from the fact that *to break out of* is still a spatial metaphor. The urgency of these undertakings cannot, however, be over-
emphasized, since the logic of metaphysics, of politics, of belief, and
of knowledge itself is based on the imposition of definable objective
frontiers and outlines whose possibility and/or justifiability are here
being put in question.

(1980, 129)

The English language carries within it the hidden agenda that
Australian assumptions are necessarily those of English thought.
And to break this matrix open is damnably difficult, some
would say impossible. Up to a point history tells us that we've
got to work inside English fences, nudging them gradually into
an accommodation with brute Australian fact. Often too, ironically enough, it is the authors of genuinely popular sympathies
who show deepest respect for the paternalistic (or maternal?)
clarity of 'good English': this last being in itself an interestingly
packaged phrase on which we were all brought up by our elders.
At the very least, you've got to use the language you're demur-
ring at, in order to convince the not-yet-converted audience.
You can't have a revolution without using the system.

To thicken up the argument a little more specifically I should
like to turn at this point to two contrasting exemplars. The
former is the early twentieth-century poet, John Shaw Neilson.
While acknowledging the distinction and delicacy of his verse,
critics have variously read his cultural posture as strong or
weak. His social credentials as a popular poet were absolutely
impeccable. Born into a very poor Scottish-Australian farming
family, he worked for most of his life as a penniless farm
labourer, never owned property, never married, lost his eye-
sight early, and seems to have picked up most of his poetics
from oral sources, particularly those of Australian and British
balladry. He seems to be the very person that the Australian
legend is all about, our New World development of Rabbie
Burns, the itinerant bush-worker of unstoppably natural proletarian talent.

Popular though his lyrics are in their forms, sentiments and
topoi, Neilson turns out to have written in perfectly correct
English, lightly literary in flavour, quite devoid of usages or

phrasing derived from Australian idiolect. Here, for example, is 'The Petticoat Plays':

Teach me not, tell me not,
  Love ever sinned!
See how her petticoat
  Sweetens the wind.

Back to the earth she went,
  Broken at noon;
Here is her petticoat
  Flapping a tune.

Have ye not ever heard
  Petticoats sing?
I hear a mourning flute
  And a sweet string.

Little silk ally in
  This her last war,
Know ye the meaning of
  What she died for?

Mourner most delicate,
  Surely you hold
Manna that she has stored
  Safe from the cold.

She had the loving blood,
  Love gave her eyes,
And the world showered on her
  Icicles—lies.

Speak to her, little wind,
  Lovable sky,
Say to the soul of her
  Brava—goodbye.

Teach me not, tell me not,
  Love ever sinned;
See how her petticoat
  Sweetens the wind!

The voice here is absolutely typical of Neilson's reticent lyric gift, yet it comes out of the traditional stockpot of Anglo-English, an observation I hope he would forgive me, as Scots Gaelic was also spoken in his childhood home.

The modern poet who has done more than any other to hear, to invent, to create, to persuade us of the necessity of a middle-

Australian voice speaking through poetry is Bruce Dawe. His plangent small lyric, 'Drifters', is remarkable for the way it captures the idiom and pacing of a common world, common yearnings:

One day soon he'll tell her it's time to start packing,
and the kids will yell 'Truly?' and get wildly excited
    for no reason.
and the brown kelpie pup will start dashing about,
    tripping everyone up,
and she'll go out to the vegetable-patch and pick all the
    green tomatoes from the vines,
and notice how the oldest girl is close to tears because
    she was happy here,
and how the youngest girl is beaming because she wasn't.
And the first thing she'll put on the trailer will be the
    bottling-set she never unpacked from Grovedale,
and when the loaded ute bumps down the drive past the
    blackberry-canes with their last shrivelled fruit,
she won't even ask why they're leaving this time, or
    where they're heading for
— she'll only remember how, when they came here,
she held out her hands bright with berries,
the first of the season, and said:
'Make a wish, Tom, make a wish'.

It will be clear that what I am talking about in this poem is hardly a matter of vocabulary at all. Apart from 'kelpie' (the sheepdog, not the Scottish goblin) and 'ute' there are no regional words here.

We might say that the freedom so many readers have sensed in Dawe is at heart a matter of phrasing, of the way his voice takes on the guise of suburban speech-rhythms, the pacing, the Lego grammar, the innocent anaphora, the rambling flattened stress-patterns no more than lightly stitched together by recurrent internal rhymes. To a native ear this poem sounds as Australian as a jar of Vegemite.

With Bruce Dawe, as with the playwright Jack Hibberd, we find that the linguistic democrat can also be an eclectic bricoleur. Not in this poem, but in other pieces like 'Life Cycle' and 'The Not-So-Good Earth', language-tone is playfully disordered. Juxtaposition ironizes the different discourses, generating comedy and dissatisfaction. Sometimes, admittedly, it is sheer parody that he is after, as in the opening lines of 'First Corinthians at the Crossroads':

When I was a blonde I
walked as a blonde I
talked as a blonde;
but now that I have become
a brunette I have put away my
blonding lotion, farewell Kim Novak
and the statuesque Nordic
me: a touching scene truly . . .

Here, too, the King James Bible raises its head; and in doing so lightly underlines my general point, that the clash of perceived systems makes for literature. The artistic writer (yes, such an archaic creature does exist) says to himself or herself, let's put more bumps and swerves in it to slow down traction. Let's play merry hell with decorum. That is the way to run risks, to lay it on thick. These are genuine surfers, not tentative paddlers in the green linguistic current.

These questions manage to present themselves very different- ly across the literary genres. A dramatist takes to versions of the regional language most readily, being able to distribute its tropes and tricks among invented characters. But the characters of a lyric poet are as a rule not actors, but phrases, lines, stanzas, actively engaged together; given that precondition, he or she may be obliged to call upon considerable impurity of diction to make the poem adequately combative. But it is the happy novelist who holds the thick end of the stick. For the novelist has a licence to create, not only a narrative voice, or voices, but the idioms of those direct speakers who are contained within the walls of the narrative. Accordingly, a powerful novelist like Patrick White can devise a narrative voice which, however quirky, belongs recognizably within Anglo-English conventions, and then go on to decant his colourful store of regional talk into his characters. He gets his linguistic pleasure, but they have to carry the bag. And White has made very good use indeed of this kind of authorial freedom from language constraints.

Back to Anglo-English, our large imperial inheritance. Cor- rect English usage is traditinally connected with social accept- ability, with power, with prestige, with assumptions of class and with the authority of educational institutions. But that sentence was written in correct English. Which side is my bread buttered on? Correct English, like Renaissance Latin, is an internation- ally transferable currency. You can carry it with you all around the global multiversity, it won't go bad in your pocket and you can keep on cashing it in. To put the matter another way, if you look at world universities you can simply ask yourself the question, did England win after all?

I can assert my national and cultural identity on the smallest scale by the sounds of my accent, not quite Crocodile Dundee's, but adequate to the purpose: on another scale I could do so by means of a liberal scattering of specifically Australian terms. But if I take this scattering too far I can only invite your assumption that my aim is comic. Suppose I were to say in a lecture that 'a bloke would be a drongo or at least a bit of a dag if he didn't cotton on to the kind of Toorak-and-ruin lingo that the gubs and ockers keep smarming us with', listeners would know that social conventions were being contravened, the linguistic contract broken, and that I could only be joking. The solemnity of genre would be mocked.

But for an imaginative writer the rules are different from those pertaining to an academic occasion. When I put my poet's hat back on I will strive to mesh my colloquial idioms with high speech, yarning with poesy, Australian English with Anglo-English, informal gestures with formal organization. Just as there was a political agenda encapsulated years ago in Donald Davie's title, *Purity of Diction in English Verse*, so there is a political stance to my demand for impurity of diction. We need to make room for Australian language within the English cultural imperium. Perhaps our national flag should feature an oxymoron. Alas, it does already.

5

The Person in the Poem

We have been warned that we cannot expect to find an author displayed on the pages of a book. The book has been made out of words, the English language, grammar, conventions, paper, printer's ink; no matter how we squeeze or cajole it, it will not yield up a live writer. The writer belongs in a realm called Life, the book in a field called Literature or, if it is a very scruffy book, Discourse.

But as pleasure-seeking readers we are equally sure that we can winkle an author, his or her distinct sensibility, out of these flat pages. A paragraph of Lawson or Stead, a few lines or Auden or Dickinson, and we know perfectly well where we are, whose consciousness we are now keeping company with. The author's nervous system, especially those features which most markedly differentiate it from others, is spelt out for us in the fall and flow of language. We call this style; but we read it for a living spirit, a spirit which can leave tell-tale fingerprints on the page.

Cart or horse, chicken or egg? One may just as well say that all imaginative writing is charged with autobiography as claim that it is all the result of previous discourse systems. The former is the more interesting reading, if the differences between individuals are more important than their family resemblance. Sure, we must locate individuals in their gridded historical terrain, but we should also allow them room to move. And to carry on.

All in all, the strongest academic warnings are, or used to be, offered against the prospect of our reading lyrical poems as autobiographical utterances. Stephen Dedalus fancied that a lyric had the character of a spontaneous cry, but in critical practice we are more apt to treat a lyric as a crafted object, like a Grecian urn. At a primitive level we are sure that the poet is expressing something of his or her own condition, but the orderly study of literature will not permit such an approach.

'The poet says' will be struck out with a red pencil and replaced by such a phrase as 'the poem suggests', or 'these lines assert', or 'what the poetry is doing here is . . . . ' Propriety is observed if we stick to formal analysis of the poem's shaping and development; or if we try to place it in social history; or in the historical development of a particular genre. To hunt for the person in the poem is held to be downright vulgar.

Sliding gracefully away from 'the old stable ego' of coherent character, modern poets have notoriously claimed impersonality for their own writing. Eliot and Hope have both committed themselves to such a position, the latter declaring that 'poetry is principally concerned to "express" its subject and in doing so to create an emotion which is the feeling of the poem and not the feeling of the poet. In this I am at one with T. S. Eliot, a poet whose poetry I cannot bring myself to like at all'. In some sense, this can be seen as a wish on the poets' part to have godlike powers, creating and setting loose in the world creatures which are self-sustaining. No doubt it is also defensive.

It is hardly surprising that the peculiar, sentient impersonality of the lyrical emotion has called forth many kinds of comment, many strained voyages of critical explanation. Peter Porter has caught it as well as any in two lines from 'The Last of England', which put the matter like this: 'Sailing away from ourselves, we feel/The gentle tug of water at the quay'. It is with great concision that he holds together here two versions of the self, and the emotion, and the capacious, insensate medium on which the whole enterprise floats.

But almost every poet has wanted at times to give a warning as stringent as Hope's in the face of readers' desires to write the presumed life rawly into the made poems. Just about every poet wants to insist on being a maker, not a squeaker. He or she would rather be praised for the judicious administration of half-rhymes than for laying bare a self-life. And this is easily understandable. As Auden wrote, art is not life; well, not *merely* life. Any art work, a poem no less than a sculpture or a sonata, is that glowing oxymoron, a subjective construction.

Which is to say, we still expect poetry to be recognizably personal. Every if the lyric may be fashioned of shining stainless steel, we expect it to bear the poet's fingerprints. Even if the universe flowed through the poem as transpersonal inspiration, we are attuned by our readerly contract to keeping a sharp weather eye open for such marks of individual authorship.

These prints comprise a whole congeries of phenomena: direct allusions to lived events, characteristic themes, vocabulary, favoured verse-forms, syntactical habits, argument with previous poems, quirks of tone such that one might almost call them a personal voice. Taken together, such evidences imprint any modern poem with the personal. If it were possible that there existed a reader who knew some Keats poems but had never seen 'To Autumn', that most impersonal of all great poems, the first two lines alone should establish it as unmistakably by Keats: 'Season of mists and mellow fruitfulness,/Close bosom-friend of the maturing sun'. The signals are all there, so strongly so that a susceptible part of one's mind goes out to accompany the identified poet on an actual, aromatic walk.

If we then pick up Keats's letter to J. H. Reynolds from Winchester, written on 2 September 1819, we can read what we naturally take to be a more direct transcription from 'life':

How beautiful the season is now—How fine the air. A temperate sharpness about it. Really, without joking, chaste weather—Dian skies—I never liked stubble fields so much as now—Aye better than the chilly green of spring. Somehow a stubble plain looks warm—in the same way that some pictures look warm—this struck me so much in my Sunday's walk that I composed upon it.

And reading into this we can easily persuade ourselves that we are walking with the poet into his autumn ode; or, rather, walking into its world, as well as coming upon the beginning of its writing. The stubble plains with their double atmosphere are those of the last stanza; the oxymoron, 'temperate sharpness', typifies the crossed feelings of the whole dense poem, loading and blessing together as it so harmoniously, even perhaps ironically, does. As for 'Dian skies', it is as though the virgin huntress were giving her name and identity to the nameless personification of autumn in the poem. We are tempted to believe that we have collapsed the division between a letter, the most artlessly personal of forms, and a lyrical ode, so full of artifice and elevated mystery.

We might go on to say that, far as we have got in walking into the poem by way of the poet's own paths, we have not laid hold of the accumulated sweetnesses of the first two stanzas. But then we could turn back three and a half weeks to another Winchester letter in which Keats shares with his young sister such luxuries as apple tasting—pear-tasting—plum-judging—apricot nibbling—peach scunching—and a white currant tree for company—

and there is a fruitful excess comparable to that which suffuses the first two stanzas, the poet's mouth seemingly as avid as that oozing cider-press.

Thus the point has been reached where one of the most triumphantly impersonal poems in the language (made, in Helen Vendler's words, out of 'linked things, linked apparitions, linked actions, linked syntax—all not arbitrarily linked, but linked by minutest design') turns out to be externally provided with doors or ladders of easy access, using which a reader may be persuaded that it is possible to find a strolling John Keats, caught at a particular place and time, generously present in the poem: every bit as much as a person can ever be present in a text. But there is no 'I' there, after all; an eye, certainly, to draw upon one of the language's central puns, but no first person pronoun. Keats has only been historically located in the poem by means of two interventions, two letters addressed to different recipients. And those letters are not in the poem; they are *around* it.

Again, if Keats is present in 'To Autumn' as in letters, questions are raised as to whether the lovely shaping of those three stanzas has served any point at all. It is the purpose of artistic form—shape, harmonies, orchestration, echoic imagery, associative concatenation, rhythmical effects—to take the utterance out of the realm of the spontaneously personal and lodge it within the impersonal stability of an achieved genre. We do not see Keats, the small, auburn-haired Londoner, in this poem after all: what we glimpse are a series of reflections on the fact that he is the most intimately known of all English writers before the twentieth century. The details of his sprightly doings are so fully adumbrated that we are inclined to resent weeks, or even days, of his floruit on which we do not know what he was doing. One day, perhaps, we shall even find out who bowled the ball which gave him a black eye on 18 March 1819, after which he slept in late the next morning and, feeling lethargic, began to conceive of 'Ode on Indolence'. Keats encourages the scholar's pipe-dream that one day we shall know everything about him: the more so since he teases our minds with his famous attachment to 'negative capability'.

In the circumstances, it is hard to reconstruct the major

emphasis of Richard Woodhouse's memorable comment on Keats's consciousness:

He has affirmed that he can conceive of a billiard Ball that it may have a sense of delight from its own roundness, smoothness, volubility & the rapidity of its motion.

To every perception there is an equal and opposite perception, it is tempting to say. We may interpret this report either as evidence of Keats's remarkable capacity for promiscuous empathy, as with the sparrow on the gravel path, or else of a solipsism within which he can imagine the billiard ball as entirely self-satisfied and self-delighting. It may even be the case that imaginative empathy comes easy to someone whose self is closely compacted: that it is from a strong, dense base of identity that one may best venture forth to enter another kind of consciousness. Ditherers are not likely to be strong poets. But this begins to draw us away from the specific question of how self manifests itself in lyric poetry.

The smuggest answer to this enquiry consists in saying that it is only by conventional agreement that any personal presence makes itself felt in such poetry. But such an answer is so banal, so conceptually barren, that it will get us nowhere. We do not sit outside language, nor romp outside culture. A critic who goes about the business of showing us how Wyatt's 'They flee from me' and Plath's 'Sheep in Fog' were made possible by their reception of certain historical conventions may well be deeply instructive; a critic who believes that these two poems are merely the products of transpersonal conventions cannot read poetry. Cannot read literature at all, I should have said.

Within the category which we loosely designate lyrical (unitary; perhaps laying claim to musicality; not a narrative; short, or at least a good deal shorter than 'Five Bells') there are many poems whose effect is varyingly personal. Tone and dramatic stance may run all the way from McAuley's lines,

I put my childish face up to be kissed
After an absence. The rebuff still stuns

My blood. The poor man's curt embarrassment
As such a delicate proffer of affection
Cut like a saw. But home the lesson went:
My tenderness thenceforth escaped detection.
                                                          ('Because')

to such elusive Marianne Moore lyrics as 'No Swan So Fine' and
'The Fish'. The McAuley lines rely utterly on embodied point-
of-view, or even on point-of-view-of-feeling, and can make no
sense unless that human location in space–time is accepted by
the reader, for the time being at least. We are obliged to believe
that there is sustantial continuity between the wounded little
boy and the poet who has made these lines. If we cannot feel
the embarrassment as having been personal the poem dies on
the page.

It is part of Moore's originality, however, to have dismantled
point-of-view. Intensely visual though her poems often are,
their language bent to naming a succession of visible phenomena, viewpoint is dissipated into something like the eye of a
mobile camera, tracking here and there, unresting, verbally
dynamic. In the case of 'The Fish', for example, the poem feels
authoritative in the clarity and precision of its language, yet it
does not provide the continuing guidance for our responses
which poetry—we believe—has traditionally led us to expect.
Readerly response has to make its own poem out of a gallimau-
fry of named perceptions which are so clearly recorded on the
page.

'In the non-committal, personal–impersonal expressions of
appearance/ the eye knows what to skip.' Precisely, except that
the reader's eye, challenged by Moore's radical art, is not so
sure after all. But 'expressions of appearance' is an oxymoron
very much to the point, and worthy of Keats as well as of Moore.
And the non-commital surfaces of her poems are peculiarly
elusive. Such poetry has generally been taken to belong over
near the impersonal limits of lyric. R. P. Blackmur, for example,
writes that 'there is no meeting Miss Moore face to face in the
forest of her poems and saying, This is she, this is what she
means and is' (1957, 246). It is lack of discernible viewpoint
about all which leads to this impression of an authorial absence.
We cannot see where she stands, in the poetic geography; we
cannot get at the poet as author. Cold pastoral, these poems
will not let us in. Their beauty involves resistance.

In another sense, however, Moore's locally dazzling poems
are full of a distinctive presence which might well be labelled
personality. They are powerfully idiosyncratic, stylistically individual, recognizable as *hers*. Gwen Harwood once lamented
her own persona (well, at least her own dinkum persona, there
having been playful others in the past), saying that she should

have had a front man with flashing eyes and floating hair. Moore certainly had a 'front man' or decoy, a seemingly genteel, even fussy, spinster, attentive to cuttings from magazines and to the surfaces of material objectives. It was behind or against this puritanical mask that a very strong poetic personality got on with its business, expressing itself in what may well be the most original, the most resistant, poetic style of our century. Is she not, in the Bloomian sense, a strong poet, crushing her antecedents into something she can use for herself and in doing so perfecting a daughter's poetic revenge against the fathers? The traces of her forebears are all but obliterated, being saucily replaced by allusions to *The New York Times* and the like. Ruskin, Emerson, Tolstoy and Yeats find themselves shrunk into merely random sources, forced to keep company with Dr R. L. Ditmars, C. H. Prodgers and the captain of the Brooklyn Dodgers. Even her notes, unlike those to *The Waste Land*, are merely notes, brisk enough to keep all the referents humble.

So there she is. If one compares the coherent voice and manner of Moore's poetry with the shilly-shallying, the multiple obeisance, dalliance and *bricolage* of Ezra Pound, it is the less-lauded female poet who surely emerges as the more powerful. In the end she can be seen as having steadily created imaginary formal gardens with a real self in them: a self strong enough to accept the world steadily without the adoption of Renaissance point-of-view. We pay tribute to a sustained toughness which creates poems in which there is no centre of attention:

If in Ireland
  they play the harp backward at need,
  and gather at midday the seed
of the fern, eluding
their 'giants all covered with iron', might
    there be fern-seed for unlearn-
ing obduracy and for reinstating
the enchantment?
    Hindered characters
seldom have mothers
in Irish stories, but they all have grandmothers.

Moreover, she carves the shapes of these poems into the blank page in a repeated elaborate assertion of will. Objectively though her images strike us, we can hardly find Marianne Moore's poetry to be marked by negative capability. She is altogether too commanding a presence.

At last I have reached the point where it becomes possible to understand a remark of Auden's which has puzzled me for many years; he concludes an essay on her poems by saying that 'they delight, not only because they are intelligent, sensitive and beautifully written, but also because they convince the reader that they have been written by someone who is personally good' (1963, 305). Goodness is hard to locate in the authorial face of literary works, hard to make sense of in such a context, indeed, but it is a reasonable way of characterizing the mixture of steadiness and strength which can be found throughout Moore's oeuvre.

Tempted as I was, then, for some time by the way of reading Moore which is summed up in Stanley Plumley's attributing to her a deep involvement in 'this essentially modern problem: how to create the authenticity of emotion without compelling the close proximity of the self', I cannot in the long haul fully believe in the division which it proposes. Rather, it would seem just to say that the poetic emotion finds itself authentically separated from the biographical self while it continues to be attached to the textual self. And Moore's textual self is as sturdy and independent as can be.

It is in other, later poets, John Ashbery and John Forbes for example, that I find this neoclassical project more deliberately carried on. In Ashbery's case the heart of the project lie in this taking authority away from pronouns, whether through rapid shifts, rather in the manner of Humpty Dumpty's song from *Alice*, or though frequent passive constructions, which serve to take authority away from human beings and yield it to the well-mannered Furies.

It is the aim of John Forbes's poems to give pleasure by withholding pleasure. They give it and take it away, the reader being placed in the position of a baffled donkey, the carrot repeatedly placed in front of him (or her, but I have a strong inkling, which could be argued through, that these are poems designed for a male aesthetic, rather than a female taste) and then abruptly withdrawn with a flourish, a formal flick of the wrist.

Formal? Yes, very formal. When the chips are down, Forbes is our most austerely formalist poet, constantly preferring construction to expression, the skill of boatbuilding to an audible groaning at the oar. He makes his request to language accordingly: 'Subtract me from the motions of my body,/my arm moves & I represent it, either calm/ or in a pink fit palmed off as behaviour'. Poets who are fond of ampersands are commonly more fond of typography than of what Donald Davie has called 'the reek of the human'. And they might well insist that nothing could be more human than printed language.

The word 'subtract' has much in common with 'abstract'. Forbes's poetry takes its place in a history of abstraction that runs from Turner and Whistler down through Ben Nicholson and de Kooning: not ideas about the paint but the paint itself— the phrase might serve as an oppositional motto for the whole line of unsentimentality. But all poets want to be abstracted or drawn away in some measure; and not just 'charioted by Bacchus and his pards.' despite 'Speed, a pastoral', a poem in *The Stunned Mullet* which explicitly evokes Keats, inviting him to dinner along with Flaubert, but rather on 'the viewless wings of Poesy'. Viewlessness would be an especially pleasing concept to Forbes, I should imagine, since his poems are full of devices which have been designed to prevent naive or mimetic reading:

The city fits the Harbour
　　the way a new suit
fits a politician like applause
as if a drowned river valley
was glad we're here, moving
tons of paper around . . .

As several contemporary poets have realized, there is nothing like the proliferation of similes to keep rude nature at bay, and to keep unreliable human nature at arm's length, into the bargain. Forbes participates in the post-modern revolt against too-suasive expressiveness of metaphor. These poems, he keeps insisting, are made out of lengths of syntax, attractive units of language. They wear similes on their sleeves like chevrons.

One of the kinds of authority, and hence of personality, which poetry traditionally claims is the authority of the line. Poems are built out of lines, and then out of stanzas; the lines bespeak kinds of strength. One of the things Forbes is up to in many of his poems is the disconcerting or rug-pulling enjambment, a rhetorical and rhythmical gesture which weakens the line you have just read by revealing its reliance upon the line which follows. Psychologically, the effect is like the repeated destruction of memories; stylistically, it is like a chain of shaggy dog jokes. These seemingly nutty enjambments have just the opposite effect from those in early Lowell: there they were signs of

a thirst to get the dramatic immediacy of present action down
on the page, by hook or by crook. Lowell's run-ons bore witness to a mimesis which was manic, inexhaustible, apocalyptic:

I saw the sky descending, black and white,
Not blue, on Boston, where the winters wore
The skulls to jack-o'-lanterns on the slates,
And Hunger's skin-and-bone retrievers tore
The chickadee and shrike.
                    ('Where the Rainbow Ends')

Forbes, by contrast, goes in quest of understatement, or of the
throwaway phrase. He is fond of ending lines with a conjunc-
tion, an article, a preposition, or between a subject and its verb.
This is one of the ways in which his grammar keeps revealing
slippage.

   In some poems, 'Baby' for example, this tactic becomes
a kind of wit in which lines change their meaning completely
as the reader moves on. Elsewhere, as in the graceful 'Going
North', the effect is that of a speaker who keeps on going, unable to do anything so authoritative as bringing a sentence to a
stop. These effects can come to seem as personal as stuttering.

   Such sliding, fainting and throwaway transitions are made the
medium of a pleasurable eloquence in 'The Promissory Note',
'Serenade' and the first ten lines of 'Missing Persons':

the planets line up & nothing happens
beneath the sheltering bowl
of your don't-have-a-clue feelings
as the day goes to pieces & you disappear
equally indulgent but almost on schedule
in the next life I am Ike
& you are Tina Turner, vibrating
between box speakers on a shelf.
next to me is a water-ball
with snow falling on Sydney Harbour

It is in the last four lines of this poem, however, that we are
made aware of a cost Forbes recurrently has to pay for the
liquidly anti-epigrammatic character of his idiom: his poems
are very difficult to bring to an effective end. Something about
their internal dynamics suggests that they should be printed on
Mobius strips, or writ on water.

   If one says of this poetry, as one might say of Ashbery's, that
its undermining of the authority of the line leads to a lack of

memorable poems, even of memorable chunks, one is probably falling into a trap. It is very much the tactic of this poetry to refuse to hand over memorable rhetorical units, strong lines or closed epigrams. Not only does Forbes mistrust mimesis and its claims but he also detaches himself from any declaration of authorial presence by such tactics as a fondness for the second-person pronoun: 'you idle around the perimeter', 'that inertia/ you cancel your career with', 'unless your brain is damaged' and 'a European sense of style/ you can always be at home in' are just a few examples of this pronominal deflection. The voice of these poems is continually off and away.

But what are these poems about, the cognitive reader will want to ask. For all the show of Paul Hogan casualness, a couple allude to contemporary philosophers (Quine and Rorty), a couple play on Les Murray's 'An Absolutely Ordinary Rainbow' and there is more concern than one would at first have thought with Australian consciousness, nervously or wittily compared with that of the Americans. 'Watching the Treasurer' is a good poem about a new, ambiguous kind of folk hero. There is a longish Oz view of European countries which mainly proves laborious but comes up with one good couplet, the stunningly deadpan 'Besides, if you remove the art, Europe's/ like the US, more or less a dead loss'. And there is a very flat dream piece which suggests that, stylish poet though he is, Forbes cannot write prose.

Mostly, though, Forbes writes as someone who wants to subvert discursive themes, escape tangentially from an audible self and avoid giving names to the creatures and objects of his Eden. If anything, he worships language itself; he kneels at the altar of its slippages. Especially he rejoices in the slithery syntax of compound sentences, sentences which run quick-silverly on like this:

I'm sorry there's only this loop to consider, no way out except the teasing but abstract pleasure a kept promise brings, like an imitation of the first day ever, or—working back the other way—as if once taken up, one's golf just got better & better.

The nearest thing to naming daily concerns in these lines is the weak phrase, 'one's golf', and the pronoun has already been undermined aurally by 'once'. Oh dear yes, Forbes is damnably hard to catch: as another poem puts it, 'I stay in a territory/ expunged or out of reach'.

It is important to read carelessly as well as carefully. If we scan Forbes's poems fast we find that a number of subjects come up over and over again. What are they? Water, money, television, fame, stimulants and the Harbour: exactly what we might wickedly expect of a Sydney writer. And their presence signals something about the writer who has positioned himself behind the poems. They tell us that his tastes are as democratic as his rhetorical figures are dodgy.

A poet like Forbes is deliberately kicking against the pricks, and gets his kicks out of doing so. Few female poets write like this, although Moore and Bishop veer away from declarations of personality into eye-on-the-object precision, while that strangely neglected strange poet, May Swenson, delights in verbal games, visual patterns, extravagent conceits and structures like 'The House that Jack Built'. Like Moore and Bishop, she has found her own way past self-expression and has arrived at an idiosyncratically compelling solution to the problem of presenting the detached Modernist personality. As she puts it in unusually declarative lines, in reference to her early work, 'To one loved, talked through/layers of masks./To this day we can't know/who was addressed'. This is a curious claim, suggesting that the poet herself can lose the initial vocative sense of her poems: personality is withheld from her later self as well as from other readers.

What some of these poets delight in, build on, is a determination to bend the poetic or epiphanic contract as far as it will go; they presume upon the reader's passive sense that anything shaped like a short poem will be simple, direct and passionate in feeling (however complex, oblique and hammered in form), in order to have it both ways. That is to say, they expect their client to be intrigued, braced and rejected by dispassionately secular surfaces of the poem; but they also expect that the client will bring along lots of traditional baggage so that he/she will read in the undisclosed passion, the smothered epiphany. The white spaces around a sparse lyric, or between its stanzas, resemble the white gallery walls around a painting or the wide piazza surrounding a Renaissance sculpture: they encourage elevation to be inferred, to be written in by the attuned psyche. Lyrics are meant to vibrate at the edges: against unmeaning space and unredeemed time. They are traditionally sacred sites.

So we come back to the main kind of post-Romantic lyric,

that is to say the poem as charm, as word-music, as apotropaic incantation, as a haunted well of language. This is the norm that even Forbes's larrikin verses, even Swenson's quaintly shaped poems, deliberately swerve away from: language so magically condensed that it is intensely personal in its affect while hardly personal at all as discourse.

Louise Bogan's 'To Be Sung on Water' will serve as a paradigm, straight and clear. Even the title comes from a Schubert song and a little tradition of barcarolles:

Beautiful, my delight,
Pass, as we pass the wave.
Pass, as the mottled night
Leaves what it cannot save,
Scattering dark and bright.

Beautiful, pass and be
Less than the guiltless shade
To which our vows were said;
Less than the sound of the oar
To which our vows were made,—
Less than the sound of its blade
Dipping the stream once more.

The distinguishing marks of lyric as tacit song are all there: repetition, lovely rhythms, primal rhyme words, lucid diction, formal tightness, a lover's address and the difficult vector between transience and circularity. Everything suggests that music is conceptually present, for all that we recognize the poem as a text. And, above all, it is difficult to paraphrase. It is lucid but not finally clear.

Generically speaking, what could be more instructive than Milan Kundera's definition of the novel as 'antilyrical poetry'? With its causal and fabulous traction, the novel is just about everything that lyric is not; lyrics refuse to tell us a story, no matter how much we yearn for such pleasure. They are a product of the intense, arbitrary tastes of modernity; we take to them among the pleasures of life in the Imaginary Museum: something in language for a quick fix. As W. Jackson Bate has put it,

Like the giraffe, we were now living off the tops of the trees. The anthologized sections of the 'best' parts of only the 'best' poets were becoming our habitual diet, . . .

(1971, 75)

And we still go to lyric poems in the hope of getting a tasty cocktail of personal affects, contained in an elegant glass. Novels, on the other hand, are pastimes.

In Australian poetry, which is virtually all modern or at least post-Romantic, there have been two main postures of lyric poetry: there is a primary lyric, or poetry of pure self, which comes to us through Brennan, and a secondary lyric, in which self is articulated through a natural Other: this line passes through Slessor, our most fastidiously mimetic poet.

Brennan wrote of his aims thus in his essay, 'Fact and Idea':

Our negative consciousness of the infinite, the void, inane profundum has for emotional aspect the aspiration, or more than aspiration: I, the Human, ought to be there—to fill that void . . .

(1962, 10)

He wanted, no, he desperately needed, to put personality back into the symbolist project. So, although he could write brilliantly about Mallarmé, and was influenced by Mallarmé, his own project was quite different. In his grand scheme of narcissism, Ego could still redeem Infans, self turning out to be a virtually inexhaustible resource: both the mountain and its springs. Brennan's classic poem on this ground is his 1897 'Epilogue':

Deep in my hidden country stands a peak,
and none hath known its name
and none, save I, hath even skill to seek:
thence my wild spirit came.

Thither I turn, when the day's garish world
too long hath vex'd my sight,
and bare my limbs where the great winds are whirl'd
and life's undreaded might.

For there I know the pools of clearest blue,
glad wells of simple sooth,
there, steep'd in strength of glacier springs, renew
the lucid body of youth.

                . . . .

If any murmur that my 'sdainful hand
withholds its sacrifice
where ranged unto the Law the peoples stand,
let this blown word suffice:

The gift of self is self's most sacred right:
only where none hath trod,
only upon my secret starry height
I abdicate to God.

That all-important peak is not, as the critics of the 1950s were
fond of saying, *there*: it is nakedly a trope for the core of self, the
invaluable core. Coming down like Moses from this peak, the
visionary poet becomes an intermediary between 'the peoples'
and God. Not only does he put others in the place with his
peremptory 'let this blown word suffice' but he is also a blocking figure between them and the deity. in Brennan's sense of a
sacred role he strenuously exemplifies Arnold's inkling that
poetry was taking the place of religion; he is even willing to
nominate the terms on which he will abdicate (royalist verb)
to God. As with Emerson, the self either expands to fill the
universe or, perhaps more accurately, ingests the universe.

Many readers have found Brennan's diction to be a disappointment, a patchy drugget in which to deck out his shining
ambitions, but there can be no doubting the scope of his ambitions. We can glimpse their lineaments on one of his remarks
on Mallarmé, that adoptive fellow-spirit;

He was that rare poet—Keats, our most splendid possibility, was on
the way to become such—who possesses a poetic philosophy, a philosophy that is entirely poetry, a systematic body of imaginative thought
wherein reality is transposed, dissolved into pure light—

(1962, 281)

Brennan's successors were not willing to follow him, either in
this quest for a non-discursive philosophy or in his great Orphic
enterprise. FitzGerald backed off from what he saw as modernist irrationality at the onset of World War II; McAuley strug-
gled with Brennan for the course of one exciting book, *Under
Aldebaran*, and then chose to make sacred responsibility civic;
Hope turned away from his passionately subversive poems of
the 1940s, pulling the ladder up behind him with the aid of such
essays as 'The Discursive Mode' and 'The Middle Way'. Only
Francis Webb persisted in the narcissistic enterprise, under
God knows what compulsion and at enormous personal cost.
The further point should be made, that it is almost impossible to
imagine a woman poet being influenced by Brennan. Can one
imagine any woman rising to the expansive arrogance of that

final stanza, that trope which can be redefined as saying that God is the son of man, whose sacred self allows him to exist?

Slessor, far more influential upon those who have come after him, works at the other end of the poetic scale; he devises linguistic contraptions to replace any possible betrayal of self. In his stylish poetry God is dead (we are allowed to glimpse His decay in 'The Old Play') and things are eloquent, indeed numinous, because they can be seen vividly. His hunger for visible, tangible things is very much like that which Hillis Miller discerned in Hopkins:

> This way of seeing things is the origin of poetry. Instead of seeing an object as an example of an abstract category the poet must see it as if it had just been created, and then the depth of his being opens up to receive, in a flood of emotion, the being of the thing he sees.
>
> (1963, 321)

Such perceptionism is even more purely present in Slessor than in Hopkins, since the poet-priest had a weakening habit of diluting his sonnets in the sestet with some explicit conclusion about the Lord or the Holy Ghost. If Slessor has a parallel weakening impulse it is nothing more than the comic irony of Modernism. Perhaps he is a type of Keats's billiard ball: sensuous and perfectly secular.

Let us return to the question, whether the speaker/singer of a lyric poem can ever be seen as identical with the poet. One could simply say no, on the naive ground that texts are not people. But being more serious and accepting the cultural heritage of the textual contract, we can say that there is too much asserted ego in Brennan's poetry for us to find a self there; and rather too little in Slessor's, except in a few outstanding anthology pieces. We can find a recognizable self in David Campbell's poetry, in large measure because—as I shall argue in a later chapter—his way of life happily corresponded with themes which had been underwritten by traditional genres. In Judith Wright's poetry we can perceive a different kind of self again: dispersed, various, unegotistical and successively, even discursively interested in the same themes and problems which have preoccupied the historical Judith Wright.

Going one step further, we may see a different kind of disclosure of the poet's self in some recent Australian poetry: autobiographical telling. In *The Personal Element in Australian Poetry*, James McAuley argued that Lowell's *Life Studies* had been influential in this development: it certainly played its part, although this more explicit telling of the self-life is surely a nat-ural late development of the Wordsworthian tradition in which the growth of an individual life is seen for a source of value. In much of the poetry of Dorothy Hewett, Vincent Buckley and Robert Adamson, poetry is concerned with the relating of the self-life, a very different matter from the traditional lyric bal-ance between closure and disclosure. Marjorie Perloff, in her recent study, *The Dance of the Intellect*, sees Palgrave's anthol-ogizing taste as central to our inherited notion of the lyrical, pointing to the procedural directions in his Preface:

Lyrical has been here held essentially to imply that each Poem shall turn on some single thought, feeling or situation. In accordance with this, narrative, descriptive, and didactic poems—unless accompanied by rapidity of movement, brevity, and the colouring of human passion—have been excluded.

(1985, 177)

From such a canon any continuing autobiographical narrative would be excluded, unless it were broken up into short epiphanic instances in the manner of Adamson's *Where I Come From*. For the most part lyric does not resemble autobiography be-cause it lacks an interest in causation.

This brings us back to the very heart of lyric. Like Humeian philosophy, it disbelieves in the necessity of causal sequence. It disowns causation and, unlike Hume, replaces it with formal or aesthetic organization, tacitly laying claim to a correspon-dence between such form and our deep psychic structures. In the beginning was the word, and in literature's beginning, the lyric utterance. Andrew Taylor, discussing Judith Wright, points to the paradox built into such a claim:

But to long for the Word alone, the Logos alone, is to long to escape from language entirely, which means to escape from the whole con-stitution of human knowledge. Taken to an extreme, her longing for 'one truth in singleness' would entail either a pathological regres-sion to a prenatal preconsciousness or a move beyond language into a mysticism which brooks no discussion. In either case it would be a regressive move toward origin.

(1987, 97)

Lyric seeks to tap origin, whereas autobiography offers us a narrative of causes and effects, telling us a plausible self-story which links persent existence with origin. One of the very rare poems which bridges these antithetical aims is Hope's 'Ascent into Hell', where the 'regression to a prenatal consciousness' is accomplished through a lyrically telescoped narrative in which time has been reversed, as though the selective film of a life were played backward, fast. 'Ascent into Hell' is one of our central poems and in Palgrave's terms it has 'rapidity of movement' (hectically so, it might be said) along with 'the colouring of human passion', but I do not think he would have admitted this harsh regressional as lyric poetry.

For McAuley, on the other hand, the impersonality of lyric was a necessary defence of cultural verities, of a coherent public world, of rational scrutiny and control. Asserting, as he so strenuously did, the values of a natural order and a normal poetry, he was perplexed by the emphasis which modern poetry has placed on 'particular personal experience'. In *The Personal Element in Australian Poetry* he sought to come to terms with this outgrowth of romanticism and individualism, to rise musically above its threatening moral. Oh dear, yes, lyric must always be an amoral art form in the end.

So we come back to the crude question of what lyric poetry actually is, what relation it bears to the self who held the pen. In the end it remains incorrigibly tripartite or three-faced. First of all, it sound like the utterance of a particular person who sounds like the poet, and so the poetry itself feels personal: this effect might be related to Antony Easthope's remark that 'Typically in poetry the represented consists in the first place of an individual speaking'. Second, if it is any good it will appear to have been meticulously crafted, put together as a formal, impersonal object, cool as a Caro sculpture or a Grecian urn. Third, the lyric cannot be divested of the trappings or aura of the sacred which still attach to it, even late in the twentieth century. And its sacred quality is surely, among other things, impersonal, unless we still want to call upon that psychological short-circuiting device, the muse. For McAuley, interestingly, the muse was, among other things, the queen of secondary elaboration, able to 'spread her net across oblivion/ To catch the luminous incoming tide.'

In conclusion, nothing on earth—nothing of earth, can bespeak the paradoxes of lyric poetry more ravishingly than Neilson's 'May':

Shyly the silver-hatted mushrooms make
  Soft entrance through,
And undelivered lovers, half-awake,
  Hear noises in the dew.

Yellow in all the earth and in the skies,
  The world would seem
Faint as a widow mourning with soft eyes
  And falling into dream.

Up the long hill I see the slow plough leave
  Furrows of brown;
Dim is the day and beautiful: I grieve
  To see the sun go down.

But there are suns a many for mine eyes
  Day after day:
Delightsome in grave greenery they rise,
  Red oranges in May.

To discuss the poetic effect of naming colours would be another bag of tricks altogether, a green thought in a green shade.

6

That Second Body:
Allen Curnow's Progress

It is easy for me to remember when and where I first saw a poem by Allen Curnow. After my father came back from the War, back from his years in Asia early in 1946, he bought several copies of John Lehmann's *Penguin New Writing:* unusual objects in a household—flat-hold, rather—starved of modern poetry except for the narratives of Stephen Vincent Benet. In *Penguin New Writing* number twenty-seven, published in April of that year, there were some good modern poems. Three were by Louis Macneice and one of these three, 'Carrick Revisited', might fairly be regarded (to refine a suggestion of Peter Levi's) as the seed from which that rich crop of Ulster poetry has since sprung.

Another was a fine poem by Allen Curnow, his by now much-anthologized 'Landfall in Unknown Seas'.* Its curiously impersonal vocative opening seized the attention:

Simply by sailing in a new direction
You could enlarge the world.

Although this elegantly self-deporting public poem was clearly about New Zealand, I did not know that Curnow himself was a New Zealander. Nor did I even know that there were New Zealand writers. Not that I assumed there were not: it was just that in those days of centripetal empire I did not think of New Zealand at all, except for geography which we had carefully learned at school. If it comes to that, for a long time I knew of no Canadian writers except Leacock and C. G. D. Roberts, no South Africans except Olive Schreiner.

---

* I had no way of knowing then that 'Landfall in Unknown Seas' had already been published in Curnow's 1943 volume, *Sailing or Drowning*. It seems that John Lehmann regarded previous New Zealand publication as no impediment to the appearance of a poem in England.

When I turned back to Curnow's poetry in the mid-fifties, beguiled by the great moa and by the bounding lyricism of 'Wild Iron', there was no need to flip a special Kiwi switch in readerly production, no call for inter-dominion adjustments, since he was already assimilated to a generation of poetry which was appealing to me strongly: that of Macneice, Auden, Bernard Spencer, Empson, and Sidney Keyes. Looking back at the poems collected in *Island and Time* (1941) and *Sailing or Drowning* (1943), one can now find much that was written *by* the early forties, in a sense that is not dishonourable or reductive: we all have to get our bag of tricks from somewhere. History does not remain passive when there are texts being produced.

Curnow's most derivatively thirties utterance is to be found in 'Dialogue of Island and Time', where his syntax gets itself caught in Audenesque cramps along with the flying line-endings of adverbial *sdrucciola*:

The third and fourth generations
Begin to speak differently
Suffering mutations,
Cannot help identity

But the Audenesque is far more spryly used in 'It Is Too Late' from the same volume, used to confront the beginning of the Japanese war with elastic rhymes and the quickness of short lines. One thing Curnow had yet to do was to move from the shepherding of plural, often abstract, nouns to the delineation of singular objects like those in the alarming catalogue, 'Baldachin, black umbrella, bucket with a hole/ drizzled horizon, sleazy drape', where metonymy leaps with all the grandeur of metaphor.

In early to middle Curnow we can see much of the then-common enterprise of assimilating late-Yeats: dialogues, choruses and large announcements; an interest in experimentally plucking available verse forms, including sonnets, quatrains, ode stanzas (in 'The Scene'), free verse, and even pantoums; and an unpastoral interest in the expressive possibilities of hardish landscapes.

By the 1943 volume Curnow was beginning to show signs of a more pervasive irony, a sardonic long view of possibilities:

Between you and the South an older enmity
Lodged in the searching mind, that would not tolerate

So huge a hegemony of ignorance

Awkward but interesting; apart from a proleptic use of that
nowadays cant term, 'hegemony', this already shows affinities with the play of wry, shouldering polysyllables in 'Moro
Assassinato', another slant on the harshness of history from
twenty-five years later:

Normality was the moment's
mixture, moment by moment
improvising myself,
ideas, sensations, among them
the lacquered acridities
of ducted air in the car,

One can readily see why some readers have found Curnow's
delivery to be cold or abstracted, but such a judgement seems to
me merely to account for surface, and not always for that.

The polysyllables that began to flourish in *Sailing or
Drowning* were taking the place of a theolog's elemental mono-
syllables, Curnow having been in fact a theology student in
Auckland for a couple of years in the early 1930s. The early
poems are chocked together from such rudimentary building
blocks: eyes, cold, stars, blood, light, soul, dry, Christ. But he
had come to see the inflexibility of these materials and had
fallen into his generation. For may we not by now think of a
generation which held their art in place by fastidious linguistic
fingering: Auden, Empson, Macneice, Elizabeth Bishop, F. T.
Prince, Slessor, and sometimes Hope? All had been released
by Yeats and Eliot from the declared self; all were fond of
impersonal forms of syntax; all could have written, 'Blood from
a conundrum: insoluble but endlessly/Amusing in the attempt'.
The heritage is foregrounded by the title of Curnow's 'Spring
1942', which resembles 'Sept. 1, 1939',* which in turn derives
from 'Easter 1916'.

Another interesting development in Curnow's poetry during
the war decade is to be seen and heard in his expressive use of
rather heavy enjambments, like these in the first stanza of
'Dunedin':

---

* It has not been noted that Auden's famous/notorious poem reappeared during
the war with a new title, later discarded. In Tambimuttu's anthology *Poetry in
Wartime* (1943) it was entitled 'September 1 1941'.

Is it window or mirror the enormous
Deforming glass propped on horizons here?
What did we see? Some town pinched in a pass
Across which stares perpetual startled sheer
Vacuous day, the kind blind wilderness,
Space put behind bars, face pushed too near:

We may see this kind of muscle-flexing versification as a staging-post on the way to the easily colloquial enjambments and waterfall lines of late Curnow: to that unbuttoned style which has reached its extreme in section VIII of 'Organo ad Libitum', from Curnow's 1982 collection.

Poems 1949–57 show some further turning points, a swerving away notably from the authoritative iambic epigrams which lie down together in the sonnets of the two previous books ('Each day makes clear a statement to the next'; 'Unhurt, there is no help for her who wakens'; 'Transport is licensed somewhere at the top'; 'This you suppose is what goes on all day'). Although such well-trodden pentametric neatness of mind was loosening up through run-on and heavy caesura in *At Dead Low Water*, readers must have rejoiced in the new formal freedoms, the range of shaping, that were to be found in Curnow's 1957 volume. Heaven knows how any particular creative imagination goes about its work, but we may think wonderingly about the fact that this volume preceded a virtual silence of fifteen years, a silence which looked at the time like the drying-up so common in creative artists once they have exhausted their first barrel of goods: the middle years' syndrome, indeed.

'Some burn damp faggots, others may consume/ The entire combustible world in one small room', Yeats declared, and it is certainly the case that poets of distinction tend to fall into two categories or life-curves: most burn up their talents quickly (a trope not included in Jesus's parable), but a few like Hardy or Yeats himself—and we take this for a mark of peculiar distinction of character—go on developing new artistic strengths into their old age. All honour to Curnow, then, who could emerge from his silence to sail on into his seventies by way of four truly impressive books of poetry. He survives amongst us, having out-lived such turbulent younger incendiaries as Dylan Thomas, Lowell, Jarrell, Berryman, and Baxter. Not merely endures, but survives.

To return to that curious threshold, the 1957 collection: here almost every poem was a fresh protean enterprise, whether into short couplets, half-rhymed quatrains, long stanzas, the broken alliterative measures of 'The Changeling', the Pindaric ode become elegy ('In Memory of Dylan Thomas'), a shrinking suite in honour of Wallace Stevens, and one lonely self-subverting sonnet of vivaciously springy step and turn:

> To introduce the landscape to the language
> Here on the spot, say that it can't be done
> By kindness or mirrors or by talking slang
> With a coast accent. Sputter your pieces one
>
> By one like wet matches you scrape and drop.
> ('To Introduce the Landscape')

The mixed diction of this sonnet also ventures far out beyond those proverb-forging habits of the late 1930s and early 1940s, years of what G. Rostrevor Hamilton called 'the tell-tale article'. Here is room in a once-colourless writer for such mandarin colourations as 'Ponderous pine wagging his windsopped brushes/Daubs Latin skies upon Chinese lagoons'. We are following a self-inventing poet who has moved far out from those modest beginnings fairly characterized by C. K. Stead when he wrote, 'Mr. Curnow, one feels, was never chosen by the Muse'.

Trees, Effigies, Moving Objects of 1972 introduces what we may call late-Curnow, whose nimble poems inhabit a post-Stevens, post-Wittgenstein and, as people are so fond of saying these days, post-modernist climate. They belong to a word-world, they textualize themselves, they joke about their own acts of mimesis, and they are manifest descendants of 'He Cracked a Word' and 'To Introduce the Landscape', poems which were already subverting the claims of perceptionism. Indeed, we may say that just as Curnow has become more and more skilled at memorable mimesis he has come to build into his poetry disavowals of the linguistic possibility of mimesis:

> A wood god botherer stands
> not fifty feet from his own
> door, calls trees by name.
>
> *Speak up we can't hear you.*

This line, the way of disenchanting landscapes and disclaiming the romantic religion of natural perception takes us on into the

leapfrog syntax of a far more complicated poem from Curnow's
most recent collection:

as you recline bare-armed looking
up the spongy firmament has begun
drizzling the paper's getting wet

put the pen down go indoors
the wind bloweth as it listeth or listeth
not there's evidently something
up there and the thing is the spirit

whistle for it wait for it
one moment the one that's one too
many is the glassiest calm an
'intimate question' for the asking.
                    ('The Weather in Tohunga Crescent')

In the work of a poet who has long adhered to the regional
against the so-called claims of the universal, a poet who has
stood for the 'local and special', these circumlocutions are hard-
won. In a very young poet syntax like this might well sound
smart or trendy; in Curnow this writing is a very late point in a
long process of renunciations in the course of which the poet
has become less and less shaman or god-botherer, and his
writings more and more provisional. The poems declare themselves to be products of a poetic tradition, of our language
games, even of print culture itself. Let me cite an especially
subversive, self-dismantling stanza from the 1982 volume, *You
will know when you get there*:

Absently the proof-reader corrects the
typesetter. According to copy
the word is exotic. He cancels
the literal r and writes an x.

All this might suggest that Curnow is no more than the lapsed
theolog turned into intellectual sceptic, that he who once believed in the fall of man now believes in little more than the
collapse of the signifier. A reading of the last four volumes of
his poetry (and I shall say nothing of his plays here) will show
that this is far from the case. His poems continue to be full of
that old-fashioned ingredient, subject-matter. As I observed
in a review of *You will know when you get there*, his striving
for intense mimesis of natural objects has grown stronger and
stronger. He strains his lines after the evanescent physical
experience, as in

```
   or ten summers
later the long breath held
   bursting under-
water in Corsair Bay
   and breaking
surface from the deep green
   dive,
              the breathless
exhalation tweaking
   the neck,
```

even if he can also turn to parodying the appeal back to fact and experience, as he does in the opening of 'A Window Frame':

```
This paper is eleven and three-quarter
inches long, eight and one quarter inches
wide, this table four feet five inches long,
thirty-two inches wide, this room
twelve feet square, this house one
thousand square feet,
```

But this is a poetry which continues to lay claim to wind, water, cloud, trees, timber, steel, traffic, and household objects, even in the very same poems in which the acknowledged limits of language keep beating the claim down.

More than this, Curnow's recent poetry continues to be strong on subject matter in a larger, looser sense of that phrase: the man in the street's sense. The two long sequences around which *An Incorrigible Music* is structured dramatize and explore assassinations: those of Giuliano de' Medici and Aldo Moro. They are in a sense echoed by 'Dichtung und Wahrheit', another murder poem, even though it derives from a fiction. Knife, gun, sacrifice, and death recur, Isaac-wise, through the seven other shorter, non-dramatic poems in *An Incorrigible Music* to the point where even the moon is described as 'cutting it fine', or to where a quaint bump of syntax produces the line, 'Millions die miserably never before their time'. This poetry is absorbed by what Anthony Hecht once called 'the place of pain in the universe'.

As well as the place of pain, there are the pains and pleasures of place. Curnow's concern with region, with rootedness and with the Adamic naming of antipodean phenomena were well known as early as the 1940s. Not only did he evince his appetite for locality on particular poems; he spoke to the cause again and again in essays and introductions, slamming the loose term, 'universal', and even going so far as to assert, 'I wanted to place New Zealand at the centre, the only possible place'. And his excellent *Penguin Book of New Zealand Verse* (1960) might be seen as a deliberate verbal mapping of a place in time.

In Curnow's most recent verse this passion for a particular location reasserts itself, although by now it is less New Zealand as phenomenon than familiar bits of coast, bay, suburb, recorded and rendered lovingly: in the process, a new joyousness makes itself felt in the poetry, the syntax becoming not merely subversive or provisional but downright jaunty. If one expects chill, hardening or sloppiness in an old man's poetry, the creative buoyancy of 'You Get What You Pay For' and 'The Parrots at Karekare' will come as a remarkable surprise. Not only are they as tautly written as anything that the poet has ever done but they have about them an air which I would call, at the risk of sentimentality, falling in love with life all over again. Their crisp phrasing combines a sense of delight with a nimble spirit of inquiry: place and time elicit the leaps of self. Language lives in the body.

Curnow is in his late seventies, and I shall make no attempt to predict what he might still do, but the excited intelligence of his recent poetry, its joy in rootedness, directs me back to a comment he made years ago, which may serve as an epigraph to his own work:

Santayana somewhere calls a man's native country 'a kind of second body'. A writer's vision may be said, I believe, to be mediated through that second body, in some sense analogous to the mediation of his personal body and the agonizing limitation of his private individuality.

7

Squatter Pastoral

David Campbell is one of those Australian writers—among his compeers are Judith Wright, John Manifold, Geoffrey Dutton, Mary Durack and Patrick White—who have come from the squatting class. It could be said that this class background, this spatial identity, allows the writer to take on both a stronger sense of social self and a firmer sense of his/her own place in the forest of genres. Such assurance about writing a self marks almost all of Campbell's work.

Let us approach Campbell's writing by juxtaposing a small poem and a passage of prose taken from one of the *Evening under Lamplight* stories. Set thus side by side they might only serve to demonstrate the difference in manners between poetry and prose, between musical contraction and loose-limbed metonymy; but they seem to me to have serious qualities in common, affinities which run deeper than a mere pleasure in creekside nakedness.

One is the lyric, 'Summer Comes with Colour', and it is a cavalier song full of luminous associationism:

Summer comes with colour,
The wheat turns yellow
And in globes of light
Hares lope through the stubble.

Where in shimmer to their knees
The trees cut their losses
And forgetting cold reason
Strip as gold as goddesses,

Give us such ease.   0
My blue-eyed lover,
Why should your beauty
Alone hide in coverings?

Here by the riverside
The bindweed invite you,
And what more do you need
Than this light about you?

The other is a section of the second story in *Evening under Lamplight* (1959; 1987). Elsie is the maid on the station owned by Dr Dalrymple, father of the three children. (In the original book, published in 1959, the name of the family was Graham, the father, Colonel Graham. In *Flame and Shadow* (1976) he becomes the Doctor, perhaps to help explain why he spends so much time in his study, a strand of some narrative importance.) Proprieties are so strictly observed that we have already been informed that Elsie is only taking the children swimming because their governess is on holiday. She is, of course, fully clad. (Well, perhaps not 'of course'.) The romantically creekside settings encourage comparison:

Billy dated Bert's fall from favour from the day Mr. Blake appeared on horseback above the creek bank.

'Ah!' said Blake from the sky. 'Having a picnic, I see.'

The effect was immediate.

Elsie sprang scarlet from the arms of the willow like a startled lover; and Janet, who had ruled for that day that bathing with nothing on was allowed, streaked for her towel and stood with it to her lips, screened from Blake while remaining naked to the rest of the world.

'It's all right, said Billy, sloshing upstream. 'It's only Mr. Blake.'

'Only!' hissed Janet. 'It's all your fault, Billy. You're always wanting to take your clothes off; and you look disgusting.'

But Mr. Blake was quite at ease, heeling his horse down the side bank and clattering through the water.

'Mind if I join you?' he said. 'Couldn't eat my lunch. Like concrete.'

Mr. Blake was the jackeroo. He had arrived a month ago under a cloud, following a telegram that read: Delayed. Expect Me Thursday's Train. Love, Blake.

'Love!' their father said. 'Love! His expectations for the next half year are dagging wethers.'

But Blake explained that some girl had sent the telegram, a friend of his sister; bought a pipe and a fast motor-bike, and looked about him.

Now, on the sand, mouth full of scone, he repeated, 'Just like concrete! How that cook makes bread like that I don't know. It's her art.'

'Oh . . . Emmy,' Elsie simpered, pouring tea. 'She's too busy fooling around with Sol to think about bread.'

Billy stared hard at Elsie, for Emmy did not fool around with anyone, unless it were God. And Blake was up sharp on his elbow, staring too.

'No!' he said. 'Not our Emmy? I don't believe it.'

Elsie flushed, as well she might, but she managed airily, 'Oh, you've go to keep your eyes open.'

Mr. Blake's eyes were very wide open, gold as the eyes of a fox; and then they narrowed into laughter.

'Well the old trout!' he said. 'I thought she died years ago.'

'Oh, you've got to get up early,' Elsie said; 'or late, in this case.'

Billy noticed that Mr. Blake's laughter came out like the tea from the thermos: the sound started at his lips and then went deeper.

'Still a kick in the tail!' he cried. 'Elsie, you're a discovery!'

He was still staring at Elsie, who was laughing too, her eyes running off merrily amongst the teacups and then returning, delighted with her lie.

'Elsie!' snapped Janet, coming fully clothed and haughty from behind the willow. 'Watch the tea. You're pouring it all over the scones.'

But Mr. Blake's laughter won the day, and soon they were all making fun of Emmy except Janet, and Elsie forgot to crook her little finger from the cup and kept offering their scones to Mr. Blake.

'Go on,' she said. 'They'll do you good.'

Mr. Blake ate them and Elsie smiled. It was a strange broad smile for the world in general; but when it met Mr. Blake's she coloured up slowly, as if he had surprised her getting undressed.

'Well, well,' said Blake, stretching and rising, 'now I know where the good tucker is.'

And he cantered off with the reins so tight that old Kismet reared and side-stepped like a two-year-old.

(1976, 17–19)

What the two passages of language have especially in common is ease. In both language affects not to be mannered, as though there were no gap between nature and consciousness, no syntactical strain required to modulate between Eros, hares and horses. Admittedly the poem, not being webbed in social comedy, foregrounds its gestures more, especially in that tiny sentence at its centre or hinge, 'Give us such ease': after which the sexual invitation begins.

Both are, I suggest, extremely polished, dare I say sophisticated, pieces of writing, but both conceal this in a laconic naturalness of manner which looks casual. In the poem, consider the Shaw Neilsonesque first line, 'Summer comes with colour', and the throwaway economic trope in 'The trees cut their losses'. In the story, look at how slyly one word of boyish whimsy in Mr. Blake's telegram both sounds quite inappropriate and proleptically signals his later misdemeanours; or at the oddly naive metaphors from rural life which characterize the children's view of him: his 'eyes were very wide open, gold as the eyes of a fox' and, a few lines further on, 'Billy noticed that Mr. Blake's laughter came out like the tea from the thermos: the sound started at his lips and then went deeper.' In each case the diction is so plain that you have to pull yourself up hard to spot how cunning Campbell has been. How simple it all seems.

Such freshness in the administration of pastoral situations implies a distinctive ability to renew what might be rural commonplaces or romantic commonplaces: implies, indeed, the tact of a poet whose pastorals stand as far as could be from Samuel Johnson's complaint about pastoral in 'Lycidas' being 'easy, vulgar, and therefore disgusting,' such writing engages us as fluent, convincing, and therefore artful.

There is a peculiar serenity, a lyrical plainness of style, which is also the expression of region and occupation, that frequently marks, indeed distinguishes David Campbell's writing. To this style or tone there could be given the title, squatter pastoral. We should look further at its characteristics in Campbell's poetry, especially in the earlier poetry, and in that suite of short stories, *Evening under Lamplight* (1959). Let me add that he seems the finest practitioner of this mode, and that he brought to it, as it brought to him, possibilities of a peculiar kind of lyrical certainty and poise.

In placing the poet in his poems, it is worth pursuing the idea of squatter pastoral, inquiring into its origins and affinities, and tracing some of its particular characteristics in Campbell's books, he having been the writer who in my opinion produced the genre at its purest and most ravishing. Let me put some of the eating of the pudding before the proof and cite a Campbell lyric which deploys the genre, or sub-genre, most clearly. In this vein we could look at poems which flaunt their pastoral lineage explicitly like 'Cocky's Calendar', with its immediate echo of Spenser's *Shepheardes Calender*, or that double-voiced recension of Raleigh, 'Come Live with Me', but we can find a subtler, prime example in 'Song for the Cattle':

Down the red stock route
Hock-deep in mirage
Rode the three black drovers
Singing to the cattle.

And with them a young woman,
Perhaps some squatter's daughter

From homestead or township,
Who turned her horse easily.

To my mind she was as beautiful
As the barmaid in Brewarrina
Who works at the Royal. Men
Ride all day to see her.

Fine-boned as a brigalow
Yet ample as a granary,
She has teeth good for laughing
Or biting an apple.

I'm thinking of quitting
My mountain selection,
The milking at morning
And the lonely axe-echoes;

Of swapping my slab hut
For a rolled-up blanket
And heading north-westward
For a life in the saddle—

For the big mobs trailing
Down the empty stock routes,
A horned moon at evening
And songs round the campfire.

Yes, I'll soon be drinking
At the Royal in Brewarrina
And ambling through mirage
With the squatter's daughter.

It could be objected that the speaker or singer of this fine ballad
offers himself as selector rather than squatter, but I do not feel
that this dramatic fiction really bends the mode at all. Indeed, it
is surely typical of pastoral to take for persons and personae
simple swains, shepherdesses, sweaty nymphs or hayseeds, yet
to locate their songs in what are implicitly very well run, harmonious estates. Even the landscape backgrounds of Poussin
and Claude Lorrain tend on examination to look pleasantly
grazed and very selectively wooded (savannahs with invisible
landlords, one might say); and Marvell's mowers, however they
may be offered as bemusedly lovelorn, measure their amorous
disorder against 'sweet Fields' and 'these Medows fresh and
gay': a landscape of prosperous grazing land. As Paul Shepard
has argued in *Man and the Landscape*, the aesthetics of successfully grazed landscapes have entered deeply into our conceptual

preferences. As for this poem, the ease of squattocracy is transferred to the young woman, and the tropes of class and style are slyly inverted so that the admiring comparison can declare

To my mind she was as beautiful
As the barmaid in Brewarrina
Who works at the Royal. Men
Ride all day to see her.

The pastoral mode is, in the last resort, a kind of synecdoche: the pains, labours, fears and mortgages of rural life (or those of life in general) get reduced to a slumbrous sheepcote, a sunlit paddock or a sequestered interval of rural music. In 'Song for the Cattle' the horseback life of drovers is diminished in complexity to 'the red stock route/ Hock deep in mirage' and 'the big mobs trailing/ Down the empty stock routes': no sweat. As well as being called a song, the poem refers to songs at its beginning and end. In sum, it combines all manner of key figures of pastoral distillation: rural harmony, glimpses of work, sexual attention, music—and drinking. Like several other Campbell poems, this adds an Australian figure to the traditional cast of pastoral song: the barmaid, envisaged as a natural addition to the resurrected golden age.

   It was over several centuries that pastoral, with mixed classical origins, spun itself out in English literature. We are not concerned with pastoral drama, nor much with pastoral romance, a sub-genre that can not be said to have much of a run in the English language despite Sidney's *Arcadia*. a much-praised, little-read book that has, by and large, been filleted for its poems: as far as a general sense of pastoral has filtered down in English it has surely come by way of poetry, through pastoral elegy, pastoral eclogue and pastoral lyric.

   Apart from its being grassy and stylishly sheepish, what can we say about pastoral mode, as we receive it? Certainly whatever is meant by the title of Wordsworth's *Michael: A Pastoral Poem* is *not* what we are concerned with here, since Wordsworth is bitterly and deliberately subverting the genre in that poem, putting paid to the *camera obscura* which could still refract world-pain into a serene, harmonious picture. The roots we seek are in a more traditional field, especially in the early seventeenth century. And above all in lyric poetry.

   The definition of the genre which titillates me most is that of

William Empson, that most bull-headedly original of modern critics. He puts the matter, brusquely enough, like this in *Some Versions of Pastoral:*

> The essential trick of the old pastoral, which was felt to imply a beautiful relation between rich and poor, was to make simple people express strong feelings (felt as the most universal subject, something fundamentally true about everybody) in learned and fashionable language (so that you wrote about the best subject in the best way). From seeing the two sorts of people combined like this you thought better of both; the best parts of both were used. The effect was in some degree to combine in the reader or author the merits of the two sorts; he was made to mirror in himself more completely the effective elements of the society he lived in. This was not a process that you could explain in the course of writing pastoral; it was already shown by the clash between style and theme, and to make the clash work in the right way (not become funny) the writer must keep up a firm pretence that he was unconscious of it. Indeed the usual process for putting further meanings into the pastoral situation was to insist that the shepherds were rulers of sheep, and so compare them to politicians or bishops or what not; this piled the heroic convention onto the pastoral one, since the hero was another symbol of his whole society. Such a pretence no doubt makes the characters unreal, but not the feeling expressed or even the situation described; the same pretence is often valuable in real life.

(1960, 11–12)

Admittedly this definition comes from a chapter entitled 'Proletarian Literature' but it will help us none the less with squatter pastoral, in which the selector can dream of squatter's daughters, bar-maids are merrily rusticated, open air nakedness is easy, and even drovers or shearers can have expectations of a *fête champêtre*, as Campbell's deliberate revision of Giorgione asserts.

The Giorgione poem is relevant at this point because it does in fact 'imply a beautiful relation between rich and poor', insisting in its opening lines on a hierarchical order ranging from two graziers down to a distant shepherd, but sliding easily to the claim that the elegantly naked young women—appropriate playthings of the graziers—display a loveliness which 'is commonplace/To drovers summering in the south.' Pastoral dissolves class-envy, in short; or to put it another way, Eros sublimates class-envy. All enters into what Leonie Kramer has called 'relatedness':

THE PICNIC

This is what picnicking is for.
Giorgione understood the scene:
A distant shedhand, flutes and wine,
Two graziers, and in the fore-
Ground such young women as Dior
Might dream of, if they had not been
So elegantly naked, seen
One from the side and one before.
Their loveliness is commonplace
To drovers summering in the south
And where's the man to take offence
At such delights of form and face
Even if you should give your mouth
To me in wanton innocence?

Not that Campbell's forte is to make simple people use 'learned and fashionable language', but rather to admit them to an exotic democracy of lucid lyrical utterance and full-sounding rhymes. And the language to which Eros is thus admitted has at the end the demeanour of the English seventeenth century, that rich field of lyric poems with a pastoral demeanour: the last four lines sound as though they could easily have come from Herrick or Carew or Suckling. The demure oxymoron which ends this poem might be seen as itself defining the climate of pastoral.

Let me add another observation here. Where sexuality in most kinds of narrative is the prime source of conflict, of dynamic confusion, in pastoral poetry the truth is that sexuality is part of the harmony: it is as though Adam and Eve had never fallen. With Campbell it should be noted that Eros performs rather differently in the verse and in the stories. In his poems even natural objects teach amorous lessons, lessons about harmony and relatedness.

Empson's proclaimed blending of the hierarchical and the democratic also runs through—indeed, gives structure to—the decalogue of stories which make up *Evening under Lamplight*. The characters have precise social status, from the squatter-cum-doctor and his wife, through manager, governess, jackeroo, a blacksmith who doubles as carpenter, stationhand, cook, and maid. But a peculiar social tranquillity which we can associate with the miniature scale of this community allows these ranks to feel almost democratic, quite matey. Two other factors help to enforce this amiably open social climate, this up-country branch line from the Golden Age.

One of these factors is the gentle dsturbance of love, felt as Marshall, the manager, flirts circumspectly with the doctor's wife and then is led to find his proper place at the comedy's end married to Miss Frost, the governess. Although Blake forgets himself and his due place, getting the maid pregnant, so that he has to be expelled from the festive circle, a suitable husband is found for Elsie, and the last story focuses on a christening party and the non-arrival of the Holy Ghost. While sexuality, as we might expect, stirs the calm surface of days and kicks the plot along, sexual love remains, as so often in Campbell's writing, a benign influence, even salvific. Despite the light of spry comedy that falls on the Dalrymple's household and property, their domain shares in the sense of love's magical power to harmonize the universe that we find asserted in the first stanza of 'Who Points the Swallow':

Love who points the swallow home
And scarves the russet at his throat,
Dreaming in the needle's eye,
Guide us through the maze of glass
Where the forceful cannot pass
With your silent clarity.

In looking at the over-pattern of *Evening under Lamplight* we might also notice how it is infiltrated by forces that do not belong to the daylight world, or at least by suggestions of such forces: much as pastoral was traditionally able to reflect the religious dimension as well as the secular, drawing its implications via the pastoral pursuits of the Greek gods, the rustic imagery of the Old Testament, and of course the emblematic figure of Christ, the Good Shepherd. While the supernatural element is much diminished in Campbell, it still faintly frames the narrative. Thus the first story begins with Billy riding the nighthorse home in darkness and it is not till the second page that we are sure that 'nighthorse' is a term more substantial than its seeming equivalent, 'nightmare'. In other stories the two elder children, Billy and Janet, are apprehensive about ghosts in the night. And in the final story a modern clergyman denies the literal significance of 'the descent of the dove', but Billy finishes by intuiting the Holy Spirit's descent upon some people, while not on others. Through the vision of children, itself a kind of pastoral simplicity, secular bounds prove capable of extension. And we have known from early on, after he has pissed on a tombstone, that Billy has a healthy fear of God.

The question arises, where did the squatter mode come from. I can offer some strands towards an answer, if not a conclusive argument. Those who have grown up in grazier's families do not automatically acquire the power to plug in directly to a pastoral tradition in literature. But there are directions in which they might well turn for influence.

There were the ballads of 'Banjo' Paterson, for instance, himself a Monaro man and loosely pastoral, at least, in his rollicking narratives. We know that John Manifold, scion of a Western District squatting family, was a lifelong admirer of Paterson, and Rodney Hall's biography of Manifold makes plain how strong his influence on Campbell must have been when they met up as students at Cambridge in 1935. Manifold, Hall tells us, was by then writing ballads on Australian subjects, Campbell having already turned to the ballad in his undergraduate writing. The writing of new bush ballads would have been one track leading into squatter pastoral.

It has frequently crossed my mind to ask how much Campbell would have known about Ethel Anderson's work. It would be very strange indeed if he had not read some at least of the poems which she published in *Squatter's Luck, with other Bucolic Eclogues* (1942). Not only was this a very distinctive book, but Anderson was deliberately pioneering new—which is to say old—modes for Australian verse. As she wrote in her preface to the second edition,

It is still my aim to perform for Australia the service the Nature poets, following a classical tradition, have done for England . . .

Some of the verses . . . spring from my desire to bring the bucolic pleasantries of Virgil and Theocritus to this new land. And Virgil is nearer to us than might be guessed. A countryman lately said to me, 'The ewes were not bearing, so I put the dog in the paddock. He chased them around at midday—that did the trick.' This is Virgil's advice.

(1954)

She went further with this vein, depicting in one of the Bucolic Eclogues a character called Mariana who has tried to conduct her own farming on the advice given in Virgil's *Georgics*! As a poet, Ethel Anderson was less assured than

Campbell or Manifold, more easily given to kinds of learned charm which can shade over into whimsy at the drop of a hat, but hers is one of the most eccentric voices in all our writing. Here is one of her several exchanges between her principal rustic swains, Eustace and Silas, and an old character called Ike Peachey. The long, swaybacked rhythms are marvellously managed:

BLONDE wheat. Lapis-lazuli sky, and umpteen candle-power
     sunlight.
Flocks of galahs in the grass. Flamingoes along the lagoons.
('Sweet as a strand of her hair,' dreams Eustace, 'the wind
     in the wilgas.')
Silas is spraying a silo; Eustace dips corn-sacks; the weevil
          —Wee Willie Weevil—the evil they intend to ex-
          terminate.

'Fifty Corriedale four-tooths, which were shorn at the Rocky
     Point shed,
Yielded an excellent average,' says Silas, 'of three hundred
     ounces,'
Then Eustace: 'At Dulla Dulla a ram twelve months in the
     wool, Si,
Gave twenty-five pounds.' 'At Carcoar, a pure-bred Corrie-
     dale cull
          Nineteen.' 'At Cardagga, quadruplets were dropped
          by a cross ewe.'

'The sire was a Corriedale?' 'Yes.' 'A 'ogget at Tumbi
     Umbi,'
Says Ike (who does not believe this tale of miraculous lambs)
'Gave birth to er litters er Tamworths; 'e wer a Corriedale,
     too
—Wher's 'e off now?'—of Eustace, who has a date with a
     damsel;
          'I'm off to buy Corriedales, Ike, If I'm guaranteed
          quadruplets!'

Some comparisons, or contrasts, with Campbell spring to mind. One lies in the breed of diction being used: Anderson's habit, indeed the source of a lot of her fun, involves cheerfully mixing up different kinds of diction, high or low, art and paddock, elaborate and simple. Campbell, as we have already noted, employs a very simple, seemingly homogeneous diction, deriving its clarity as much from late-Yeats (who was still in full production when the Australian went to Cambridge) as from any other literary source. Anderson gets her comedy from the kinds of disparity she foregrounds: in her work we encounter Empson's 'clash between style and theme'. In Campbell it is as though the imagination has already done part of its work on experience, so that the poems have merely to sing a world in which squatters, drovers and barmaids exist harmoniously in a *fête champêtre*, in which they can go about their work without getting mud on their boots or slops on their blouses.

James McAuley in *A Map of Australian Verse* strenuously denies that Campbell wrote literary pastoral (except in a few earlier poems, which he sniffs at) and cites the poet's own remark, 'I do not think of myself as a pastoral poet'. This comes from an impish introduction to the 1973 *Selected Poems* in which Campbell went directly on to say 'a poet thinks with the images nearest to him'. But where is near, for a writer, a text-maker? Do images come from literature or from raw life? The door swings to and fro.

At this point one might well come back to Douglas Stewart's early trope: can a pastoralist write pastoral? Unlike Anderson, and unlike such offspring of squatting families as Manifold, Judith Wright and Patrick White, Campbell returned to the land, to grazing, to being a squatter. The relevant images remained 'near to him'. But the hurley-burley of a grazier's life continued to be refined, harmonized, eroticized in the manner to which I have given the appellation, squatter pastoral. Variations of this lyrical genre pass down through 'Droving', with its lovely image of the cattle as 'The flower-fat mob', through the boisterous 'Chansons Populaires'. In *Deaths and Pretty Cousins* (1975) the vein is thinning out, yielding to poems of ironic or even minute observation. But it still makes itself heard in 'Serranilla', 'Two Song with Spanish Burdens', 'Descent to Brindabella' and in a small poem which is surely its pure distillation, 'Hairbell':

Hairbells like punched out
Pieces of sky leaving
Starshaped spyholes,
Nipples of Aphrodite.

Hairbells I set in
Your softer than touch hair,
Blue snow on the crest
Of your mount of Venus.

And naked we walked where
The hills were breasts and
Your breasts bare hills
Astonishingly round.

When we lay together
Your eyes were blue
Hairbells, madonna
Of the moment's paradise.

To see 'the moment's paradise' embodied in the world around him, to find that world at once erotic and at peace, to sing its peculiar stillness, these were David Campbell's great gifts. And the assurance with which he made poetry and prose out of such imaginative priorities argues a very sophisticated art on his part: an astute craftsmanship that didn't just fall off the back of a horse.

8

Vincent Buckley and the Poetry of Presence

The story I have to tell is one episode or one phase in the long history of the desacralization of lyric poetry. As such, it is a story of resistance. We can read it as an episode in macro-history, in mezzohistory or in microhistory. When we think about Australian cultural consciousness in the post-War years, we may well choose to read it at the mezzohistorical level, but I will try to locate the issues in question within larger and smaller mental gardens.

On the largest scale, we are intersecting with a long process of secularization and demystification of those miniature texts characterized by their intense verbal music, those texts which we call lyric poetry, or often, more simply, poetry. This combination of words and the lyre, words and the drum, words and the music sticks, words and the tribal dance, stands in a shadowy way behind each modern lyric poet; poets as private and print-bound as Mallarmé or Ashbery are still laying claim to a privileged space for their little texts because of the tradition which they continue to evoke in swerving away from it, a tradition which goes back to the Orphic mysteries and to nameless tribes far beyond, a tradition which continues to inscribe itself in those lingering names, ballad, sonnet, ode, song, chorus, canto and so on. Although the inner light of Protestant faith became in time the inner light of romantic self-scrutiny (and, even later, the prismatic inner lights of the post-symbolist poem, which guiltily dismantles the authority of each of its own mimetic gestures in succession), the short poem continues to demand privilege and power, almost on the basis of the white space which surrounds it on the page. Closure and white surrounding space are signals of lyric authority just as clearly in the ending of John Forbes's linguistically sceptical 'A Loony Tune' ('As the clear air breathes a big Hullo/Echoed by the bodies

turning over below.') as they are around the fullness of a poem
by Gwen Harwood or Vincent Buckley.

But in my very naming of these three poets, the two elder so
strongly contrasted with the self-dissolving Forbes I move to
the mezzohistorical scale of my argument, generated by a clash
between two streams of Australian poetic theory over the past
twenty years; or, more accurately, by two streams of poetic
practice and the occasional billabongs of attendant theory. The
phenomenon represented by 'A Loony Tune' sets itself at
almost every turn to dismantle the syntax of mimesis, while
even naming the island of Crete is no more than an experiential
bell-wether, a phoney signification. So much for its stylistic
category. But why is the text thus? First of all, the text refuses
to allude to recognizably Australian experience, whether that of
generalized cultural discourse or that of particular inscape.
Such a refusal of Australia might be claimed to be merely
symbolist or merely deconstructive; however when we examine
the recognizable signifiers out of which these abstract poems
are crafted we can recognize that they are partly derived from
Modernist art but usually from American television, films and
pop music. Stepping aside, we can find that Forbes was also
writing a thesis on the New York post-Modernist, Frank
O'Hara, whose broken metonymy plainly exerts its influence.

Again, let us look at how Forbes's poetry was marketed. He
was one of the poets promoted by John Tranter's combative
anthology, *The New Australian Poetry* (1979.) The editor's
introduction to this anthology truculently insists that the
enterprise it displays is that of trying to revitalize 'a moribund
poetic culture'. We are being told that the poets represented
here are the goodies, whose job it is to displace the baddies,
Nothing new in that: many anthologists are up to such tricks;
but it is worth pausing over several points of emphasis in this
introduction. Firstly, Tranter writes that a major influence on
the poets he approves was the arrival of two American anthol-
ogies in the early 1960s: Donald Allen's *The New American
Poetry* and Donald Hall's *Contemporary American Poetry*. He
sails on to claim that these two books 'showed the local writers
that there was a real and vigorous alternative to the world of
Henry Lawson and A. D. Hope.' (xvii) The bracketing of these
two names is perfectly ludicrous *unless* we take it for a complete
rejection of Australian literary culture. Tranter has arrived in
the late 1970s at the same position which was occupied by the

much-derided Professor G. H. Cowling back in the 1930s: that Australian writing has not generated anything that is a classic, even for its own purposes, and that the way forward can only be found through close attention to the achievements of a foreign, imperial culture. (By calling the United States of America 'imperial' I am not passing a censorious political judgement, merely reflecting on the ruthless power and pressure of its culture in Australia, and in other 'small' countries.) Secondly, Tranter insists that the poets he has selected belong in either a post-Modernist or a sadly delayed Modernist ambience; and he insists that the core of this late Modernism is to be found in the poets' rejection of mimesis and in their replacing it by verbal or conceptual reflexiveness. He exemplifies this claim by explicating John Forbes's poem 'T.V.' Incidentally, it should be added that at least four of the poets in his anthology—Beaver, Viidikas, Taylor and Wearne—write with a thoroughly mimetic approach, whatever the influences on them may have been.

Thirdly, Tranter constructs for himself a very curious straw enemy. It is a kind of crude prose poem constructed from 'a selection of phrases used in two typical reviews of a well-known and highly-regarded contemporary Australian poem, Vincent Buckley's "Golden Builders".' These are phrases of approval, elevated, solemn, humanist, perhaps pompous, and the editor categorizes such language as entirely inappropriate to the kind of poetry he wants to publicize, suggesting that it represents the spilt religion of the academies. It is significant that Buckley was the obliquely displaced target of this attack. We shall come back to the definition of his role shortly.

Tranter's introduction to *The New Australian Poetry*, although entirely innocent of literary theory, takes up a historical posture akin to that of many recent literary theorists or meta-critics. That is to say, he sketches a cultural world in which mimesis proves naive because of the necessary instability of signifiers, in which 'liberal humanism' is derided as empty pomposity, in which post-Modernism keeps problematizing the authorial subject and in which texts are sited at a busy crossroads through which keep moving other kinds of discourse, powered by God knows what, unless it be a mass of older discourses as heavy as the nightmare of history. In this complicatedly sceptical climate three kinds of presence tend to be disallowed. The first is the presence of the author, whose authority is of course dismantled. The second is the evoked world of contingent experience. And the third, not surprisingly, is God or any dimension of supernatural sanction.

At this point in my tale I am bound to turn to a larger, almost procedural consideration, one which keeps putting me in mind of that old historical argument about 'socialism in one country'. It is this: To what extent should we read the stages of cultural history as being inevitable and universal? Those who assume that they are will naturally assume that Australia should have reached the stations of Modernism, post-Modernism and so on at the 'right' time, and has only failed to do so because of wilful stupidity, blindness or pigheadedness. The confluence of causal factors which fed into the Modernist revolution in the arts of Paris, London, Petrograd, Berlin and New York will be read as generally applicable to advanced countries (the mere phrase begs the question) and as having been blocked only by provinciality of mind. But it may be that such a totalization of cultural process can be regarded from within Australian discourse as yet another example of the Cringe. This debate tends to pulse with that throbbing 'and yet . . . and yet' which Paul Kane recognizes in the conclusion of his Melbourne dissertation, 'Origins and Absence: Romanticism in Australian Poetry'.

If our stress is on the particularity of Australian cultural process, then terms like Modernism lose their talismanic power, their capacity to order other kinds of experience. We may then stress instead that various clusterings and concurrences have occurred here and there in our short history to which *ismic* titles will one day be given; and we may still want to sketch this map of Australian culture even as we recognize that successive eclectic bundles of foreign writing have played a large part in influencing Australian poets and novelists. Everyone is influenced by a host of texts; those whose work is admirable tend to swerve hard away from their sources; some will combine a determined attachment to the naming of present experience with a swerve against succumbing to some proclaimed international demeanour. Among the poets who have exemplified resistance to post-Modernist scepticism about signification I would name Gwen Harwood, Vincent Buckley, Les Murray and Robert Gray, and I will focus on Buckley's peculiarly impassioned presentation for the rest of this essay.

Without a doubt, Buckley's poetry has always concerned itself with manifesting some kind of numinous *presence*, but what kind of presence that might be has changed very con-

siderably over the past thirty years or so. Still, the title which he
gave to his third book of literary criticism, *Poetry and the Sacred*
(1968), is a deliberate sign, a signal which can remind us of how
all his poetry asks to be read. Early or late, this poetry is
solemn, elevated, hieratic: a poet who proclaimed his identification with the text he had made, through a particular musical
eloquence, kept proclaiming the sacred character of the named
experiences. Over and again these poems are like charms: they
lay claim to magic or to epiphany.

The early poetry which Buckley published in *The World's
Flesh* (the very title an appropriation of the figure of Christ
incarnate) was expressly religious. Poems treated explicitly of
the Holy Ghost, the Virgin Mary, St Catherine of Siena,
eucharist, ritual and the Flight into Egypt. The language is
richly overwrought and self-assertive, also marked—as one
reviewer observed—by the trope of catachresis. Uneven
though the poems are, there is everwhere an impression of
verbal *force*, as though the very language were being bent
toward some gnostic apprehension of reality. Phrases like 'the
dewy fallen universe', 'a hard nothingness', 'her murdered
convenant' and 'the thundering/Of axles of their tombs' might
be said to cut themselves wilfully adrift from contingent
experience, from what R. P. Blackmur called 'behaviour'. Con-
notation runs rings around mere denotation: transcendence is
everywhere. Attention should be paid, though, to the last
quatrain of one of the tightest poems in the book, 'Death by
Cancer':

> And we, to whom time was familiar things
> Moulded by friendly hands, a presence curled
> In light, recall how once and fierce it stings,
> And shudder with this shuddering of the world.

Time here is not process nor abstract concept, but a presence.
Before the death it was 'a presence curled/ In light' but even
after it has been darkly metamorphosed it is defined as a fierce
or stinging presence, a force which has helped to engender the
world's new shuddering.

Whether Buckley had much impulse to persist with a diction
so often marked by archaism and incantation I do not know.
Many factors were certainly against it: the main currents of
Australian poetry in the 1950s, Buckley's increasing wish to
particularize the details of eloquent landscapes, his growing

sense of an expressly Australian art and the stress in university
literary criticism at that time on specificity, concreteness and
enactment, the last two being great hurrah-words. His second
volume of poetry, *Masters in Israel*, was published in 1961; the
title, in which irony wars with triumphalism would be unthink-
able nowadays. 'Borrowing of Trees', a lyric celebration in five
quatrains, epitomizes the new mimetic particularity of this
book. It looks back in some measure to the tree images (I
almost said, the tree-spirits) of Judith Wright's early poems,
'For New England' and 'South of My Days'; it also brings to
mind the fact that Les Murray and Geoffrey Lehmann were to
publish their first book of poems, *The Ilex Tree*, only four years
after *Masters in Israel*. Buckley's reafforestation of his childhood landscape in Romsey, Victoria, is a worthy precursor of
Murray's poems in praise of Bunyah, New South Wales. It is
Buckley, too, who is clearly the more concerned with aural
intensities in the landscape of memory:

BORROWING OF TREES

I was born under a continual
Movement of trees, bred in their gathered light,
In the high scything rhythm, the stopped flight,
The sea-sound urging through the timber wall.

And have been held. The laurel's dense glitter,
The elms at random over the hill's shoulder,
The willows with their hidden taint, the bolder
Cherry dying of isolation, fritter

Their substance, are cut one by one, and burn
Sharply or fragrantly so I'll remember.
A heritage, surely. Something which every limber
Landlord of wings must emphasize in turn,

Even the unremarkable plum, or the peppercorn
Too normal for the secretive child. And the hush
Of pines, pines, their dominant slow rush
Rides on all my summers. I was born

Under this usury of trees: Their noise
A lent wisdom of guardians talking together
Blent like husband and wife in the rusty weather
Or wound like a vine about this timbered house.

A historical point should be made at this point about
Buckley's dealings with landscape, natural objects and the local
habitation. As his early critical essay, 'A New Bulletin School?',

signals, he kept his distance for a long time from those poets who saw it as their prime task to depict the natural environment; he liked to keep at a wary distance from the work of Stewart, Campbell, Robinson, and even in some ways from Judith Wright. Yet some impulse gradually brought him back closer and closer to plants, local waters, air-smells, earth-smells, to the wish to lovingly evoke details of

> a land that in its steeped
> Peach-dark fruits,
> Resin,
> Pods,
> Is warm as blood.
>   (Places)

and often to evoke them as here by seeming to draw the land into the speaker's own body, earth becoming blood, perceptions quivering in the nerve-ends, synaesthesia everywhere.

About 'Borrowing of Trees' I would note just a few other things. First, the delicacy in the title of the participle, 'borrowing', in which the poet reveals an awareness that he cannot actually *take* natural objects for the sake of a striking text, but can do something more provisional, more qualified, more clearly circumvented by life itself. Secondly, like Adam in Paradise, the poet is at his business of naming things in the garden, in his own first garden. Observe how plainly the nouns are assembled in their catalogue: laurel, elms, willows, cherry, plum, peppercorn, pines. Can the names of particular species themselves function like tiny poems? Specificity is always attractive, even after it has been taken to ludicrous hyperbole in the 'Cyclops' chapter of *Ulysses* with the bosky wedding of Miss Fir Conifer of Pine Valley, and in other associated catalogues there.

The other striking thing about the poet's borrowed trees, however, is that none of them is native to Australia. This is both a comment about Australia farmyards in the old days and, more broadly, about Australia's colonial inheritance: linguistic, cultural and horticultural. Except for a scarlet bottlebrush in one poem, Buckley's textual world does not contain indigenous plants. Even the peppercorn tree was imported from Mexico, all the others from Europe like the language which holds them. It would be hard at this point not to remember that Buckley's geographical *axis mundi* had two poles, one surfacing in Australia and the other in Ireland, as many recent poems and one book of prose have testified. Perhaps, too, like many poets before him he found it hard to celebrate the names of plants which do not have the literary mulch and tilth of centuries heaped around them.

In the poetry of his next book, *Arcady and Other Places* (1966), Buckley had recourse again to those trees and to the role they played in embodying childhood memories like wood-spirits. Reading the harsh, seven-part sequence called 'Stroke' which traces the process of his father's dying we come upon this epiphanic recovery of the country childhood in section III:

Oaks, pines, the willows with their quiet
Terror; the quiet terror of my age;
The seven-year-old bookworm sitting out
At night, in the intense cold, the horse
Tethered, the stars almost moving,
The cows encroaching on the night grass.
The frost stung my lips; my knees burned;
Darkness alone was homely. The hawthorn tree
Glimmered as though frost had turned to language
And language into sharp massy blossoms.

The slippery chiasmus of those last two lines will remind us that the poet was in no wise innocent of modern subversions of linguistic verity, but some of his deepest allegiances remain chthonic and arboreal. The phrase about 'the intense cold' (in a region where it doesn't even snow, as a rule!) will remind us of one of the most striking preoccupations of Buckley's poetry, early or late: a concern, almost amounting to an obsession, with the temperature of the air about him. His almost neurasthenic sense of heat, cold, smog, draughts, humidity, creates a peculiar theatre of consciousness: that of a man who seems ill at ease in his body, frequently stirred, easily put out—and one who has to place great reliance on the magical verities of earth, water and air. Place and atmosphere keep being depicted as parts of a salvific presence. As in Hopkins or Lawrence, landscapes are valued not only as repositories of aesthetic pleasure but for the ways in which they testify to the immanence of spirit. In an ABC broadcast Buckley said, 'I think at a certain psychic level Australia belongs to the Aboriginal people'.

Frequently the poetry testifies to a Coleridgean reciprocity between this immanent spirit and the perceiving poetic consciousness. We find both that 'Scent forms/ at the brain's base, from a twig of/ oakbuds, tiny, clustered,/ seedlike as pearls' and that 'One more day of my life/ was dying: the yellow bloomed in every pavement/ and the cool rang through every/ nerve and surface', toward the end of 'Golden Builders', indeed at the very point where anguish begins to give way to a pastoral coda. The poems keep positing two delicately interacting presences, that of the natural scene, which tends to be the more active as well as providing spiritual succour when the self falters, and that of the self, hypersensitive, pained, responsive, but capable of giving names to non-linguistic depths or sources of experience.

'Golden Builders' may be the place to which one should go to see how these transactions are played out in the social and historical fabric of a known city, but I prefer to turn at this point to a late poem called 'Theories'. Nowhere before this had Buckley dealt so explicitly with questions of the generation of language, with pressing towards the roots of any possible text. I should also be noted that in the title of this poem he was partly fending off the pressure of 'literary theory', which in the academies presents itself as the handmaid (or perhaps ring-master, depending on your sense of gender and priority) of post-Modernism. At the same time, the two sections of the poem begin with phrases which are significant variations on William Carlos Williams' dictum, 'no ideas but in things': the poem is both mimetic and speculative, both local and locating itself in a modern tradition. Williams' phrase comes from book one of *Paterson*, a transcendentally local poem, like 'Golden Builders'; and Buckley had expressly praised Williams for his ease of language, for his 'sense of meaningful factuality.'

I

Those are not selves, but things.
The summer nights begin to float
machine noises weird as kites
over the balconies of the Home Units
in which some transient, motorbike-crazy,
slamming and starting, revs the whole house.

Nor are they symbols. But, dribbling
precious water into the scoops of earth
around the shrubs that burst and die
of sheer scent, you might call them
metaphors, they stick so close to the mind.

To the mind, and to the real.
Most urgently in mid-evening
when, hot still under the fern,

the sparrows cling to the water
and the front garden shines dry as bran.

II

No things but in words.
Scandalous the leaves rustling
hot and hoarse, not in but against
the lisp of my language:
rolls like a pebble
on the road, stark coming
down with its dogs
all barking, and the man's voice
working set as a ratchet.
Here or in Kildare
that's how the world wags:
No X but in Y.
The roots of language
definite as the wind-cry.

Not only does the poem's questioning of signifiers waste away
to the minimalism of 'No X but in Y', but syntax collapses in the
last part of this poem in a way which it virtually never does in
Buckley' writing. Yet the last two lines defiantly assert an affin-
ity between language and nature. Buckley did not care much for
Wallace Stevens, but here the American is an audible ally.

How does one talk about *personality* in poetry? How would
one ever demonstrate that it was there? The answer is not cast-
iron, but a throng of signals suggests that the authorial presence
in Buckley's poetry is constantly asserted, early and late, in
good poems or bad. It is felt in the suasive rhythms, in the high
rhetorical tone, in eccentrically braced adjectives (ochreous,
drowsed, peach-dark, superb, cancerous, foxy, slimed, glare-
lighted, hairless, faunal, androgyne, thrawn . . .), in the poet's
insistence on his threatened individual body, and in his almost
complete disinterest in dramatizing alternative viewpoints. The
poems have changed over thirty years but they go on bespeak-
ing the same author—as sufferer, impressionist, bard, prophet,
magus:

And hard-faced men, who beat the drum
To call me to this Cause or that,
Those heirs of someone else's tomb,
Can't see the sweeter work I'm at,
The building of the honeycomb.

That's how the voice of assertive presence sounded in the metrical cadences which he employed in the mid-1960s. By the mid-eighties those metres have given way to an easier kind of voice, lightly built out of angular phrases; but the authority is still very much in evidence:

If peoples were still named after their weapons,
we would be called
the Projectile-people, *or* those who kill from afar,
or Spitting Poison-people, *or* Anthrax-minders.
On the great lowlands rugged with grass
we squat beside snout and muzzle,
we are growing moustaches
and learning laws of trajectory.

The inventions in those last lines, from 'Soft War Poems', are akin to the kind of thing Les Murray's imagination might have come up with; but in a Murray poem the invention would have come across as broadly good-humoured, even ludic. Buckley's preoccupations were darker: he may well remind us of E. M. Forster's observation that modern poetry tends to be minatory.

Two general paradoxes seem to me to emerge from this discussion of Vincent Buckley's work, paradoxes which also bear upon the poetry of Murray, Harwood and Gray. In the first place, I am struck by the fact that details of landscape, foliage, sky, water and light are frequently the subject of writers whose outlook is primarily a humanist one. Secondly, material objects are remarkably often foregrounded, depicted, lovingly lingered over and insisted on as real lumps in what is, after all, a text by poets who are not materialists. These are, I'm afraid, questions which belong to the general history of post-Romantic literature, and we can all think of the ways in which such terms as *symbol*, *epiphany* and *image* have been used as desperate hinges to close up such dilemmas of emphasis.

There is a much larger problem about poetic mimesis which both troubles and entertains me, however. It is one which will also return us to the scraggy, much-nibbled field of post-Modernism. It goes something like this. If poets believe that they can depict or imitate the brute matter of existence through language, why does that language need to be worked up into elaborate artistic arrangements? In what ways does a poem release the signified life to us? Can it be the case that ordinary language is opaque and cannot really signify any clear presence, whereas highly crafted language becomes somehow transparent and therefore makes the signified world available? Surely at the base of the modern poet's craft we have a choice of two positions: the atavistic one, that poems are a form of magic and thus have powers to transcend the ordinary limitations of discourse; or the sceptical one, that no language consists of accurate signs for parallel units of experience so that all one can do is to construct whole poems, contraptions whose elaboration is so subtly done that it can mime a block of experience as merely linear language can never do.

So at the end of my tale there is no clear ending, but two paths leading on. The poet is both archaic and sophisticated, both god-botherer and linguist, both a lucid namer of the world's things and a desperate magus, well aware of the ambiguity of his/her signs and gestures: their doomed inadequacy. In such an ambiguous role, Buckley signalled that he was aware of post-Modernism's Nietzschean messages (if not enamoured of them), but he continued to write in a high romantic posture, imprinting the poems with signs of his personal presence (we call these his style) and claiming to display on a printed page the presence of named objects, winds, clouds, people and creatures, not least among them being racehorses.

Buckley's reliance on a mimetic contract with the non-verbal world, as well as his passionate regionalism, has been declared in his remarks on Ireland and Australia in a radio interview. His comments here are so natural as to be very strange indeed:

> I feel a distinct linguistic break between my attempts to get Australia into poetry and my attempts to get Ireland into poetry. One difference for example . . . is the matter of smell, because all through the spring and summer in Australia you're surrounded by smells of the most powerful and delicious kind.

It was particularly daring of Buckley to single out smells for comment, for of all kinds of sense experience they are the most powerfully connected with promptings of the *mémoire involontaire* and at the same time they are the experiences to which linguistic signs bear the most arbitrary and unsystematic relations. They are presences without fixed names, even in a thoroughly conservative linguistic world.

9

Intimations of Secular Grace: David Malouf

Poets go in quest of the good time, the great good place. Poems are non-causal, resistant, enchanted, when compared with the moral and sociological traction which novels have to offer. Each short poem offers to its readers the possibility that it will annihilate all that's made to a golden thought in a verbal shade. Read me, it says, and for a while history will come to a stop.

The disingenuous poet engages in a double game, pretending that he or she has danced sideways out of self into a realm of pure art, which is to say pleasure, but believing at the same time that this artefact testifies to a unique authorial personality. It is an old game: perhaps its time is running out, but I hope not.

For centuries a prime model for poets in English has been Horace, in large part because he offers an imitable way to mediate between self and art, between the voice of a genially hospitable countryman and the marmoreal text. Of all great poets, he would seem to create the least anxiety of belatedness among modern epigoni: as a father, he writes himself into the culture as entirely benign. Like Collins Street farming, he gives us access to a secular form of grace.

It is the Horatian model, especially the tones and topographies of the *Carminum*, which springs to mind when I take a retrospective view of David Malouf's poetry, a prospect made possible by his *Selected Poems*. 'View' is right, for these are poems which, over and over again, celebrate the influence of benevolent places, concurrences of time and place in a world of serendipity. They even analyse the process:

Which is to say, that where we are is always
where we meant to get to, the time being

ripe, the place sufficient, a mild terrain
with a climate, like all gardens, propitious for

the full life of each fruit, its blossoms, rind,
and fall.

('Ode One')

Well, yes, it is a broad, post-Christian serendipity which finds
room for the *felix culpa*. And a stanza which can end with
the phrase, 'the time being', points us to another strong—and
at the same time Horatian—forebear of these poems, W. H.
Auden.

Malouf made a full avowal of how much Auden means and
has meant to him in a long review of *The English Auden*. In the
course of that review he not only declared his allegiance to the
late, sober-toned, discursive poems over and above the early,
coruscating work, but also declared the force and fascination
which the early work held for him in writing that

The Malverns still reads to me like a brilliant and deeply felt poem,
marvellously evocative of its time and the tensions of its time, utterly
secure rhetorically and rhythmically, extraordinarily—perhaps even
fatally, Auden might have thought—attractive and memorable, as
indeed all those famous and rejected poems prove to be.

(1978, 40)

Still, it is surely the urbane, almost whimsical dispassionateness
of the late work which has most affected Malouf, rather than
those brilliant sparks thrown off by the word-magician of the
'thirties. And there is one major difference between the two
that leaps to mind, Malouf's being so much a poet of memory
where Auden held so firmly to the Blakean hunch that memory
and nature are, at root, enemies of the imagination; think of
that wisdom-utterance from *Paid on Both Sides*, 'By loss of
memory we are reborn/ For memory is death.' The division runs
deeper still, of course, for Uncle Wiz long courted the muse of
psychology, whereas Malouf is hardly a psychological poet at
all, being a memorialist of mixed Arcadias.

It has not, I think, been recorded just how powerful and
pervasive Auden's influence has been in Australian poetry,
but the attractions of his work have taken on among us like
blackberries or sheep. His example seems to be strongly present
in the poetry not only of A. D. Hope and Peter Porter, but also
in J. R. Rowland, Evan Jones, Peter Steele, Les Murray and—
distilled through his team of New York disciples—John Tranter.
Indeed, Auden's shadow falls across the poetry of the late
twentieth century to an extent which must astonish those who

thought he had written himself out by 1940, but it is not my task
here to pursue his versatile exemplariness further. Suffice it to
say that

The silly fool, the silly fool
Was sillier in school
But beat the bully as a rule

and that Auden's apparent foolishness was part of his amazing
survival power. It enabled him to outflank decorum and pre-
dictability over and over again.

David Malouf's poetry was first picked out for special attention by Jones in a review of *Four Poets* (1962), and it was
highly-wrought formal glitter which surely distinguished his
poems in that collection. Only three of those lyrics are re-
produced in *Selected Poems*, including the frequently-admired
'Epitaph for a Monster of Our Times' and—placed first in the
book—'Sheer Edge', which serves as a textual sign-post, being
a close rewriting of the title-poem of Auden's *Look, Stranger!*
(1936). Never again will he stand so explicitly close to the fore-
runner, however much his poems may broadly resemble
'Goodbye to the Mezzogiorno' and 'Homage to Clio', or other
such relaxed disquisitions from Ischia and Austria.

From *Bicycle, and other poems* (1970) on, Malouf's poetry
does not seem essentially to have changed, however much his
assurance may have deepened and developed; but then why
should it? By what precept in the deification of the sick goddess,
Progress, is it enacted that we must keep changing? Presumably
so as to provide sustained intellectual diversion for the pushy
reader. At all events, Malouf's work over these last twenty
years looks pretty homogeneous. I wonder, indeed, whether
there is some relation between the vividly static quality of the
vignettes which are juxtaposed to make up his poems and his
apparent preference for stasis on a larger scale. A poem like
'Stopping to Drink' in which the uttering voice is that of a man
who physically acts, rather than of one who merely sleeps,
reminisces or *inspires* (to draw upon the title of his longest suite
of poems) is an exception to the prevailing demeanour. And
even in this finely crafted lyric we are presented with an action
of almost Rilkean gentleness and self-abnegation. Compare,

Taking all this in
as the water takes it: sky,

sunlight, sweet grass-flavours
and the long held breath
of children—a landscape
mirrored, held a moment,
and let go again.

with Rilke's

By the road that is used to the sun, in the
hollow half of a tree-stem that has
long been a trough, ever softly renewing
a surface of water, I quench my
thirst: taking the water's serenity and source
into me through my wrists.
To drink would seem too much, too distinct;
          ('*An der sonngewohnten Strasse*')

In both cases, present action aspires to a stillness which is like
that of dream or of a formative memory. Here, as elsewhere,
Malouf reads landscape, especially its small print, for signs of
time regained or at the least retained.

It is no wonder that so many of his poems are built upon
trains of things in apposition: appositional structures are among
the least wilful, least dynamic of syntactical organizations.
Within such trains ('shinbone, brian-pan, clavicle', 'the positively committed, politicos,/ madmen, Leavisites') disagree-
ables evaporate and even the horrible messes of history can be
verbally tamed, a procedure which Europe—Malouf's present
chosen ground—constantly calls for. It must be admitted that at
times his hunger for the strictly equivocal can generate a merely
confusing sequence, as it surely does in 'The City of God':

          the sores, the fleas, tribes with a taste
for buggery, and witches who would lead us there by millponds,
a short cut flying at night between their thighs, the narrow way
for Paradise, the broad way leads to Nottingham, its dark
satanic shopping-malls.

This addresses itself wittily enough to the museum-system we
call Europe, and Wallace Stevens called 'the dump', but the
grammar has become rather lazy.

Mimetically speaking, poetry is a Janus-faced business. It
says both, I can acquaint you with this experience, and, I can
acquaint you with the teller: I have something to tell and I only
am escaped to tell thee. The bundle of signs which a poem

assembles points in two ways, while we as readers sway between finding, say, a landscape rendered for us and asking, in Auden's words, 'What kind of a guy inhabits this poem? What is his notion of the good life or the good place? His notion of the Evil One? What does he conceal from the reader? What does he conceal even from himself?' (1968, 51)

The experience to which Malouf's poetry turns is characteristically involved with landscapes and slices of landscape, occasionally with room interiors, and it has to do with the good minutes harvested from living, whether in European cities or in the benevolence of Australian space. His first two novels clearly delineate the areas which the poetry also inhabits: *Johnno* is a bricolage of all sorts of random-seeming bric-à-brac hauled out of a personal past (one poem, 'The Judas Touch', actually overlaps with the book), while *An Imaginary Life*, history rendered timeless, becomes with some assistance from Marguerite Yourcenar's *Memoirs of Hadrian* an old-world myth in which to mirror the light of yearnings—above all the yearning to stand outside time in a shaft of light.

In the final chapter of *An Imaginary Life* we come upon, are drawn into, the kind of romantic epiphany which is so often, and increasingly, a point of focus in the poems. Ovid, the Roman poet with the big nose, is rapt in his vision of the Child, a Scythian boy who is travelling across the unbounded summer steppes with him:

The stream shakes out its light across his ankles as he wades deeper, then climbs on to a smooth stone and balances for a moment in the sun, leaps, leaps again, then wanders upstream on the other bank, which is gravel, every pebble of it, white, black, grey, picked out and glittering in the late sunlight as in a mosaic, where he pauses, gathers one, two, four snails, and with the stream rippling as he steps in and out of it, walks on, kicking at the gravel with his toes and lost for a moment in his own childlike pleasure at being free.

(1978, 151–2)

It is an evocation which partakes equally of freedom, space and light: it is that state to which Freud gave the name, the oceanic feeling, and claimed unconvincingly, puritanically, that he had never experienced it himself. Configurations like this, signals of the oceanic feeling, are of key importance in Malouf's mature poetry and they are again and again signalled by the same cluster of words, a cluster which certainly includes 'stars', 'light', 'glass', 'water', 'frost', 'snow', 'drawn' and 'grass', the last aurally so close to 'glass'.

At heart far less ironic than Horace or Auden, Malouf gives us whole poems which celebrate lapsing out into momentary transcendence. Curiously, he does not display much concern to explore the epistemology of these 'moments of inherent excellence'. There are signs, however, that their origins are frequently sexual; by the time we reach such later poems as 'White Days, White Nights' and 'Inspirations', placed side by side among the selections from *Poems 1975–76*, the romantic declarations of sexuality have become far more explicit. What is testified to here is a realm where 'Eros guides', where the very air can be described as 'unzipped', and 'We are conductors of an absolute music'; its moments of stasis and illumination are most vividly epitomized by the stanza,

In my body's depths a shining
as leaves turn, a boy reads over
a young man's shoulder
in an empty field, white, borderless, at noon.
                    (White Days, White Nights')

Those who proclaim a 'New Romanticism' in our poetry might well claim Malouf for one of their exemplars.

Caelum non animam mutant, qui trans mare currunt.* Malouf has spent a lot of time in the Old World, and now lives in southern Tuscany. One of his problems, one which he shares with his fellow museum-haunters, Peter Porter and Murray Bail, is how to avoid the poor little colonial's sentimental overvaluation of things European; like the other two he has resort to wry fragmentation, 'Postcards of travel' and the like, but he does not for long indulge in Porter's dryness (despite 'The Little Aeneid'), let alone Bail's hilarious subversion of the whole seductive Grand Tour. He is none the less aware that the Grand Tour is verbal as well as touristical, as he signals in a sequence called 'The Little Panopticon', the titles of whose poems are the names of eighteen great cultural works, almost all of them books, from 'The Elements of Geometry' to 'Elective Affinities'.

In an ABC interview on Radio Helicon, Malouf had a number of things to say about his choice of residence in Europe and

---

* 'They change their skies but not their hearts, who shunt across the sea.'

antipodean contrasts. One of his comments was particularly revealing, especially in the teeth of his saying how comfortable life in Australia is:

Because Australia is so isolated it never knows how far it should be going, in any of its revolutions, whether it's a sexual revolution or a literary revolution, and it often in fact finds itself going further than most other places because it doesn't know how far is enough.

There is something not far from fear in this utterance. And what it brings us back, or around to, is Malouf's deep-laid conservatism, something which I was suggesting in my earlier comments on his recurrent imaginative preference for stasis. A muse which is so strongly planted amongst remembrances is likely to resist change, novelty, disturbances to the psychic economy. Also, is it this cast of temperament which has led Malouf to leave out of his *Selected Poems* one of his most dynamically inventive lyrics, 'A Charm against the Dumps', while including so many whose chief impulse is memorial?

Formally, too, the poems are conservative, in a perfectly honourable way. Their shapes are neither very free nor yet part of the new, experimental testing of fixed forms that one finds in poets as different as Murray and Tranter. His measures are freeish, with an occasional interest in the seven beat line; his stanzas fairly regular, unemphatic, pellucid in their effect; they are like string bags into which as many as possible of the world's things can be packed. His syntactical units are longish and discursive, but wherever possible the discourse is crowded with tangible examples, with 'a jetty's planks', 'Your green travelling clock', 'satin and witch hazel', 'flotsam cafe tables', 'the stoat's unhinging metal shriek' and

Behind a wall of pintucked
silk the embryo,
poor hairless ape with nine
fingers and a giant's
ponderous head
('Before the Revolution')

It is the accumulated security of all these gathered things which holds his world in place: that, and his stylish equability of tone, the civilized voice which he creates and which reads so well.

Civilized, *civilisé*, yes, and like so many of us in the poetry game nowadays Malouf is a poet who celebrates a great many artists and art objects; in modern poetry the fetishism of commodities runs rapidly and by partial reaction into becoming the fetishism of artistic production. All too seldom do any of us explore, let alone celebrate, the politicians, generals, business-men, lawyers, doctors and Uncle Tom Cobleys who shape our world; for us they lack aura; we slip back into art about art, feeling that the aesthetic object is still, however privately, numinous. Thus the crowdy things in Malouf's poetry include a great many glimpsed statues, paintings, famous buildings, musical performances and, as evinced in the titles I mentioned earlier, books.

There can be no doubt that he knows the cost of those beautiful products he cites with such love, knows that those splendid cantatas or murals cost the lives of a lot of foot-soldiers and the birthrights of a lot of peasants. Such poems as 'Before the Revolution' and 'Theologia Germanica' face up most im-pressively to the blood and pain, counting the cost. Neverthe-less it is hard to guess how much Malouf would make of what the dangerous, doomed poet, John Berryman, wrote in gall and wormwood about the glories of Western civilization:

> culture was only a phase
> through which we threaded, coming out at the other end
> to the true light again of savagery.

But then, what do the rest of us make of it, and how could any writer keep writing if he sat down and numbly believed something so blank? Before we ponder that question, we should at least be able to respond with pleasure and gratitude to the harmonious things Malouf has made out of words, out of the time-flux. And we need not, I think, puzzle too much about the curious chronological relationship between the *Selected Poems* and his later/earlier collection of poems, *First Things Last*, the very title of which may be a publishing joke.

10

The Loud Posters of Kamala Das

The career, or part-career, of Kamala Das has that exemplary quality which is common to many important modern writers. But when I call it exemplary that is not to describe it as a model of moral virtue, to be viewed as we view the lives of More and Milton, Wordsworth and George Eliot. Instead, it is the impression of excess, the vulgarity, the sense that we are being admitted to a sexually scandalous world, which is precisely what is exemplary about the poetry. The constructed subject is alarming and is meant to be so: that is our way into the poetry.

On the dustjacket of *The Old Playhouse and Other Poems* (1973) there is an elegantly rounded line drawing of a woman sitting hunched up, naked, her knees drawn up and her long hair flowing in arabesques around her left breast, thighs and feet. She looks longingly off to one side. We are tacitly invited to identify this figure with the un-ironized speaker of the poems in the book. In turn we are to construct that speaker as being the poet in person: there are no signals, except perhaps for embarrassment, to tell us not to do so.

Then again, there is Das's authobiography. If some critics are ill at ease with the poetry, most would prefer to forget about the prose. P. Lal, who published her second book of verse in 1967, was to write that, 'One (liberated lady), Kamala Das, got a full-page spread a couple of years ago in the pages of the newsmagazine *Time* with the publication of her 'sizzlingly candid' autobiography *My Story* (1977), an atrociously written work that has become a bestseller'. Atrocious or not, *My Story* is part of the process of assembling a poetic life that will arrest and affront. It is easy to remember that Das belongs to the same generation as Plath, but we can return to this comparison or contrast later.

This apparent identification of the speakers of Das's numerous lyrics and monologues with the historical poet is encouraged in a poem which is firmly called 'An Introduction'. It seems like a

gangplank leading directly into a verifiable life. Early in the
poem we find the seemingly documentary approach of

> I am Indian, very brown, born in
> Malabar, I speak three languages, write in
> Two, dream in one. Don't write in English, they said,
> English is not your mother-tongue. Why not leave
> Me alone, critics, friends, visiting cousins,
> Every one of you?

The passage begins by listing apparent facts in a metonymic
chain, linked by commas; the rhythmical flatness is underwritten by nerveless enjambments. The rhetorical intensity rises
in apparent argument: an argument which explicitly bears on
Das's role as poet. Significantly, *critics* are lumped together
with friends and relations. Mandelstam once observed that information was the real business of prose, and these lines are
both informative and unformed. They are prosy.

But if we look further at 'An Introduction', it will become
clear that it is the business of this poem to be systematically
unformed. First glances are deceptives; it looks on the page like
a monologue by Browning: sixty-eight lines long, no stanza
breaks, capitals at line-beginnings, and the look of blank verse
to it. But this last look is deceptive, for no metrical pattern is
established, only a dominant count of eleven syllables to the
line. Like Marianne Moore and Auden, she has turned to the
weak emphases of a syllabic measure, but where they seek
impersonality in syllabics she is after an impression of restlessness; they use the legato rhythms with an elevated, consciously
aesthetic diction, but she combines them with jagged, sometimes vulgar, emotional speech like 'my limbs/Swelled and one
or two places sprouted hair' or 'Don't play at schizophrenia or
be a/Nympho.'

Yet, just as the apparent orderliness of the poem on the page
masks disorder, the rhetorical disorder of its process is finally
drawn to a kind of order, to a satisfying closure. The last seven
sentences, echoic and contracting, do not merely affect us as
aurally powerful. More importantly, they keep reinforcing,
questioning and dismantling the pronoun, 'I', the central word
in Das's poetry.

Few of her poems are not scored again and again by the
columnar capital I. Five of the last twenty-seven lines of 'Blood'
begin with it; two of the eight lines in 'Contacts' actually *end*

with it; three of the last four sentences in 'Gino' begin with 'I shall'; and 'A Hot Noon in Malabar' saves it carefully up for the last line. Sometimes it rhymes immediately with 'die' or 'lie'. Part of the sub-text of that powerful poem, 'The Looking-glass' is to be found in the way the first-person pronoun has become 'you', just as a mirror transforms the not fully visible self into another who (or which?) can be scrutinized. Indeed, the images of self and other in this poem proliferate extensively with the aid of mirror images. Thus, the self advises herself—that is to say, 'you'—to stand 'nude before the glass with him' so that he, the lover, can see both mirrored bodies in close comparison.

This poem is particularly acute about a traditional Romantic problem: the relation between that which can be clearly seen and that which can be known and loved. Ruskin thought that there was no problem, but the Romantic poets were aware that there was, knew that the keen scrutiny profits from distance. What is the line between intimacy and complete detachment in these arresting details?

> Notice the perfection
> Of his limbs, his eyes reddening under
> The shower, the shy walk across the bedroom floor,
> Dropping towels, and the jerky way he
> Urinates. All the fond details that make
> Him male and your only man.

Fascinating, yes, but in the main traditions of love poetry we do not look at 'all the fond details'. The loved one is not a life study. It is the business of love to generalize and to idealize. The large metaphor of burnished or tarnished brass which ends the poem is far more like the stuff of love poetry.

Of this final trope, let me just add that burnished brass is a reflective or gleaming surface, much as a mirror is. So the loving body both gleamed 'under his touch' and was another version of the looking-glass. As Anne Brewster has observed, an important dimension of Das's poetry lies in the contrast between surfaces and depths. The eye perceives surfaces.

The undeniable force of Kamala Das's poetry fights against and is to some extent a product of multiple displacement. First, of course, there is that displacement or dislocation that all modern writers feel: their loss of grip on a coherent body of experience, real or imagined, which went by the name of tradition. Secondly, there is her awkward distance from that imperial language in which she feels the need to write. As R. Parthasarathy has written.

The Indian who uses the English language feels, to some extent, alienated. His development as a poet is sporadic. And it is partly because of this that there is, today, no perspective at all in which to evaluate this phenomenon.

(1976, 3)

Not only poetic careers but individual poems are likely to have a sporadic air in a situation where the language is politically as well as psychically alienating. Das's lacunae, her little rows of dots, are surely, to some extent, acts of resistance. Defiance of linguistic decorum is one way of standing up for yourself. Syntactical swerves also have flags of significance to wave.

The third kind of displacement is that inherent in the poet's being female. And we can be sure—despite Sarojini Naidu's large career—that the norms of poetic expectation are no less masculine or phallogocentric in Indian writing then they are in Western literature. This poet acts accordingly, reacts, constructs the poetic subject differently from our expectations. Where we expect progressive argument,' she gives us rough transitions. Where we expect full stops, commas. Where we expect irony, crude contrasts. Where we anticipate some kind of conclusion, odd suspensions, as in 'Contacts':

Only
The world shall die
Shall die, and I
Remain, just being
Also being a remaining . . .

or in 'Loud Posters':

Click-click, click-click tiresomely into your
Ears, stranger, though you may have no need of
Me, I go on and on, not knowing why . . . . . .

Incidentally, 'Loud Posters' deals specifically with the question of how to construct or reassemble a self, a coherent subject, an ego capable of finding some true space in the interstices of an overbearing print culture. The speaker, inside out, displaced, records her desperate career as a pin-up and as a product of typewriters. The tropes of her anomie are fragmentary, contradictory, successive; they range from inversion to poster to alley cat to mind-body gap to two-dimensional image to mechanical domination and voicelessness. They could, it seems, like the last line 'go on and on'.

In an unpublished Ph.D. thesis, Clara Elizabeth Lawson has argued that a 'slanted view' may be detected in the work of major female poets of our century, that this slanted approach to form, syntax and discourse represents both their alienation from the dominant tenets of a male-dominated literary culture and their tactics for coping with that culture. A discernible eccentricity, she suggests, is both the symptom and the medication. She argues her case, with varying persuasiveness, about five poets, American, English and Australian. As I have already been suggesting, it is surely a case we can make out to explain the peculiar force and ostensible carelessness of Kamala Das's poetry. And we can see that such poetry represents a series of flank attacks, not merely on masculine discourse, but also on an imperial language, one of three languages available to her but the one she has chosen to write her major poetry in and to subvert. Her tactics are guerrilla ones; she writes that 'They are lucky/Who ask questions and move on before/The answers come,' and 'my only freedom being/the freedom to/discompose.' She also manages to obtain as much power as possible by rendering sexuality into language while pointing in the same poems to the weakness of language:

> Betray me?
> Yes, he can, but never physically
> Only with words that curl their limbs at
> Touch of air and die with metallic sighs.

What this poetry, with its assertions, plaints and elisions, keeps building or flaunting is a poetic personality. This personality is marked by excess; it is Rousseauseque or Byronic. It assembles the texts as evidence of a rather shocking self: and it invites us to use the assumption of that self as a key to reading those texts. As I suggested earlier, this Byronizing of the poetic subject may well lead us to associate Das with Sylvia Plath, as Anne Brewster has explicitly done. The distinctions between these two contemporaries should also be clearly noted. At the level of subject, Plath presents violence, whereas Das presents sexual desire ('It's only/To save my face, I flaunt, at/Times, a grand, flamboyant lust.'). Plath's poetry is vividly metaphorical, whereas Das's tends, as I have suggested, to work more through metonymic accumulation: true, some of her poems gain their order from sustained tropes of glass, the sea, fire or houses, yet metaphor cannot be said to be the mainspring of her verse, as it is in Plath.

But there is a difference of essential strategy between the poetics of these two writers. Plath began with, and never forsook, the well-made poem; she accepted the artistic ideals of a male culture even while the discourse of her poems assailed and derided it; she was willing to subvert the decorum of masculine poetry, but not its form, not its shapeliness. Even late poems like 'Tulips', 'Sheep in Fog' and 'The Arrival of the Bee Box' are conventionally beautiful pieces of literature; even 'Daddy' is meticulously well made.

Only rarely does Das conform to our traditional expectations of making and shaping. Perhaps she most nearly does in her celebrated micro-madrigal, 'A Request':

When I die
Do not throw the meat and bones away
But pile them up
And
Let them tell
By their smell
What life was worth
On this earth
What love was worth
In the end.

These rhymes, this closure, these are atypical in Das. As I have been suggesting, she is always breaking the pots, always giving the jagged impression of life-talk. She likes, and often uses, the off-beat measures of syllabics. She certainly prefers poetic forms which do not enjoy the balance and symmetry of stanzas; instead she gives us a solid-looking slab of verse on the page, but one which proves to be internally divided by its voices of contrasting moods, contradictory reactions, the tesserae of psychological impressionism. Her poems often start with an utterance which is abrupt, yet given a temporal location, as with 'There was a time when our lusts were/Like multicoloured flags of no/Particular country' or 'I have a man's fist in my head today' or 'There was then no death, no end,' or 'Nani the pregnant maid hanged herself/In the privy one day.'

What this combination of formal ease, abruptness, conversationality and specificity about time guarantees is that Kamala Das's poetry is above all, dramatic. Whether it evokes another person or turns inward and activates a 'dialogue of one', it gives an effect of rapidly succeeding scenes played out in the theatre of the psyche. Its very loudness or excess is a quality of drama, rather than of lyric. No wonder that she called one of her collections *The Old Playhouse and Other Poems*. In the play-house of self the actors must always struggle against the imperious nature of language, using language to do so.

11

The Textual Self

The world that revealed itself in the book and the book itself were never, at any price, to be divided. So with each book its content, too, its world, was palpably there, at hand. But, equally, this content and world transfigured every part of the book. They burned within it, blazed from it: located not merely in its binding or its pictures, they were enshrined in chapter headings and opening letters, paragraphs and columns.

Benjamin

Before the self fully was, there were texts. They were ranged like vertical gods along father's and mother's walls. And before the self had ever come to read, there was typography, with its magic of authority.

There are books, authors, painters, composers and the like whose excitement is a longstanding erotic charge, incapable of being damaged by any hostile criticism, any laboratory session of the practical critics, any blast of theory. Their elixir has already flowed too deep in me to be amenable to rational dispersion; their grip feels like something pre-cognitive. And at the other extreme from these there stand at parade those creative artists whom I have had to learn to admire—Tolstoy, Wordsworth, Bach, Verdi, Michelangelo among them—and who seldom grip me very deeply, not reaching through to the innermost strata of affects at all, however 'great' they may be. They are solemnly acquired tastes. There is something rather external about greatness; it shares a frontier with pomp.

The former, magical group of artefacts and artificers hold a privileged position within any reader's psychic terrain. To them are the high hills, the rushing streams and the arrows of desire. The very names in catalogues or lists generate excitement. They provide references for all I do. Their murmured titles or bright bookjackets bring consolation.

One rides within onself. Sometimes, too, one stands outside for a while, leans aside or flies aloft, trying to get a look at that self. We sway between asserting the ego as prince of freedom and as imprinted. For a bookish child or a child from an arty, text-haunted house the modes of textual imprinting are myriad. The texture of our lives has been articulated by patterns from a host of sources. And into that crooked bar between the signifier and the signified, life has already interposed a tacit information system which will later go by the arcane names of Baskerville, Garamond, Bodoni, Gill Sans and the magisterial Times Roman.

Let us turn away from the power of typefaces awhile. In our house when I was a small boy, and later, there was a picture which struck me as particularly eloquent. It was, in fact, a commercial print framed behind glass and was a reproduction from that master of illustrative illusion, N. C. Wyeth. Seductively coloured, craftily drawn, it represented Balboa (or was it Cortez? I cannot tell for sure now and have blurred the fact with schoolmasterly accounts of Keats's ignorance of the distinction between those two *conquistadores*) atop a hillock, the blue Pacific main beyond him, his cinquecento clothes rather splendid in a sensible way, his clustered men a little lower down that slope in Darien so that they reached only to his waist and could not yet see their goal. Over the Pacific there floated like galleons several mounds of glided cumulus clouds. Gorgeous grammarians in golden gowns, perhaps?

There are clouds very like this in Titian and Giorgione's *Banquet of the Gods*. This strikes me as self-evidently a very great painting, but how far is this a comment on the etiology of my own perceptions, on the fact that Titian and Giorgione were my re-presentations of N. C. Wyeth, a Wyeth laid down in the mind's art gallery by my childhood self, to be forgotten often but never to be displaced? And not even to be displaced now, when I detest Wyeth's work in general.

It is clear that this particular print belongs in the category of precursive works, those texts or structures which set down the fabric of taste and judgement within (as we spatially aver) my consciousness. As such it is located with the more abstract text of 'Greensleeves', a tune whose priority is evident to me, its power more or less unabated, whenever it is heard. Or with *Puck of Pook's Hill*, a text which inculcated a passion for Roman Britain which may confidently be expected to last me for life. It may well be the priority of Kipling's seductive book, too, which left me with my unargued conviction of the greater glamour of Rome than that of Greece. Whenever I probe for the roots of this preference I come to the conclusion that it is somehow pre-rational, like my predilection for nectarines rather than peaches.

I have with me now a little book with a worn spine, bound in navy blue. It is an edition of Palgrave's *Golden Treasury of English Verse: With Additional Poems*. In a wobbly copperplate hand it is inscribed 'To Mummy, Happy Birthday with Love from Kit, 5th May 1947'. The next day I would be thirteen, my birthday following Mum's by one day. Except that I bought the book from our local newsagent, the occasion, even the year, has blown away like smoke. But this pocket-sized text remains.

This book has remained in my parents' last house until quite recently. When I open it a time-casket is unlatched. Flicking over the pages, I can recapture more or less freshly what these poems felt like when I first tried to read them and—the matter is not simple—later in my childhood and adolescence. The type is very black, almost bold, on these crowded pages, the book being a product of wartime austerity conditions: designed, it may be, for the use of His Majesty's Forces. It was cosy to read in the garden, or on the carport roof later on.

All too easily, reading myself backwards now, I can see how some selections, those of Keats, Marvell, Yeats, Pound and Macneice for example, laid down pleasures and preferences which would stay with me for life, so it seems now. These were the kinds of cathexis Harold Bloom underlines in a passage where he broods upon his own development:

Meditating upon these splits or gaps in my own theorizings and practical criticism is not an activity designed to make my own work more acceptable or even useful, whether to others or to myself. But I have a design, and it may transcend even a drive for self-demystification. I became cathected upon poems very early, when I was about ten years old, and I have spent forty years trying to understand that original cathexis. Every love, including a love for poetry, requires reductive examination, even if, with Stevens's Mrs Alfred Uruguay, reduction can lead to our wiping away moonlight like mud.

(1983, 16–17)

Other such preferences would sway me for some years into adulthood before I managed to outgrow them: Davidson and Flecker come to mind. The dullness exhaled by the selections from Sidney, Wordsworth, Hardy and the steadily hateful Tennyson is perceptible still, even though at great pain over the

text-haunting years I have learned to admire Wordsworth and
to love Hardy.

According to what I shall call the law of conservation of
cultural materials, all those old affects are still present, clogging
around these poets and these texts. And the roots of such
feelings are most readily discernible when I turn, as I have
here, back to the original book, the original typeface. Or, to put
it the other way, all my critical readings are also psychic history.

So this small volume encapsulates and can release large
territories of the bookish past, the past as poems felt upon my
nerve-ends. It can still yield up its goods from a miniature
tablet, as mosaic as Marcel's miraculous Japanese paper flowers
which open under water. Regrettable as it may be, within these
flowers there resides a power that fewer and fewer poems
discovered in later years can generate. These foundation
poems, Marvell's 'Bermudas', say, or Thomas's 'Adlestrop', or
Pound's 'Villanelle: the Psychological Hour' (which is not a
villanelle at all, but which contains bits of what may be one, but
why should I care, who would not for years have a clue what
villanelle meant?), have all the advantages of relative primacy.
They are kings-of-the-castle. They are prior determinants of the
name and nature of poetry.

Thus I could say that a small dark-blue volume of verse long
ago inhibited my freedom to read objectively (whatever that
may mean) or at least detachedly, were it not for the fact that
for every reader there are, somewhere, other such moments of
primitive romance laid well down in the substrata of personality,
giving a focus both to defence and to cathexis. In these prior
texts subsequent reading was written small. For some readers
they may lie buried metres under ground like the skeletons of
Herculaneum, but they still pervade the present with their
eloquence, determining which later texts are, in Auden's
phrase, sacred objects, and which are merely secular stretches
of inscription.

Accordingly, thinginess for me is always determined by the
Hopkins of 'Pied Beauty' and the Auden of

Here at the small field's ending pause
Where the chalk wall falls to the foam, and its tall ledges
Oppose the pluck
And knock of the tide
And the shingle scrambles after the sucking surf, and the gull lodges
A moment on its sheer side.

Such poems as these established criteria of desirability which would lead me in Form IV to parts of *The Rape of the Lock* and in Form V to Keats's 'To Autumn', the latter already familiar. In verse, I was not to seek discursive continuity but everything that bumps, jolts, glitters, freckles, twitters or, in the critical cant of later years, seems to *enact*. It was the Browning poems in this same anthology which were, in similar fashion, to set my standards for ebullience, even if I had to play the Browning card very close to my chest when, as an undergraduate, I was taught by hectoring Leavisites.

The Yeats bundle in *The Golden Treasury* was especially disconcerting and beguiling. There were a couple of his early poems which left no imprint at all and then, seventeen pages later, six utterly heterogeneous poems, whose very disparateness it was that played so large a part in preparing me for the punching and counterpunching of discontinuities, as well as establishing my taste for his work. To find 'The Hawk', 'Byzantium', 'The Delphic Oracle upon Plotinus' and 'Two Songs of a Fool, II' standing side by side in semi-scrutable succession was indeed to be teased by allusion and verbal authority; who on earth were Plotinus and Bland Rhadamanthus? who the fool who 'slept on my three-legged stool by the fire'? where in the mind did Yeats's Byzantium stand, and how could I unwind the tangles of chiasmus which made up such lines as this?

Before me floats an image, man or shade,
Shade more than man, more image than a shade;
For Hades' bobbin bound in mummy cloth
May unwind the winding path;
A mouth that has no moisture and no breath
Breathless mouths may summon;
I hail the superhuman;
I call it death-in-life and life-in death.

One thing I learned from this poem was the fact that syntax is capable of astonishing degrees of orchestration and syncopation.

From here I cannot tell when or how often between the ages of thirteen and twenty I returned to the well of this book, but a number of its thin pages (the type shows through the paper) still have a redolence of madeleine. It was ever so often a sub-text on which my school English teachers had to build with their Coleridge and Kipling, Flecker and Pope. And, come Pope, how ugly, cribbed, tenement-like his couplets looked on the page, compared with the spacious stanzas of that half rhymed pair, Keats and Yeats, or with the staggy free verse of Pound.

Of course *The Golden Treasury* was not unique: its impact is the effect of many books in synecdoche, but it remains especially telling as the first book of poems I know myself to have read, let alone gone out and bought. And it has flown back faithfully to my hand, rather like that boldly coloured American marine print which hung in our homes for some thirty years and which my eldest son strangely went and bought from a Bundoora flea market, not even knowing that it was the very same picture, right down to the frame.

In so far as we manifest ourselves as flesh and blood, we are largely bundles of genetic determinations, but in so far as we reveal ourselves in texts, as script or as print, we are largely the product of other texts. How we do stagger about, carrying on our humped backs such a mountain of books, poems, articles, paintings, epigrams, tunes, hymns, and even advertisments. And the products of this mountain tumble over into our oral selves, and into our reading selves, as well as guiding the pen of the writer within us.

There are, of course, those in whom the archaeological stratifications are far less rich, far less deep. They did not have the serried childhood bookshelves which most of us enjoyed or feared. These are they of whom Emily Dickinson wrote, 'How do most people live without any thoughts?': a patronizing sweep of the pen, that one. But the fine eye of a keen and acculturated critic could also begin to determine *their* textual selves, the heap of little texts which, however trivial by high literary standards, have gone to make them, to build what organicist criticism calls their sensibilities.

There is a good, if harsh, comic poem on the subject by Bruce Dawe. In this poem, 'Enter without So Much as Knocking', he envisions the construction of a suburban self, the building materials being the stacked-up phrases and hectic cliches of the electronic media; we overhear the signature tags of serried announcers, the whole torrent of shaky optimisms, which have gone to make the gone man.

In the long, circuitous haul we are all—readers, writers or just plain livers—determined by a greater host of things than we can ever put a name to; and since we cannot put all the names to them we behave as though we had free will.

Nevertheless, we can at times come to terms with large clusters of personality determinants, especially if we concentrate our efforts within one information system, as J. L. Lowes did with Coleridge's absorption of literary and topological texts in *The Road to Xanadu*. However radical their gestures may seem, books connect systematically with other books within the larger frame of language and the tightly organized information system which is print culture. Even if it be the case that we agree with Proust's Marcel that 'A book is a huge cemetery in which on the majority of tombs the names are effaced and can no longer be read', we can always read some of those names immediately, and with time and care restore many of the others. When we examine ourselves, we know which books it was that did the damage. It may take us time in self-exposition, fingering the scar tissue, hunting for the key in darkness, pressing after the repressed materials, but because they belong to the Great Library we have some kind of Dewey decimal system by which we can find our way to them. The text-inheritance is both powerful and relatively scrutable because it is organized by a clearly arrayed scheme of scaffolding: contrast the part played in our psyches by smells and tastes; the mnemonics of spring's first cut-grass smell are virtually unknowable and hence insidiously powerful.

But with verbal formations we have a certain amount of system to go by. We can find our way back linguistically, fumbling our way informedly enough towards the source: towards those roots of which the French poet, Alain Bosquet, writes,

Au fond de chaque mot
j'assiste a ma naissance*

And indeed it is the case that verbal influences can be sufficiently atomic to reside in single words. Some verbal influences would seem to reside in rhythms. I do not know, for instance, why so many imaginatively charged words have the same dactylic rhythm: assegai, amethyst, Borneo, Dandenongs (misheard in childhood as Dandelongs, first cousin to those prolific yellow lawn flowers or weeds), Gundagai (reinforced by a popular song of the thirties), lanoline and Rechabite. It may be that three syllables prove just enough to make a little tune,

---

* At the source of each word I am present at my birth.

sometimes even enforced by a rhyme, as in that comically circular name, Amsterdam. Carraway; peppermint; cadmium: how rhythm enforces magic; or, to put it more pussyfootedly, how rhythm enforces a sub-rational suggestiveness attaching to certain words, phrases or lines.

I should like to press on a little while longer with these examples of the acquisition of cultural sub-strata. Not only will a further display help with this process of what Bloom called self-demystification, but it will lay stress on a far earlier period of cultural formation and on an example which is morphologically rather different.

As I have noted in another essay, there were certain children's books in the rented South Yarra house of my pre-War childhood which laid down their sediments early. One of these, powerfully formative although, as it turns out, only partly read, was *Letters to Channy: a Trip around the World*, a book or collage by Heluiz Chandler Washburne. Published in the year before my birth, it has an eye-catching frontispiece, a double-page map of the world framed by lozenges in which are stars or, alternatively, silhouetted figures emblematic of world travel. In the foreground, between South America and Australasia, there stands a little boy in shorts peering into the map through an opened envelope. His back squarely towards us, he recalls Yeats's pen-portrait of Keats:

I see a schoolboy when I think of him,
With face and nose pressed to a sweet shop window,

The boy is Chandler Washburne, aged seven, who stayed in Wheeling, Indiana, while his parents travelled round the world: hence the book. This visual trope alone signifies an attitude to reading of some importance, it being a window into maps of a reality far more exciting and exotic than the merely contingent world.

When I rediscovered this book recently in the Bodleian Library I came to realize that as a child I had only ever read some of the early chapters—those on Hawaii, Japan, India and perhaps China. In the rest of the volume only occasional brisk illustrations were familiar. The one detail which has resurrected frequently over the years is that source of my childish puzzlement, the fact that Channy's sister Beatrice was 'called Bice (pronounced *Beechay*)'. The exoticism of this information long haunted my linguistic psyche. (It springs, by the way, from the

very beginning: from sentence two of the Foreword. The beginnings of texts have especial incantatory power, of course.) Both
of the other passages which stir specific recall also share in this
macaronic quality. They are 'Hawkshaw, a big strong Hawaiian
boy', and 'In Calcutta we went to see a great scientist who
studies the life of plants. His name is Sir Bose'. I take it that any
passage which disconcerts the consistency of the linguistic code
in play is likely to stick like a burr in the childish imagination.
Resistance is more important than traction.

Letters to Channy helped to lay down a taste for the
fragmentary, the improvised, the interrupted narrative which
has carried right through into my present critical appropbation
for *Ulysses, Such is Life, Tristram Shandy, The Road to Oxiana*
and *La Vie de Henri Brulard.*

But the direct effects of *Letters to Channy* are slight, lying
partly in the fact that a few of its details remain marked with a
mnemic accent and partly in fostering a taste for discontinuous
texts. To another fragmentary narrative, *Puck of Pook's Hill*,
published in that lovely little Macmillan uniform edition in navy
and gold, with an inopportune swastika or fylfot on the spine, I
remain indebted for a more powerful imprinting, as I have
partly suggested already.

Puck of Pook's Hill which I delighted in, read and reread
for years, yielded an ironical interplay of primary narrator,
secondary narrators and characters, and also, with great charm,
a sense of the historical layering of the English landscape. (As
a result, you might say that it prevented me from reading
Australian literature for a further thirteen years or so.) Although Puck's narrative and legerdemain begin with the Norse
gods and then proceed to three chapters on Norman England
before tracking back to 'A Centurion of the Thirteenth', it was
Roman Britain that seized me then and does so still: to such an
extent that any text or artefact alluding to Roman Britain
remains erotically charged for me in a way which no other slice
of history can equal—not even Mughal India nor the Highlands
during the Jacobite uprisings, both these sediments having been
laid down in my heart-floor by somewhat later influences; my
father's wartime experience in India in the case of the Mughals,
and sentimental schoolteachers for Bonnie Prince Charlie and
company.

I am not sure not how far familiar atheism also lent a hand,
when I think that my passion for Hadrian's Wall and the legions

was long shored up by a long dislike for the Malorian Middle Ages. It was with almost inexpressible delight that I first found Arthur translated back from wispy chevalier to sturdy Latinized Briton. And much greater again was to be my delight when, as an adult, I found in the Norse sagas a great, non-Christian mediaeval literature. One's history is always a chapter of accidents, an odd mosaic of cut-off and snub-nosed texts.

I am on the brink of laying aside this memoriousness for more general speculations, but let me just note that such speculations about influence as these must always tread the borderline between what Richard Rorty has called 'texts' and what he has called 'lumps'. We are professionally concerned with 'texts', which are distinguished by their being 'phonetic or graphic inscriptions', but our textual selves may none the less be deeply affected by 'lumps', ranging anywhere between lumps of landscape and lumps of shortbread. Where do I draw the boundaries in defining the Indophile strata of my imaginative predilections between, say, *The Jungle Books*—also, conveniently by Kipling—airletters my father sent back from India for four years or so, the Indian artefacts and objects he sent back, ranging from ornaments to *kukris* to bolts of cloth, and the knowledge, orally acquired, that some of my relations had fought in the Indian Mutiny (not as mutineers, of course)?

There is the textual self I am sketching for your attention, then; one who has gone on to become not merely a general reader but professionally engaged in literary criticism while still believing with Auden that

All imaginations do not respond to the same sacred beings or events, but every imagination responds to those it recognizes in the same way. The impression made upon the imagination by any sacred being is of an overwhelming but undefinable importance—an unchangeable quality, an Identity, as Keats said;

(1968, 55)

Thus for me a sacredness of being, or cathectic charge remains permanently attached to the poems of Yeats, Macneice and Marvell. It must have required subsequent renewal, otherwise Dowson and Flecker would also have stayed in there, rather than falling away: I shall return to this question later. It attaches even to the cover of a book by Yeats or Kipling or Auden. (Yeats was the same age as my paternal grandmother; Hardy, Furphy and Henry James were the age of my grand-father; the thirties poets a little younger than my father: I sometimes wonder whether they wrote with 'a decade's voice' which I have somehow recognized familially.) And this cathexis so irradiated Empson's 'Description of a View' as to prepare me for my long-subsequent encounter with cubism, as well as offering the rack of diction I would draw from when I came to be absorbed in psychomachia and the poetry of mental structures:

Well boiled in acid and then laid on glass
(A labelled strip) the specimen of building,
Though concrete, was not sure what size it was,
And was so large as to compare with nothing.
High to a low and vulnerable sky
It rose, and could have scraped it if it chose;
But plain, and firm, and cleanly, like stretched string,
It would not think of doing such a thing;
On trust, it did not try.
My eye walked up the ladder of its windows.

A last self-characterization: what all my reading has long had in common is inattention, inattention combined with bursts of feverish concentration span. Did I become a rapid reader because I could not concentrate for long, or vice versa? I wonder how long ago I fell into my present habit of reading between six and twelve books at once. Somehow, I cannot allow myself to become confined to one book, however good. I need others waiting at my elbow, like good servants. You might say that I need a seraglio of books. The textual experience is not only every bit as absorbing as what we call 'life' but it is also something I orchestrate in order to produce the greatest possible excitement, the greatest charge, the erotics of a multi-course dinner. The excitements which I crave are still to be provided by those texts which have long been sacred. And by certain late recruits, but that is a further story: a tale of metaphor and metonymy.

Very well, then. What general principles begin to emerge from this account of the formation of a textual self?

The first is that if the determinants of taste, preference and even interest prove to be so utterly arbitrary, then the critic's first duty is to put as many cards as possible on the table. The only way to cope with one's irremediable subjectivity—or idiosyncrasy of formation—is to be deliberately and openly subjective about it. Having deconstructed the notion of a free, coherent readerly self, we immediately have to reconstruct it again in order to have the only basis for critical discourse which is not mere conventional agreement.

This declaration of a readerly self serves two purposes. The more simple one is thereby enunciating what one's readers and auditors need to know about the grounds on which a series of utterances are taking their stand: only extreme provisionality should be honoured as a posture, although I must confess that we will frequently be seduced by sheer style.

But the second purpose is this: that by setting down as clearly as possible the far-off processes by which a self has been constructed the critic may come nearer and nearer to the hidden, even repressed, determinants of his or her position. As in the clinical dialogue of psychoanalysis, the critic is subjecting (I like that verb) himself or herself to a continuing pressure that progressively uncovers the sentient machinery which is being brought to bear on a succession of texts, and trying to do them justice without being either a blind juryman or a hanging judge. The critic has somehow to strike an appropriate posture, neither rushing nor slouching, in the elastic medium of time, for criticism is in a sense the work of active memory and

> ... the mneme ... is conservative and progressive, in the same time, for its function is the conservation of progress ... (mneme) occupies the middle ground between instinct which is of a generally conservative nature, and intelligence, which is progressively directed.
>
> (W. Stern, in Rapaport, 1950, 121)

That is where criticism is, surely, balancing awkwardly between conservative responsiveness and the keen joys of progressive subversion. A balance must be struck in the most enabling possible way for the critic, where he or she stands in history, bearing always in mind Proust's—or Marcel's—dictum that 'Every reader, as he reads, is the reader of himself.'

Manifestly, each textual self is going to be an entirely different cultural formation, even if developed within a culture as Babylonian, centralized and hierarchical as that of France, for instance; as we all know, French critics are a strikingly diverse mob. And so are we all. Each self has been imprinted quite differently, put together from different textual and experiential raw materials. Our common ground, apart from the grid of language, which we just can not get out of, is a matter of conventions, some of them heavily laid on us, some gleefully accepted, some so insidiously and widely implanted that we seldom glimpse them at all. We can all see that Cambridge moralism or *nouveau* Marxism is a matter of convention, readily open to critical debate. We are much dodgier about the conventions of logic; we can see that they do not mirror truth of the world in any way, but go on imposing them on our students as part of a contract we share not only with teaching institutions but with broad traditions of Western discourse; I try to write logically about the fact that there are no grounds for logic. Other examples cut even closer to the quick. I recall asking a very impressive radical critic in England whether she thought that the concept of correct spelling was an authoritarian imposition on individual freedom. To my surprise, she did not see the point.

As regards what reading and discourse can finally get a grip on, I do not see that we can get any further than David Hume's remarks,

All probable reasoning is nothing but a species of sensation. 'Tis not solely in poetry and music we must follow our taste and sentiment, but also in philosophy. When I am convinced of a principle, 'tis only an idea, which strikes more strongly upon me.

Critical discourse might seem to have become impossible for those who have taken this point, and agree with it. And yet two centuries of thinkers have gone on doing so. Scepticism about absolutes does nothing to bring the game to a stop. Marxists, radical feminists, principled solipsists, all go on behaving institutionally and even linguistically in much the same way as the staunchest academic tory. Even if they have glimpsed the abyss, they go on giving lectures which are fifty minutes long, writing grammatically, and scrawling 13½/20 on the final page of students' essays. They also go on preferring some books to others. We declare our philosophical scepticism, but go on living from day to day by conventions which we know how to see through. And we welcome competing theories not because they will go further towards illuminating 'truth' but because they shake us out of lazy habits and because they offer us new insights in which we can take intellectual pleasure, which is also instinctual pleasure.

I presume, alas, that academics have no choice but go on working within such conventions, whether they be called the

M.A., the Ph.D., the staff seminar, the conference, the review, the critical essay. Without conventions we are done for, thrust back into the bottomless sceptical solipsism which most of us have clearly glimpsed but which, taken solemnly, leaves us merely back up the creek. The last utterance in that direction is that of the disarmingly honest Nietzsche, on the very brink of the madness which finally claimed him, writing to the authorities of the University of Basel,

Dear Herr Professor, when it comes to it I too would very much prefer a professorial chair in Basel to being God, but I did not dare to go so far in my private egoism as to refrain for its own sake from the creation of the world . . .

After that, madness and silence, which is the cost of electing to be God. And since most of us prefer, or have no choice but to prefer, not to be God, and mad, we vote to work within conventions and systems, vote to operate somewhere in the range between a manifestly inadequate empiricism and a manifestly mendacious over-arch of theory. That way, discussion, debate, teaching, and even society become possible. Or, to put the matter rather differently, the language system, in which we are all constellated, subverts our attempts at a rational scepticism, much as it subverts the humanist continuities.

Let me turn now to take up a thread which was laid aside earlier. It has to do with the law of conservation of cultural materials, which is in truth only an echo of Freud's 'nothing once formed in the mind could ever perish, . . . everything survives in some way or other'. The problem here is not to do with those things which are remembered or rediscovered, but with the vastly more spacious domain of lost, forgotten or repressed materials, all those thousands of lost texts which also played their part in making the textual self, the responsive adult sensibility. How can we talk about what we cannot discover? We are surely in the same *mise en abîme* situation that psychoanalytic theory frequently is, with its stress on the repression of significant materials, on the deformation wrought in them by condensation and displacement, and above all by its insistence that the most important experience is likely to be the most deeply buried, like a treasure chest on some unmapped Treasure Island. Yet psychoanalysis does not despair, and nor should we. There are methods of self-scrutiny, paths of association, hermeneutic systems, which will gradually reveal the nodes and corners where it all happened. As Lacan explains in 'Function and Field of Speech and Language',

> The unconscious is that chapter of my history that is marked by a blank or occupied by a falsehood: it is the censored chapter. But the truth can be rediscovered; usually it has been written down elsewhere. Namely:
> —in monuments: this is my body. That is to say, the hysterical nucleus of the neurosis in which the hysterical symptom reveals the structure of a language, and is deciphered like an inscription which, once recovered, can without serious loss be destroyed;
> —in archival documents: these are my childhood memories, just as impenetrable as are such documents when I do not know their provenance;
> —in semantic evolution: this corresponds to the stock of words and acceptations of my own particular vocabulary, as it does to my style of life and my character;
> —in traditions, too, and even in the legends which, in a heroicized form, bear my history;
> —and lastly, in the traces that are inevitably preserved by the distortions necessitated by the linking of the adulterated chapter to the chapters surrounding it, and whose meaning will be re-established by my exegesis.
>
> (1980, 50)

Some of Lacan's categories are, as usual, far less clear than others, but it is demonstrably the case that we partly and increasingly recognize the buried as well as the visible textual determinants of our present reading selves. And that we must keep on feeding our new access of knowledge, our new glimpses of self, into the process which call critical reading. The act is full of past performances.

Finally there is an analogy between the attraction or dark potential felt to be lurking in one's own lost experience and the seductive power which a work of literature, a lyric poem, say, exerts by seeming to withhold experience from us. Readerly desire becomes aroused by the poem's concentrated reticence, its resistance to critical translation.

In the last gasp, in the run home, I find that theory, however bracing, collapses. For what I want in and from literature is mystery: the withheld, the unexplained, the plangent, whose secret name is Death. And whatever it is that dances on the thin roof of Death's house. As the romantic poets, from Keats to Stevens and Slessor, knew all too well, language dances on that roof with peculiar eloquence. Stevens wrote that 'death is the mother of beauty', and what clse is beauty but another name for the mystery, that return of the repressed which we as readers so often desire? I do not know, by the way, why the world *beauty* has remained unfashionable for quite so long; I suppose it took too much boosting in the nineteenth century and, consequentially, too much of a shellacking in our own time.

Ah, yes, the return of the repressed. Given that I am especially drawn to these poets and to their sense of the sorcery of Thanatos, can it be any accident that the first poem which I know myself to have been taught at school—I was six years old at the time—was Thomas Hood's deadly,

I remember, I remember
The house where I was born,
The little window where the sun
Came peeping in at morn.
It never came a wink too soon
Nor brought too long a day,
But now I often wish that night
Had borne my breath away.*

'That *night*' or '*that* night'? Relative pronoun or demonstrative adjective? I am sure that this syntactical ambiguity added grip or expressiveness to such a creepily slight stanza, enabling it to brood away there in my psyche for decades, like a heavy stone.

But we shall all have noted the final paradox here for the reader as critic. In so far as he or she manages to reduce that residual mystery he or she is thereby the more powerful critic, the wielder of greater critical authority. But in so far as the critic not only respects but evokes a sense of that unanalyzed residue the resultant criticism is thereby a more seductive guide to the aura or to the expressive powers of the work. There we are, then, and there's the pity of it. Surely we are all bound to work within the toil of two countervailing scepticisms, as Hume recognized when he recommended 'carelessness and inattention' as the only way of getting by with one's doubts.

---

* I find belatedly that the syntactical ambiguity which teased me for all those years does not exist; the seventh line simply ends with 'the night'. I wonder, then, why I needed to produce that crux.

12

Swaying in the Forties

Ration books, whatever became of ration books? Those little
brownish pocketbooks, the coloured tickets and a neat pair of
scissors tied to the shop counter, these are so deeply ingrained
in my childhood as to seem inevitable, not memorable. They
have a routine quality, like *Champion* or 'The Search for the
Golden Boomerang' or visits to the flicks on Saturday arvo,
hoping against hope for a film marked out by June Allyson's
distillation of sweetness. And opposite the deep naturalness of
all these—in the mind's other eye—are to be found the forties'
inherently surrealist artefacts: gas producers on the left front
mudguards of cars, slit trenches in front lawns, gas masks and
midget submarines, all worthy the starkly graphic imagination
of an Eric Thake.

When, a few years ago, I cobbed together a series of
reflections on 'my' 1930s the job was easy, the problems of
selection few, for my best-loved screen memories were just
sitting up there like Jacky, waiting to be made use of, waiting to
be strung together. The forties come harder, since in dealing
with that faraway but far larger memory-field I have to take
account of questions of causation and chronology.

They have their music too, their distinctive flavour, none the
less. At one end of the dial sound the sweet beguiling strains of
'Lili Marlene' and 'The Lady from Twentynine Palms' (or was it
Fortynine?), familiar occasions for escape. At the other end
were darker musics which I did not yet know how to hear. Like
this, for instance:

Nietzsche respected the great god Plumb
That lays his pipes in a baby's tum.
Beneath our logic's pure avowals
He heard the murmur of the bowels.

(James McAuley, 'The Family of Love')

Or the fact that another unknown, Judith Wright, was declaring
that 'The trains go north with guns.' As a schoolboy I knew

nothing of the peculiar utterances of the modern arts; my classmates still called Picasso 'Pig's arse-o' and Dad was to tell me on one occasion that a poet called T. S. Eliot had written that 'The sun was setting like half a tinned apricot into a sea of junket'. And, ah yes, I did know the private collection of our grandest friend, Hilda (Mrs R. D.) Elliott, a personal gallery which displayed Orpen, Brangwyn, Degas and the wrong John, Elioth Gruner and Blamire Young. Of more interest to me was the fact that she kept kangaroos in her Toorak front garden.

I have on the desk beside me a copy of the *Herald* for Thursday, 4 January 1945. The day was warm, 82 degrees F.—poor old Fahrenheit, I still can't do without it in these diminished Celsian days—and we were probably on summer holidays at Black Rock, now a mere suburb: it was the only place we ever had our holidays, I do not believe we ever said 'holidayed', during the War. But it is the front page of this newspaper which brings rushing back my common childhood terms of reference: 'NEW ATTACK ON NAZI WEDGE', 'ALLIES ON MANDALAY RAILWAY', 'CANADIANS PRESS ON N.W. OF RAVENNA', 'TURKEY BREAKS WITH JAPAN' and 'NEW GREEK LEADER FORMS CABINET AS GUNS ROAR'. No wonder we all knew so much geography in those days; one of my exact contemporaries still remembers the capitals of all the countries in the world, as they were in 1939.

It was not only a World War: it was also a war world. Come August 1945 and the flurry of VJ Day, my main source of puzzlement was to be what on earth they would put in the papers now it was peacetime. You cannot get much media mileage out of the return of Jack Baird's pace bowling to the Carlton team, nor out of such items as 'Mr J. D. G. Medley, Vice-Chancellor of the University, is spending the holidays at Khancoban and will return to Melbourne on January 15.' The editors do not seem to have been troubled: politics is just a way of continuing war by other means.

Let me place a figure in the picture, my own. I begin the decade as a small boy going off with his mother and younger brother to share an aunt's timber house at the seaside because Dad has sailed away to the impending war in Malaya and will not be back—except for one brief compassionate leave—for five years; I end it as a lumpish youth of sixteen scraping through a science Matric by the skin of my teeth and finding

a job as Junior Technical Officer at the Royal Mint, William
Street, Melbourne, there to work amid the buying and smelting
of gold, the smelting and stamping of bronze or silver coinage.
The intervening period is stuffed full of schooldays, full of
sustained routines, inkblots, nicknames and only rare showings
of memorabilia. I begin by going from one small school, Yarra
Bank, to another, and then on to another, where we start
French at six, Latin at seven. There's history for you. I move to
a very large school indeed ('The biggest boys' school in the
southern hemisphere'), where one-and-a-half thousand boys
could be loosely deployed in picturesque landscape settings,
and stay there for eight years and more. For nine years, after
Black Rock, we are crammed hugger-mugger into a tiny flat,
just off Toorak Road. Only reffos or bachelors are meant to
live in flats; ordinary people have, or rent, houses. My mother
ignores this palpable fact, willing to put up with being a sardine
for the sake of a toffy address. Having no garden, we play in the
street. An old tennis ball bounces interminably against brick
walls.

It was my mother who had some awareness of what moved
artistically. Before the war her friends had included pianists,
potters, painters and printmakers, but that global melodrama
and the need to look after two boys had switched off her
cultural input. Once he had escaped from the jungles of Burma,
a thousand miles on foot, lost for much of the time, Dad had it
much easier. Stravaging around India, Persia and Lebanon, he
could wallow in costume drama and ruined temples, devour
exotica, imagine the sweep of tribes, peoples, dynasties through
the Krac des Chevaliers or the Red Mosque, and keep alive
in his heart the ideals of Norman Lindsay and the great il-
lustrators. Fortified by a century of illustration, his response to
most modern painting was an easy one: 'The bugger can't
draw.' But I was only to hear this line in the latter half of the
decade. Until then my father was the faraway source of photos,
flimsy airletters rich with oriental travel details and curvilinear
gifts from China or India. He was geography personified:
already I could see how he idealized Ptolemy the Great, Asoka
the Furious, Alexander—not the British field marshal but
Iskandar himself.

History diffuses as much as it classifies; indeed, it dissipates
aura because it classifies things and places them in sets or boxes.
It is mute household objects, humble tastes and modest smells

that by their maverick or mongrel qualities retain their eloquence. So the 1940s are for me still encapsulated in chops, cauliflower cheese and the sparsely fluted metal containers in which were served the chocolate malted milks I loved so well; in the wooden grid that floored the central area of trams; in the smell of a summer northerly bearing malthouse and Rosella tomato sauce flavours richly over from Richmond; in dust and fallen tickets by the wicket gates on railway platforms; in thin, flat wafers of beechnut chewing gum, the currency of our American invaders; in aeroplane scrapbooks; and in the prickly feeling of grey worsted suitpants against my sweaty legs after a lunchtime spent playing some hectic game in the school grounds. Zinc, chromium, manganese . . . in those lost days I became obsessed by the chemical properties of metals.

It was a time of displacement and imaginative subversion as well as of common participation in that abstract solidarity which we called 'the war effort' or, later, 'reconstruction'. People were moved from place to place in oddly random ways. Not only was Nolan sent off to the Wimmera, there to discover newly expressionist landscape images; not only were Harold Stewart and McAuley sent south to Victoria Barracks, St Kilda Road, there to give birth to that gaudy bell-wether, Ern Malley; not only was Patrick White sent to the Aegean and Slessor to the Western Desert. Whole schools went up country to escape from incipient Japanese bombs. Whole industries changed their identities. And many familiar products vanished from daily life. Most surreal of all, there were a few years in which, for the first and last time, it was patriotic to be a Communist.

Whatever the war effort was doing, it was also peeling back piecemeal the sunlit surfaces of daily life, revealing mental flora as bizarre as Albert Tucker's *Images of Modern Evil* or such lines as these, hatched from A. D. Hope's usually-Parnassian imagination:

Full sail the proud three-decker sandwiches
With the eye-fumbled priestesses repass;
On their swan lake the enchanted ice-creams freeze,
The amorous fountain prickles in the glass
And at the introit of this mass emotion
She comes, she comes, a balanced pillar of blood
                    ('Morning Coffee')

But nothing of this was visible to a boy growing up, quietly enough, reflectively enough, sportingly enough, through the bipartite forties. The only real artistic flurry I can dredge back from those years was the journalistic brouhaha over the Archibald Prize for 1943. For my rapid-reading machinery it was a span of time that began with William, Biggles and *Puck of Pook's Hill* and ended with an undifferentiated mishmash of Mark Twain, Keats, mathematical puzzles, Neville Cardus, *Eyeless in Gaza*, *The Rape of the Lock* and *Ulysses*. The one thing I was clear about was that all nineteenth-century prose was unreadable, an extended hoax foisted upon us by adults: well, by some adults.

By the end of 1950 habit-sets were slipping and sliding. I went for the first time to surf beaches instead of the flat, tepid waters of the Bay. I had sharpened up my net game, but my backhand was still my weakness. The local municipal library—for we had changed to an outer suburb—proved to be marvellously rich in Bloomsbury colourations, Gide and Stendhal; I not only read *Aspects of the Novel* but excitedly followed up all Forster's tips, nothing but the bulky *Moby Dick* failing to make an impression. Summerily suntanning daily, I waited for news about my impending job. Communists were bad once again, Korea improbably offering itself as a potential flashpoint. My father was now working for General Motors–Holden while remaining a steady advocate of the Chinese communists against 'that bastard, Kai-Chek'. I and my peers knew all the models of shiny Yank-tanks while our hearts burned for natty little English sports cars. England still produced quality products and the Japanese cheap, tinny junk. I bought a brown pork-pie hat and some army disposals shirts. It was time at last to start working in the city: all those marvellous hours of reading on the train.

Soon, for the gap before night school, I discovered the Hoddle, a basement eating house with a studenty queue all the way up its terrazzo stairs to Little Collins Street. It was the first Italian trattoria I had ever encountered. It had an aura, a very modest aura, which remains with me still, as clear as day and as thick as evening. Thick white table-cloths, thick white china, thick white bread with hard crusts and, it goes without saying, densely brown minestrone for starters. I was now fairly launched in the city. The National Gallery and the Public Library waited under their flat grey dome, prepared to swallow me up.

On summer's afternoon I went to visit Jack Bellew and his daughter June in their modern house on Banksia Street hill. On their living room wall there hung a most arresting image.

Queerly simplified, done in shiny enamels, it depicted a dark Ned Kelly with his tincan head, riding across flatness towards the viewer. It was impossible actually to like this painting, but I soon came to realize that it was the most extraordinary, the most unforgettable picture that I had ever seen. Somehow it hacked an icon out of real life. It had to do with life, but was more than it. And, miracle of miracles, here was modern art which actually had an Australian subject.

At this, my whole understanding turned over.

13

The Quaker Graveyard in Carlton

Off to the Baillieu Library we would go, waiting for, hankering after the latest literary journals from the United States. Ah, the American magazines . . . My theme is the way in which the modes and manners of American poetry struck us—and they very distinctively did—in the course of the 1950s. I am both speaking for my own reactions at the time and trying to indicate how my reactions resembled those of other poets, other readers, of my generation. Our sense of British poetry came first, however: inevitably. We were haunted by the British poets still, and we misunderstood them grossly. America was capitalist, exotic and politically wicked. But it was only beginning to take over the role of crushing parent from England, and could still seem no more than a glamorous stepmother.

Cringing, strutting or wincing, any writer has mixed responses when he or she looks back on predecessors and forebears. On the one hand, they are the figures who by their example (which we misunderstand, of course) made our existence, our activities, possible; on the other, they are the burdens or stumbling-blocks who prevent us from being ourselves. Their ancestral voices sound through us, even when we would be most acutely individual. As Marx said, recognizing the force of such anguish in himself, 'Past generations lie like an incubus upon the living', and all literary exemplars play out a role for us which is at first enabling and later stifling. When their authority is further derived from their having belonged to a power-broking colonial culture, their pressure upon us is redoubled. The creative spirit hankers to rebel.

We can find in the writings of Freud grass-root descriptions of such a process or maturation as this, since the obvious chain of connection is with the way a child develops: his or her profound ambivalence towards the towering figures of the parents. In a little essay of 1908 called 'Family Romances', Freud writes:

The liberation of an individual, as he grows up, from the authority of his parents is one of the most necessary though one of the most painful results brought about by the course of his development. It is quite essential that that liberation should occur and it may be presumed that it has been to some extent achieved by everyone who has reached a normal state. Indeed, the whole progress of society rests upon the opposition between successive generations . . .

For a small child his parents are at first the only authority and the source of all belief . . . But as intellectual growth increases, the child cannot help discovering by degrees the category to which his parents belong. He gets to know other parents and compares them with his own, and so acquires the right to doubt the incomparable and unique quality which he had attributed to them. Small events in a child's life which make him feel dissatisfied afford him provocation for beginning to criticize his parents, and for using, in order to support his critical attitude, the knowledge which he has acquired that other parents are in some respects perferable to them.

For those of us who were beginning to write poetry in the 1950s the situation had a number of readily distinctive features. It goes without saying that the literature we had been taught at school, university or teachers' college was English literature. T. S. Eliot, as he would dearly have wished, was thoroughly assimilated into English poetry: it was only well after graduating that I realized how many of his early poems are essentially about Boston life, rather than the London we firmly located him in. Ezra Pound, who fascinated me almost from the start, did not seem American either; he seemed rather to belong to Europe, the cosmopolitan world of Modigliani and Stravinsky, Valéry and Matisse. Conversely—such can be the distortions of antipodean readings of imperial cultures—it seemed at the time possible to see Beckett as sharing the Anglo-Saxon grubbiness of Amis or Larkin.

The copyright agreements which covered book distribution affected our reading habits in ways that are unimaginable today. Since the American copyright *imperium* was entirely separate from that of the British Commonwealth (with the partial exception of Canada), American books were only available in Australia if they had been published, or republished, by British houses. Then, as now, some bookshops broke the prevailing rules, but all this meant was access to a few Meridian, Harvest or Galaxy paperbacks. The general picture was that American poetry was filtered through to us by the taste and judgement of English editors. Faber was king, of course, and its imprint made Stevens, Marianne Moore and the young Robert Lowell available to us. A few other firms played their part also: Eyre and Spottiswoode for instance with the Southern Agrarians. But our sense of American poetry remained limited and selective.

So, indeed, did our sense of America. In those high, polar years of the Cold War, many of us reacted to its encampments with a sense of 'a plague on both your houses'. America was, for us, the land of Gresham's Law capitalism, where trash was free to drive out quality, the all-powerful source of comics, hit-parade songs (not until the Beatles did pop music become acceptable) and the corny, flavourless movies of MGM and Paramount. The phrase, 'Coca Cola culture', which appeared in a *Meanjin* article, described something which most of us recognized. Grudgingly, we generally conceded that the models of high culture and intellectual endeavour were derived from England, or at least from Europe. The socialist principles which, more or less diluted, a great many of us held played no small part in this instinctive preference.

Into this sort of climate came, not only the books of those few individual poets I have mentioned, but also Geoffrey Moore's *The Penguin Book of Modern American Verse*: for its time, invaluable.

It has often struck me that, with rare exceptions, critics have had almost nothing to say about the physical format in which poems are encountered first up. For example, I do not know how anyone can get the same kind of pleasure from a roneoed poem as from one on good paper in a decent typeface. More specifically, one's memory of a period is likely to be intimately bound up in particular books, certain physical and typographical objects in which the poems have a different aura than when we encounter them again elsewhere—even if it be in a well-printed anthology. Certain books, then, yield up my sense of reading in the 1950s: a slim Faber crown octavo with blocky black type, containing a fine little selection of Pound's poetry, and, in its matt purple and red dustjacket, Robert Lowell's *Poems 1938– 1949*, where I encountered for the first time that dense, astonishing monologue, 'Falling Asleep over the Aeneid'. Similarly, the first edition of *The Penguin Book of Modern American Verse* has for me a recapitulatory power like Marcel's tea-dunked madeleine: between its sombrely laurelled covers we first had access, we felt, to the poetry of the United States.

As this and other collections became available from the early fifties on, young Australian poets could feel they were in touch with something which released them from their postures of filial ambiguity towards British poetry, and from their Australian forebears. It is still possible to recapture that first welcome shock of *strangeness*, that new access to habits, attitudes and voices which lay right outside our habits of learned response. This was a different distillation of the Modernist movement and its aftermath from any we had learned to make; it is intriguing to ask what it was that seemed so stimulating or diverting in such poetry. Alex Craig has done something of this already in his admirably concise account of the period in his introduction to *Twelve Poets*, but I want to hunt the quarry further.

Wise after the event, some commentators have suggested that one turned to American poetry for ways to be more open, democratic or committed. Except for the case of Bruce Dawe, whose creative impulses were strongly demotic for all the richnesses of his diction, the reverse was generally true. Australian and English poetry (think of 'the Movement' and its plain worsted verse) were at the time deeply committed to plainness and good sense: it is only now that he is dead that we can see how powerful, weird and estranging the *oeuvre* of Philip Larkin turned out to be, how far he went towards inventing a new kind of post-surrealism in which, as Bayley has claimed, 'the world of elsewhere is also the acceptance world'. In the fifties, Larkin still appeared respectively dowdy. Time transforms texts.

Looking outside the family circle, we hungered for something quite different, and in Geoffrey Moore's very catholic anthology we found it.

Among the immediate attractions of this American poetry, then, was the fact that it seemed not merely exotic but even mandarin. Stevens, Marianne Moore, Ransom, both the Bishops, and others as well were zany, dandyish poets of an elevation that Australia has only known in Slessor and Lex Banning. An Australian reader knew nothing that resembled Robert Horan's marvellous, Kafkaesque fable, 'Suppose we kill a king', let alone the consciously trendy decadence of H. Phelps Putnam's 'Hasbrouck and the Rose':

Hasbrouck was there and so were Bill
And Smollet Smith the poet, and Ames was there.
After his thirteenth drink, the burning Smith,
Raising his fourteenth trembling in the air,
Said, 'Drink with me, Bill, drink up to the Rose'.

But Hasbrouck laughed like old men in a myth,
Inquiring, 'Smollet, are you drunk? What rose?'
And Smollet said, 'I drunk? It may be so;
Which comes from brooding on the flower, the flower
I mean toward which mad hour by hour
I travel brokenly; and I shall know,
With Hermes and the alchemists—but, hell,
What use is it talking that way to you?
Hard-boiled, unbroken egg, what can you care
For the enfolded passion of the Rose? . . .

This poem is callow stuff, to be sure, a winsome example of
what Yvor Winters used to call 'reference to a non-existent
plot', but its aestheticism had connections with that of Horan's
poem or, more largely, with that of Stevens and Marianne
Moore. The Americans showed a manic delight in the fact that
they inhabited an Imaginary Museum—as André Malraux
called it—in which all the artefacts of past and present
coexisted in their jumbled glass cases. And, at the same time,
they were consciously interested in foregrounding language
itself, in all its stubborn artificiality as well as its expressive
verve.

Archibald Macleish, often a boringly rhetorical poet, was
also represented by a lyric which struck home because of a
kindred mandarin charm. This was the misleadingly named
'You, Andrew Marvell'; the evocativeness of this has nothing to
do with the Metaphysicals, being far more like the simple
yearnings of Dowson and Symons represented in wry modern
dress. This poem has no main verb and no real point of view.
Here exoticism is all, as a few stanzas will demonstrate, jointed
by their exigent conjunctions:

And now at Kermanshah the gate
Dark empty and the withered grass
And through the twilight now the late
Few travellers in the westward pass

And Baghdad darken and the bridge
Across the silent river gone
And through Arabia the edge
Of evening widen and steal on

And deepen on Palmyra's street
The wheel rut in the ruined stone
And Lebanon fade out and Crete
High through the clouds and overblown

And over Sicily the air
Still flashing with the landward gulls
And loom and slowly disappear
The sails above the shadowy hulls

And Spain go under and the shore
Of Africa and gilded sand . . .

This is poetry as spell or mantra, all decked out with the signals of incantation. And such importance as it has resides in the fact that it recalls for us the magical or apotropaic origins of poetry itself.

Another kind of pleasing strangeness, however, lay in the striking regionalism of American poetry. Since Australian poets had developed very few regional characteristics—beyond overt reference to place—it was very puzzling to encounter poets who had no shared sense of a common reader, no broadly recognizable kind of audience. The homespun mid-western pieces from Masters' *Spoon River Anthology* had nothing at all in common with the large Californian rhetoric of Robinson Jeffers or with the elegant South which Ransom, Tate and Penn Warren so lovingly and craftily reconstructed, linking it by sheer sleight of hand to the ironical complexities of the New Criticism. And were not all these three kinds quite alien to the New York humour of Delmore Schwartz? Schwartz could, occasionally, articulate a world which was to become much more a subject for fiction: the muddled, threatening world which surrounded and entangled the *schlemiel*. Only one poem really caught it, that unforgettably wry piece of dualism, 'The heavy bear who goes with me'.

The heavy bear who goes with me,
A manifold honey to smear his face,
Clumsy and lumbering here and there,
The central ton of every place,
The hungry beating brutish one
In love with candy, anger, and sleep,
Crazy factotum, dishevelling all,
Climbs the building, kicks the football,
Boxes his brother in the hate-ridden city.

Breathing at my side, that heavy animal,
That heavy bear who sleeps with me.
Howls in his sleep for a world of sugar,
A sweetness intimate as the water's clasp,
Howls in his sleep because the tight-rope

Trembles and shows the darkness beneath.
—The strutting show-off is terrified,
Dressed in his dress-suit, bulging his pants,
Trembles to think that his quivering meat
Must finally wince to nothing at all . . .

This felt like modern poetry in exactly the same measure as it felt like a self-text. Its wit made disclosure possible, its bear metaphor became a textual self.

I should also mention the spark of sheer experimentalism in some poets. Cummings had already left his mark here and there. A laboured-at density could be felt to be part of the genuineness, the depth of both Lowell and Hart Crane, both of whom had much influence in this country: first upon Francis Webb and latterly on many others. Crane's 'Voyages' has struck many people, myself included, as a seminal poem, especially in its musical organization of syntax. By 1954 John Berryman, too, was experimenting with syntax in curious ways, which were about to give us that powerful *tour de force*, *Homage to Mistress Bradstreet*. The time was yet to come when Harold Bloom would devise a modern poetics in which the motive power, the admirable strength, of poets could be seen as narcissism: we were still commonly moralists in the fifties and looked for evidence of social community in the poems we admired. We were psychologically naive about literary affect, about the libidinous sources of lyric force. We thought that poems could wear their politics explicitly even while holding that the final, made poem was aesthetically a free-standing artefact. (The art of sculpture has long been my favourite model for apprehending the constructions of poetry.)

In retrospect it is clear that the core of the attractiveness of this poetry lay in its solipsism; or, more strictly, in the American poets' acceptance of the narcissistic self as the necessary heart of their poetry. Where English poets like Auden, Robert Graves and the young Larkin were disposed to use tonal control as a means of keeping subjective assertion in harmony with social values, one found in Americans as different as Crane, Roethke and Lowell a poetic force, a passion which declared its raw subjectivity. In Lowell it was, to be sure, entangled with the language of religious tradition and New England history, but his syncopated language was still the voice of the raw self flailing against the world's restrictions: the cool novelistic tones of *Life Studies* still lay ahead of him; and, as we all know by now, the stabilized poise of *Life Studies* and *Near the Ocean* was not to be available to Lowell for long.

Roethke, whose *Words for the Wind* came from Secker and Warburg in 1957, was a poet of exceptional fascination to readers in the 1950s, even though, or because, his *oeuvre* was so narrowly idiosyncratic at root. Here was a poet who made the contemplation of simple natural objects become a strange music of psychic dislocation. Free of the common irony of the times, he could borrow the styles of other poets all unabashed: and not to create cultural perspectives at all. It was as though he had not noticed what he was doing, much as his poetry showed almost no sign of noticing the existence of other people—except for the missing father whose unavailability haunts 'The Lost Son':

The way to the boiler was dark,
Dark all the way,
Over slippery cinders
Through the long greenhouse.

The roses kept breathing in the dark.
They had many mouths to breathe with.
My knees made little winds underneath
Where the weeds slept.

There was always a single light
Swinging by the fire-pit,
Where the fireman pulled out roses,
The big roses, the big bloody clinkers.

Once I stayed all night.
The light in the morning came slowly over the white
Snow
There were many kinds of cool
Air.
Then came steam.

Pipe-knock.

Scurry of warm over small plants.
Ordnung! ordnung!
Papa is coming!

In this astonishing work of psychomachia, the insulted and fragmented self was dramatically articulated. Freudianism was an enabling influence in Roethke, helping to liberate his plangent music, his vulnerability.

But Roethke was also, like many of his fellows, a poet of great technical abilities. The same poet who wrote the unaffected greenhouse lyrics and the experimental 'Lost Son' invented a new kind of elevated love poetry in the end-stopped lines of 'I Knew a Woman', and wrote the only good villanelle of a decade which was unaccountably given to that stupefying verse-form.

The solipsism that could be felt in Roethke and Crane was something more than the charming strangeness of the dandies. It was a kind of romantic liberation from worldly terms and scales of reference. It could be felt as a-social, unrepressed. And it could certainly produce intensities that were particularly attractive to young poets reading their work. It must have played its part in the exultantly eclectic dandyism of the young Randolph Stow, the most narcissistic magician of all my con-temporaries, a collector of exotic bric-à-brac in local settings. His poem, 'Dust', remains inexhaustibly fascinating and its attraction is very much like that of 'You, Andrew Marvell', at once all of the surface and a matter of magical suggestion. This baffled, lyrical strength of feeling communicated itself strongly to a reader, even while it remained foreign to his normal imaginative priorities.

The time was still ahead in which the dandy and the solipsist would coalesce, becoming one in the frigid, evasive wit of John Ashbery. I have been reading Ashbery attentively for decades now, looking for kinds of resonance and reference that are not there and glimpsing orders of rustic piety which one could hardly have suspected were there. In the end, he is probably the only poet in history who becomes less and less available the more one reads him. And I should like to remain an innocent enough reader to think that this is a bad thing. Or is there always the baffled, genteel sentimentality of a lost farmboy trying to get out of Ashbery's strangulatory syntax?

I find my conclusion in Les Murray's passing comment that 'art is the intimate memory of nations'. Twenty years ago I was fascinated by modern American poetry, its various and scintil-lating performances. (I even remember being roundly scolded by Jim McAuley for my interest in a body of literature which he regarded as vacuously subjective and formalist.) By now I am chiefly struck by how strange, how completely American it remains: one returns in time to one's own familial needs. As far as we are concerned, most American poetry might well have been written on the moon. That is its secret; this is its charm.

14

A Tour of Dreams in Space and Time

It is the end of December, and sunny, tree-crowded Madras is an introduction to tropical India at once colourful, thronged and hospitable. Near at hand, too, are the many carved temples of Kanchipuram and the display of history in stone at Mahabalipuram, running right to the sandy shore.

A crowd of visitors stood outside a temple and I was asked, 'Shall we light a candle in your tomb or in his'? 'Arr, piss off'! I replied.

The following weeks find us in the drabber, more metropolitan spaces of New Delhi, reading Indian history, seeing mosques and forts, coping with our tummies and with taxi-drivers, not to mention conference-going.

I heard an announcement, from I do not know what source, that in South Africa mathematical accomplishment is hereditary.

There was a long, slow customs and security check at Delhi airport in the small hours before we left for Israel, and it was only a few hours since we had finally arrived back from our ten-day motor tour of Uttar Pradesh. Now we are in cold, windy Jerusalem, our surroundings completely westernized again.

It seems that I am waiting at a Customs counter in Australia and a group of Orientals are arguing with the authorities about access to Japanese Officers' Village, an area of Melbourne which is immediately recognizable to all and which may possibly coincide with Olympic Village. Later the same evening, I heard a voice say, 'I would have thought anyone would be glad to give a man shekels to hold the gate of his car for only forty minutes'.

Our first days in Athens wear two contrasting faces: that of classical antiquity and that of having to cope with evasive police about the theft from our suitcases somewhere between Tel Aviv airport and the baggage belt here.

I discovered that all Athenians carry transistor radios around with them so that they can listen to the arguments of Socrates.

It is a pleasure to arrive in Rome, despite the outbreaks of violence between students, unionists, Brigate Rosse, neo-fascists and police—there is difficulty in drawing up the lines clearly. It is also good to see A. and S. again, even though they seem quite bewildered by their travels.

In a morning minidream I saw a man handling tangled rope, and either heard or spoke the Kraus-like utterance: 'He who ties a knot around his thumb has other knots up his sleeve, for himself'.

After the point-to-point of so much journeying, there is something secure about our having our feet on Florentine cobbles, feeling our way little by little into the daily life of this city with its hundred sandstone faces and soft narratives of fresco: a brief week in the pensione, and now we are into our flat by the river. My dreams remain curiously verbal, epigrammatic:

'How many of those who play a game in the struggle really take part in the struggle?'
In an afternoon minidream, I was being shown a grassgrown Roman amphitheatre by a bloke who said, 'The thing is, it's simply a bourgeois thing; not in the simple Adam-and-Eve sense, but a bourgeois thing'. And again, 'He's done all this in the mistaken belief that Christ is one of the Democristiani'.

G. arrives and the three of us head off by train to the sweet green neutrality of Switzerland, its peaks and parks and pines. One result is that politics vanish entirely from the dreamworld, though language is still hyperactive; Zurich provides me first with something that might well come from *Finnegan's Wake*.

'Le black means water, especially on teeth, and Herr Fils means desert boots rolled up.'

Another starting-point comes from a nasty little dog that bites me at Langnau:

I find myself in a New South Wales country town in khaki shorts and bare feet. I am picked up by the driver of a taxi-tram who promises to take me a few blocks. Instead he drives me northwest up a winding gravel road, much eroded with small watercourses, to the top of a dry range of hills. As a result, I have to get out and walk back. As I do so, he points out that the road surface is thick with small, sharp pieces of bluemetal. I cut across country to save my feet. It is mainly smooth earth between the low eucalyptus scrub, but I keep a sharp lookout for snakes. As I go along, a small cat rushes out and bites me savagely.

Paris in the springtime and the rain. We arrive there on my birthday and stay for a week in a little hotel near the Sorbonne.

After a week here, I dreamed that I had missed M.'s birthday on 21 May, thinking it to be in October, and she became extremely upset. In fact it *is* in October.

The train takes us back along a rainy Ligurian coast to Florence and fine weather once more, balmy days for picknicking on the Belvedere's quiet lawns. In W. J. Bate's fine biography of Keats I find this sentence: 'The numbness of near-dream, as so often in Keats, is associated with a diversity of strong impressions where one activity shades into another, and where . . . different possibilities still remain in suspension'. (1963, 503). Such a convincing account of hypnogogic and hypnopompic images.

More such fragments come as we head off on the train to Venice through a hot, bright afternoon. Train motion is very good for recurrently nodding off.

'Being asleep with glasses on, you might bite your tongue.'
On the very verge of wakefulness, I saw a vast railway yard full of coal-trucks pointing in all directions. To some extent this was just Padua station. How far? And how far the boundless landscape of dream?

After the intrusive chimes of Trastevere and G.'s departure for Australia, we head south into the peace, elevation and extraordinary beauty of Ravello, poised above the Amalfi coast amid steep hills of limestone and forest. Luminous summer is coming in.

I was trampling over a goldfinch in the dry grass, just missing it with my left foot and I looked down and saw it there in the grassroots, its colours very bright. 'I thought that goldfinch was almost dead,' I exclaimed.
'Dead?'
'No, *almost* dead!'

It should be noted that there are many more varieties of birds to be seen at Ravello than in the Tuscan landscape, where they are much thinned out.

Back at home in Florence, I find myself succumbing to a few

patches of sleeplessness in the early mornings, largely induced
by literary paranoia and the lack of certain anticipated letters.
One such morning, I get this long, plotty dream:

M. and I were in the flat, looking out of a window at a flat opposite.
First one and then another youth, then more, started to break our
windows and to make a dreadful rumpus, apparently carrying out a
vendetta against the residents of our building. At this, I warned M. to
keep out of sight. Lethargic, hippyish, one of these young men entered
our flat carrying many large pipes. I felt like a smoke and asked him.
He offered me one, cutting up hunks of black pitch, adding sugar and
one other ingredient. 'What, don't you have any tobacco?' I asked.
Then we had a musical performance going on, and I sprung some of
these fellows sneaking off with all the handbags. I grabbed one and
took from him M.'s second-best bag; he had my bag down his back,
inside his coat, so I hit him, knocked him down and we wrestled for it. I
bit his ear savagely and got the bag. Then I had lost both bags again
and wandered the streets of (by now) Paris, looking for the thief. I saw
him put them down on the pavement and we hurried towards him, but
were too slow. In desperation we followed him into a tunnel which
led under the Seine to a sleazy, colourful Left Bank. There were penny
arcades, bars, sailors, and a two-headed woman, vividly made-up, of
whom I asked directions, which led us to an old broken-down swimming pool in a marquee; it was run by a tall, crewcut Negro. The ladders and steps were broken, so that we had to jump down . . .

One evening, just this phrase,

'Per . . . per . . . if somebody doesn't stick that up their arse . . . '

At this stage my blent irritation and anxiety about Australian publishers and editors is reaching one of those overseas
climaxes, even though I cannot know yet that worse is to come
the following morning with R. M.'s letter, putting paid to this
optimistic scenario:

An unnamed Melbourne publisher had rung to say that he has offering me a room to work in at their city office. Negotiations were very
complicated, but I was delighted with their offer. I went to visit the
firm, going through large, white, oldfashioned outer offices, meeting
members of staff on the way: dark, polished woodwork and very good
carpet. Then I was taken through double-doors into the editorial
office, where B. H. was dictating to A. G., whimpering and flattering
all the while; opposite them, J. S. and another woman sat working at
their desks. Here the dream cut to the building where my office was
supposed to be: it was an octagonal structure, a cross between the
Baptistery and McCaughey Court, set well apart in a dark-green, large,

sequestered college garden, all set about with ivy, and nearby cypress and gum trees. I am delighted by the setting.

Months later, I realize that this garden was virtually the same as one I encountered in another vivid dream of a year or two ago.

The following night, one sentence:

The flat was all cut down, in the shape of half an egg.

This was followed, toward morning, by the self-reflective:

I've written two poems which may become dreams at the end of my bloody life.

It is one of those halflight mornings when I have two dreams in rapid succession, or so it seems: the dark bedroom is apt to keep one in suspense, guessing at the degree of daylight.

I was standing on the margins of R.'s farm at Boolarra and he needed his clothes. For some reason I had a big shanghai with me, so I rolled the clothes up one at a time and fired them high towards the house. As each went skyward, I worried in case it was going to land somewhere inaccessible. In the other, we had a diminutive B. H. in bed with us, or so M. claimed. I looked down at the flat middle of the bed, there being a little silver hair on the pillow, and asked, 'Where is he?' M. explained that he was too little to be visible.

At the end of June we set off on a long, but certainly picturesque train journey up to the along the French Riviera and thence south into Spain, heading for that scruffily distinctive city, Barcelona. Doing my homework properly, I reread *Homage to Catalonia* on the way, and sleep, and wake, and sleep.

It would be essential before arriving to find out how much a kilogram was in Spain. In the end I worked it out by cutting a goodish slice off a (slightly pressed) person, kindly making sure of not having to slice him again by making the piece a little too big in the first place. A child stood, unprotected, on a high balcony, even standing very close to the dangerous edge—his/her mother not seeming to care at all. At a bullfight, could it have been?

One morning, in the Barcelona hotel room, which lacks any window onto the outside world, I enjoyed three clear dreams, the first two of which I retain clearly on being awakened by M. having nightmares, but lose again because of dropping off for a while longer. Rising, I can remember only the third.

We were at a theatrical performance, leaving at interval to get something to eat. Outside, we walked into a dark, bustling street-market,
stopping at a stall to have meat and buns cooked over a brazier. M.,
not finding the man on the job, pinched some meat from the opposite
stall and brought it over. Just then, D. came along with H. S. We had
met D. already, but to his companion I merely said, 'Hullo, H.' and
nothing else, as though I saw him every day. I felt strongly that I was
cutting him in this.

There is, of course, an abrupt contrast between the metropolitan realities of Barcelona and the seaside pleasures to be
found in one of those prettier little beach resorts up the Spanish
coast: wide yellow beach, castle, little twisting lanes, *sangria*,
paella, forty-cent champagne and a host of German or York-
shire tourists in sandy bathers. Holiday noises everywhere,
with a mixture of slim brown bodies and fat pink legs.

I was at some musical occasion and, standing by the drums, decided
to play them. Afterwards, I looked out the window into darkness and
saw three Chinese-European couples returning from a party. Of a
sudden, they fell into argument and decided to punch one another.
Then they slunk shamefacedly away in single file. I then picked up a
roll of paper, deciding to play the trumpet on it: this I did by bending
one end almost flat, then mouthing the trumpet sound into it. I suc-
ceeded in producing one blare only . . . [At this point I was woken by
M.'s laughter at the noise I was making; I explained, and she said,
'What were you doing earlier? Playing the drums?' 'Yes.']

An interesting point about the duration of dreams is that she
thought it was about two minutes between these two external
signs: pretty much what I would have thought within the dream.
Yet some people claim that dreams are all over in a few seconds.

While reading on the balcony, I slumbered momentarily and added
half a sentence of Ayer on Russell: ' . . . but I would, had not the
serpent impeded my interpretation'.

Back in Italy, where we have for week my dear old friend,
R. A. S., staying in the flat with us, all agog at being back in
Europe after twenty years. Many dreams over these nights—as
far as I can judge—most of which I could not recall, or did not
try hard enough to recapture on waking.

I was standing in a busy street, watching a procession go by, among
whom the Prince of Wales—Later Edward VII—was driving his tiny
red racing car. King George VI came up and asked, 'What are you
doing here, then?' 'I'm a visiting poet from Australia. My name is

Chris Wallace-Crabbe.' 'With that name, your father would have been in the German forces during the war.' 'No.' I replied. 'He was in the Australian forces—during both World Wars.' In one clear fragment, I was sitting in my room when B. D. H. came up the stairs after lunch. 'How was the city?' I asked. 'Beaut,' she replied, continuing up the stairs with a new carry-bag from some shop. Also, while still awake one evening, I had one of those disturbing re-visions of a landscape once seen long ago in dream; imprecise (a village with white mud or stone walls, crossing lanes, a thatched roof, grass, chooks, etc.) and yet more real than landscapes known by daylight, giving a strong sense that it connects with everything else.

In another dream, a stern debate with the rigidly Leavisite A. D., in which he accused me of shoddy critical principles, but I dismissed his agruments firmly and cheerfully.

One of the things that most catches the eye about Verona is the river, rushing like mad down from the Dolomites between high limestone walls and under ancient bridges. When we visit the Duomo, a service is starting and when we go to hear their massive *Aida* in the Arena, the last scene is washed out by a downpour.

I was looking for the Isle of Ely and found it in a river valley, not surrounded by water, but demarcated by a change in the colour of herbs and grasses inside its narrow borders. Then P. M. rang up and M. said to me, 'If that's P. M., tell him we're not interested in his plans for shipping poetry'. We opened the doors of—we thought—two university rooms, but they proved to be the two ends of an ancient (Veronese?) chapel in which a priest was saying mass. Then we ambled through ruins towards the countryside where P. was waiting for us, lying on a grassy bank at the side of a castle; we took it easy.

A striking feature of Garda is that so many people here are insistent on speaking German whenever possible; the Italian dialect here is also a very strange one.

With no particular aim in mind, I went out to the piazza in front of where I was staying. There, squatting on the cobbles, I was greeted in Spanish by the priest from the church opposite. I did not understand, and he responded by saying (in which language?), 'That's the trouble with you English—you never take the trouble to learn a foreign language'. I explained in English that I do know some Italian and French. He then said, 'I'm pleased to meet you. I'm Junior Johnson'. (Apparently a well-known West Indian writer.) I told him that we'd had George Lamming to visit last year, and did he know the whereabouts of my old friend Patrick Johnson.

An utterly tranquil weekend at D.'s house in a tiny, end-of-the-road village atop the Appenines.

All of us were in some theatre, about to be rounded up by the French security police. I hurried outside, but they were already guarding the door with sub-machine guns. So I brazened my way past them, and then something else of importance happened which was driven out of my mind by bells from the next village.
The following morning, I was in the midst of a discussion with B. about what should be done to look after Alec Hope when he came down. B. was being fussily paranoid about the matter and I was having to be rather brusque with him . . . when D. knocked on the door to wake us up for the trip back to Florence.

Some of the above remind me how often the events in dreams are such as to be connected with 'and', how seldom they seem to call for 'but' or 'yet', let alone 'Meanwhile' or 'just as'.
    A fragment of a song, with a trick avoidance of rhyme:

'In the Bongo of the Bill
I am falling down the . . . . slope'.
In Santa Croce while a chap was playing Bach on the organ, I dozed for a moment, my eyes fixed on a distant fresco, and heard in the mind's ear, 'Do not believe that it is a dog, or a pig, or a porcupine, you fool. For when you look, when you look, you are only looking at yourself'. In the first dream of a morning, I was walking in a Melbourne garden suburb. An old man, unnamed, drove up and gave me a lift. When I asked him where he lived, he said next door to Dad's place—or I deduced this from the address. On getting there, I saw that he did indeed live next door, but behind a plot of pink blossoming fruit trees which obscured the house. I walked up to Dad's front door. He was out, but the door was jammed open with a large parcel, which I recognized as our parcel, long awaited, from Jerusalem. But when I examined it, I found that it held strata of different books and clothes, some we took on our travels, some we left at home, and some dating from years ago: a veritable archaeology of belongings.

This image has a good deal in common, it seems to me, with Freud's metaphor for the psyche in *Civilization and Its Discontents*: the ruined city in which evidence of past and present experience stand together on the one spot.

In the second dream, I found myself in a pretty, rather English countryside. I went to my brother's tiny, gabled cottage, seeking a place to sleep the night. He put me in a cramped attic, but when asleep I fell gently through an open trapdoor into his room. Then I set up my bed again, further over, taking care lest my bed should fall off a loading ramp which opened out at the other end of the attic above a pictures-que, darkened farmyard. At dawn I went out into the fields and heard gunfire. Walking over to a hedge not far from the cottage, I asked people who were running away what was going on. They explained that Gordon Barton was out shooting pigeons, which felt oddly threatening. I made my way gingerly along the hedge and then saw him, riding fast in the sky (on a cloud?) firing his gun.

It is a time of strikingly pictorial and atmospheric visions, their landscapes and light very fully detailed, very strongly charged. The loveliest of all, and recognized as such, even before waking, is the following, partly occasioned by a very impressive new 170 lire stamp.

I was taken into the *cortile* of a beautiful school building. It was des-igned in a c.1920 style, combining somehow elements of our mud brick house, the Campo at Siena and the picture on the new stamp. Standing there, I just kept staring around at those ochre-and-brown walls, that fluently irregular display of windows and exposed beams, in unabating delight: it has that kind of stunningly simple, organic originality that one associates with the le Corbusier chapel at Ronchamps. Then my mentor, a neat, older man, took me upstairs; following him up a cir-cular, bronze-painted iron staircase, I fell behind and found it harder and harder to climb right to the top.

It gives me pleasure to read this in Proust's ever-haunting 'Overture': 'When a man is asleep, he has in a circle round him the chain of the hours, the sequence of the years, the order of the heavenly host'. This quiet August in Florence finds the dream-world caught up in such richness.

One morning two long, plotty, very dull dreams—punctuated by a visit to the dunny with diarrhoea, but nonetheless continuous—full of a literature conference in Sydney, my critical strictures on *The Golden Bowl*, prettily antiqued little wooden steamers on Sydney Harbour, a couple sleeping in a tiny dresser, resuming my room at Melbourne *and* the Chairmanship, finding that G. had left behind a grog cupboard (low, like the one the couple were sleeping in) with banana cocktail, sherry, etc., in fancy bottles. A lost dream containing one Finnegan-punning sentence, with much play on 'King', 'Queen' and 'Kerr'.

This recalls to mind a long, rather heated argument we had with A. A. the previous month about whether he should go to a reception in Rome for Sir John Kerr. We were bitter over his announced intention of going along to see what Kerr was like. Four nights later, it is Australian history that comes to the fore.

Sitting an Australian History exam, I asked A. D. H., one of the super-visors, if he would go out and xerox what I had written so far. He did so but with ten minutes to go I realized the xeroxed sheets were frayed and fragmentary. It seemed that I now had two answers to write in a few minutes; however, one of the supervisors pointed our that I could include the essay, or project, I had done on the explorer, Kennedy, during the year. So I put my head down to write a rapid answer on 'The Rights of Man and the *Equo Canone*' with a brief account of Thomas Paine and the American Declaration of Independence for starters. Thinking of Singapore, I dreamed, 'One is sometimes permitted to decline one's duty and one can say, Not tonight pineapple'.

A longish patch with no clear, remembered dreams inter-venes here. It is high summer in Florence, but the hot weather gives way to a series of rainy days. The mail services have be-come very bad indeed during August, for reasons at both ends of the world. We are eating more than is good for us, I'm sure.

My arsehole had fallen out, so that I could not hold my faeces in, with the result that I did not eat. I had to last out a day before the opera-tion, extraordinarily painful by repute, in which they would stitch my arsehole back in. Everyone was sympathetic, but nothing diminished the prospect of several days' pain.

We were in a grey Gothic cathedral of a distinctly northern type. We went up to the altar rail during the service and found ourselves kneel-ing there beside the Pope. A simple-looking little nun got up into the pulpit and began reading the Gospel story of the Passion, which proved too much for her emotions, so that she broke down in tears. We were a little contemptuous of this. I argued with G. B. as to whether *All about H. Hatterr* in the end recommended 'a return to suburban values', which V. B. had once claimed in an article I could not recall. G. made the critical point about one scene that 'The language one learns at a philosophy conference is no use other than at a philosophy conference'. This sounded very convincing.

September, with autumnal brightness, visitors, heaps of let-ters and a trip to Rome, puts a bit of action back on the screen, the month opening with several multi-dream nights, too many to record, indeed.

There was a schoolroom in one, a veritable storehouse of arms, rifles, *mitre*, bombs and a kind of artificial hand with an inbuilt trigger. Some fugitives got out of this room and were running away across a large park. Those of us who remained were trying to shoot them down as they ran. Then the viewpoint become that of one of the fugitives, Elvis Presley by name. He (I) ran across the park, then, coming to a huge marquee full of dismantled furniture, crockery, etc., took refuge nervously in this as the pursuers ran by, and then set off back of the school-room in quest of revenge. Next day, *inter alia*, the line, 'The hart has swallowed the king's bright lance'.

Dreams are still coming in droves, especially in the course of a few nights when I am kept restless by a sore throat. One satisfying development is that by now a few are coming to me in Italian.

The football season has started again here, after a remarkably short summer recess. We are becoming great enthusiasts for soccer.

To my astonishment I was chosen to play left-back for Arsenal. When the game got under way I kept up surprisingly well and/or my opponents were pretty weak. The ground was narrow and damp, the light bad. Our opponents several times looked like breaking through for a goal, but failed, and we scored once. At half time I was back but the coach didn't mind. Out again, same direction, white jerseys, very clear against the dark turf.

So nine months of dreams have passed by, intermeshed with nine months of wandering across the world in search of images of change or new patterns of old shapes.

Very well then, a time of travel has been charted against concomitant events from the sleeping world, the continual private cinema of night. Dream is a variety of remembering, too. And what does this little anthology of dreams disclose about the Australian writer who was travelling *à deux* through India, Israel, Europe, in 1977? Something about my interest in sardonic yarns, no doubt; also about my fondness for word-play, for the world of public display and for the imagery of modern painting.

In the above discontinuous narrative, I have endeavoured to juxtapose the appropriate day residues with the purified, cubistic, non-discursive stories of my dreams. Surely such juxtaposition will generate comparison and contrast, revealing something of what we call self along the fault-line.

It will immediately be objected that the dreams recounted here are verbal and discursive as set down, and that their chains of association have not been traced back into the dense personal forest. Certainly their non-discursive, iconic originals were lost in secondary elaboration before they were plucked and transcribed. Such is the cost of discussion. Language sits upon more language, which sits on the dream of a pre-linguistic self. These dreams are made of language because they have been written down; but they are also full of language because the remembering process required them to be captured in a linear form before they slipped away with morning ('They fly forgotten as a dream/Dies at the opening day'); but again, they are verbal because I am a wordsmith, the sculpting of language being my métier. Lastly, it would seem more than likely that the especial concern of these fifty-three dreams with utterances was spurred on by our residence in countries where we needed to understand something of the local languages, just to get by: for example, arrival in multilingual Switzerland triggered off a macaronic dream, a surreal proverb which included words from French and German.

The connection between dreams and epigrams is like the resemblance between jokes and lyric poems noted by Wittgenstein. In each case concentration—or condensation—is required. Discursive material finds itself excluded, tossed aside into the Too Boring basket. The wit of dreams stimulates and revitalizes us; only afterwards does it demand reflection and unpacking. Sometimes the dreams even warn us of the dangers, the potential crudities of such unpacking: 'Being asleep with glasses on, you might bite your tongue'.

Another dream here admits to the family relationship which I feel between dreams and poems, speaking of 'poems which may become dreams.' And it is true that I am far less sceptical about this relationship than A. D. Hope showed himself to be in *The New Cratylus*. Yet my defensiveness about these links has revealed itself in the fact that the only complete poem which I have ever dreamed and remembered (and it was not on this journey: not in France at all) was in French. The foreign tongue helped me to avoid confronting the dream poem in its nakedness, held it at arm's length, in mental italics. Moreover, it was a dream poem about the nature of dream; a similar reflexiveness or seemingly Modernist circularity marks a number of the dreamed sentences quoted above: their sibylline tautology tends to cut them off from re-entry into the daily world. The hypnagogic phrase, 'had not the serpent impeded my interpretation', is pertinent to all these dreams. The serpent is the agent of ellipsis, intervening to prevent too plain a daylight interpretation of these miniature dramas.

Yet we are trying to read this suite of dreams, if not to interpret them, at least to understand them as evidences of a sclf in motion: of a particular Australian writer being exposed successively to a number of foreign cultures. Foreign situations. Nor are we naively assuming that the 'I' who is active or passive in these dream narratives corresponds at all simply with myself. In this unpublished manuscript, *Dreams at Work*, A.F. Davies has issued a warning against that kind of reading: 'I'm afraid we have to be shockingly brutal and indeed quite demolish protagonist. He's a phoney, a fiction; in fact, the supreme fiction that recipient and author concoct between them'. True, but to go further, both recipient and author are emanations of mine. We cannot avoid the fact that all the stuff in these dreams comes in some way out of my wardrobe of experiences.

If this is granted, then we are free to do what we so commonly do, to read the dreams without psychoanalytical rigour for their surfaces, their images and their little stories. Even in this amateurish light, they will prove informative.

It is telling, for example, that the very first dream confronts the dignified antiquity of Indian temples with a classic piece of Australian larrikinism. And that my early Italian dreams keep taking in material about terrorist and radical organizations, about the politicization of experience in that country. Interestingly, too, the dream-epigrams turn up thickly in the restless early part of my travels, fading away as I, or we, become more accustomed to European surroundings. The frequent appearance of harmonious and sympathetic landscapes here is very much in tune with my poetic preoccupations; nor is it surprising that the role of specifically Australian landscapes increased after some months away.

What these dreams, spawned by the restlessness and the anxieties of travel, so commonly share is the belief that a proverb, an epigram or an announcement will solve things. They believe in the power of language, the curing whip of syntax. And their syntax has a tendency to work like a satirical couplet, with the second half of a sentence twisting around in such a way as both to complete and to subvert the first part. As in both the Santa Croce song and the generalization about philosophy conferences, they find pleasure in ironic closure. My subconscious scriptwriter keeps hovering between poet and joker; he is also less overtly concerned with anxiety than with action.

So we could go on, but of course this brisk literary overview yields relatively little if it is compared with the exhaustive, exhausting ramifications of systematic free association. In this my discussion resembles so much in the modern love affair between the humanities and psychoanalysis: we want the bold insights, the sweeping connections, the shuntings of surreal logical connection, the claims to inwardness and the glimpses of remarkable sub-texts. What we do not really seek and could not even match are the clinical sessions, with their painfully slow piecing together of the whole picture, the tangled and trampled spoor which leads back through the symptoms to the long-buried trauma.

Indeed, classical psychoanalysis is quite indifferent to the aesthetic form of dreams, to their dramatic shapeliness. Going the whole hog, Freud even claimed that 'From the point of view of analysis . . . a dream that resembles a disordered heap of disconnected fragments is just as valuable as one that has been beautifully polished and provided with a surface'. True enough for analysis, perhaps, but for any common dreamer what a disappointment such a remark must be. All of us prefer stories to chaos, climax to jumble, compelling narration to bric-à-brac: most of all the writer and the critic, beings whose very bread-and-butter is narrative. Beautiful fictions are what we need and value, best of all beautiful fictions which are also true. Unlike the bossy Plato of *The Republic*, this is what we expect of literature: that it should be both beautiful and true, even when generically fictive.

A few of these dreams, especially those of the bag-snatcher and the English cottage, strike me as being superior tales. I wonder why they turned out better as stories than the others did. It may be that my editorial morning self recognized their greater depth from the start and did some quick work on them to make the most of their resources. And it may well be true, as Davies has suggested, that the 'best' dream narratives are the most narcissistic, much as the circularity of neater dream-epigrams has a narcissistic quality to it, of the order, 'Just watch me put one more twist in its tail'.

Richard Wollheim has observed that dreams lack a grammar, a reference system. True, but their mode of dramatization has an intriguing narrative power which we can often recognize as akin to the power of daylight stories. It would seem certain, too, that our dreams have learned a great deal from modern literature. We have now been trained to allow surreal juxta-positions as a plus in artistic effect. My travel dreams share in this juxtapositional structuring and my morning self has not tried to iron it out: such zigzags are precisely what I value, and even pillage for my own literary purposes. As one of the dreams so roundly declared, 'He who ties a knot around his thumb has other knots up his sleeve, for himself'. I cannot tell whether 'for himself' here is beneficent, or minatory.

15

Lost in Wonderland

The scene was taken from some expressive, technically old-fashioned movie. Gouts of steam poured from the ceiling, puffed and circled around, faded downwards into the aisle. Passengers, mostly Russian and Indian, wandered in search of seats, their bewilderment palpable. They kept on trying to stuff fat bags into the small lockers overhead. Several Sikhs carried uniformly long tapedecks which went somewhere under their seats. The stewards, chubby, bemused, began trying to get their act together; the tall hostesses resembled romantic actresses cast in gloomy parts. Confusion continued, it being a Soviet tradition; the ceiling dripped; motors whined; and still the steam squirted down. But as we began to taxi backwards all steam vanished, which could only be described as a relief. When he came to demonstrate the safety-vest the plumper steward looked desperately unhappy: it may be that his digestion was giving him hell.

After these first expressionist images the trip was smooth and pleasant, with much reliance on lolly water, although not yet on Pepsi Cola, Richard Nixon's bequest to the Soviet Union. I only saw the Himalayas once—or was it the Hindu Kush?

When you set out to travel to the Soviet Union you have, not so much bureaucratic difficulties, but a veritable Himalaya of clichés to overcome. These blocking clichés are massive. They include everything from the Kremlin, the KGB, an impenetrable bureaucracy (it was far easier to get my visa, in fact, than it had been going to the United States twenty years earlier), gerontocracy and a powerbroking Writers' Union through to caviare, drunkenness, uproarious merriment and anti-semitism. Such caricature elements are so powerfully reinforced by the media that they sink in firmly. Like most clichés they are sometimes true and sometimes not; it would be hard to shake them out in a fortnight.

Blessedly, Aeroflot did not provide in-flight movies. Our prime diversion was provided by an Indian in his thirties, tall, besuited, public-schoolish, handsome in the Omar Sharif style, who sat himself down beside a pretty young woman with curly black hair and speedily went through the first third of his bottle of duty-free Scotch. Soon he ran wild with the hostess call-button, pressing it again and again. Out would come patient hostess or tense little steward, while the ratbag demanded a second dinner. 'One ticket, one dinner', they kept pointing out to him. On and on he performed, insisting finally on seeing the captain. 'At the end of the flight', they would reply. Sometimes he even hunted them out from behind their curtains. In time the captain had to be rousted out: he was enormous, built like a Richmond ruckman, nodded his head with a grim sort of smile and gave no satisfaction. As a result of all this, the suave male-factor resorted to using the button to call for frequent glasses of water. We were all in stitches. This comedy ended at Delhi, where I also got off the plane unadvisedly and earned myself a pleasant walk back across the tarmac; after the Sikh troubles, the authorities were not encouraging transit disembarkations.

Back in Australia a younger, Marxizing colleague had com-plained bitterly of his first experience with Aeroflot. I had put this down to his being merely a Boudoir Bolshie, and not liking the real thing. By the end of my return journey from Moscow I would have reconsidered the justice of his view: by then I would be bantering to Russian travellers about 'Aeroflop'.

There was lots of snow around Moscow. We landed at Domi-dirov, back of Woop Woop, instead of being allowed to fly into the international terminal. We stayed on the tarmac for three hours, looking at snow and birches. Out there the fox says good morning to the hare. Finally we took off again and flew into Cheredmetov, where they left us next to a Libyan plane at the edge of the airstrip to look at more snow. Arriv-ing at last, I was whisked through customs by our interpreter, Natasha, immediately noticeable in her bright pink parka.

It was a slushy drive into town, not much catching the eye until we finally swirled past the World Trade Centre, crossed the Moskva River and I was lodged in the heavy Chryslerish ziggurat of the Hotal Ukraina. The building was full of for-eigners: some from eastern Europe; a few from America; a number from the Middle East or the Maghreb. The concierge on my floor asked me for foreign cigarettes; I apologized for not being a smoker. In the first twenty-four hours I had two anonymous phone calls. The former was to ask me the meaning of the word, 'powerhouse', and the second the ask me whether I was Algerian. Not being Neddy Seagoon, I did not think up witty replies to these questions. Otherwise all was comfortable, the hotel breakfasts quite magnificent, and my bottle of John Jameson's a pleasant cure for jet-lag.

Those first two days I walked the streets and avenues a lot, growing used to the contrasts between a large physical scale and the narrowish range of consumer goods. Disparate things caught my attention: the rush of women to buy a couple of crates of limes from a fruitstall when it opened at 8 a.m.; kids on their way to school tormenting one another with an exact Russian equivalent of 'Cowardy cowardy custard'; the many big sweet shops helping to use up the Cuban sugar cane harvests; newspapers stuck up on noticeboards, along with posters for a monologue about Tsvetaeva, another by Okhudzhava and an exhibition of Arvi Aalto's architecture; and more people than I had expected in stylish winter clothes.

By now I had met up with my fellow travellers who had flown in, Olga Masters from London and Tom Shapcott from Belgrade. Olga and I had stravaged around the Kremlin and down the shopping displays of Kalinin Prospect, looking at women's clothes and fur hats in a department store. But it was time to get down to business.

Serious matters began with our morning visit to the Writers' Union in its rabbit-warren of an old mansion, sprawled out around a garden with Tolstoy's statue in the middle. The format of our meeting was one that would soon become familiar to us: sitting around a table, three or four a side, solemn introductory speeches gradually leaching down to more relaxed conversation, Natasha usually kept on her toes translating, although many of our counterparts (if that's what they were) proved to be at least bilingual. General briefing, solemn greetings, much cultural exchange talk, the scent of hierarchy in the air. After this we went on through passages, tunnels and staircases to lunch (with beer and soft drink, for the new semi-prohibition laws were taking effect), laughter and jokes, along with some speculations about the coming millennium of the Russian Orthodox Church. Questions were asked about the intellectual climate in Australia, and Kuznetsov, one of our hosts, smilingly said, 'The Italian delegates told us about their interest in structuralism and literary theory. I told them that we had been through all that, and had gone beyond it'.

The Writers' Union building is an expansive sort of club. After lunch we struck some eccentrics. One was a primitive expressionist painter who was exhibiting his pictures in one of the reading rooms; he showed us round garrulously, and then gave us copies of little children's books which he had illustrated. Then a very sozzled young woman, seemingly a poet, took a fancy to Olga and Natasha, proving quite hard to shake off. Upstairs we went, past Lenin and photos of a hundred male notables of the Union—and one female. We did see a show of paintings then by a woman artist. 'I think her drawings are good,' I commented. 'Oh, yes,' came the reply. 'She is a qualified artist'. Nervously fingering my poet's diploma, I went on.

For some combination of reasons we met a number of artists during our time in Moscow. There was one who painted a mixture of mystical paintings and Breughelesque bawdry: his art mainly appealed to people on the embassy circuit. Another, the jovial Yuri Vasiliev, restored icons and made etchings of old churches in their landscapes. Another illustrated children's books. And another, Boris Messerer, produced paintings and lithographs of wonderfully bold construction, sometimes making use of the fluted patterns of old gramophone horns. He works as a stage designer and showed us several maquettes of theatrical sets, intricate sculptures in their own right. We did not meet any artist who practised in the social realist manner. Indeed, in a Tashkent art gallery one of our guides peeped into a room and said to me, 'Oh, it's only social realist art in there. Let's go on to another room where there's real art'.

Jokes are a major genre in the Social Union. Everybody makes use of them; everybody enjoys them. My favourite was the one about the man who is arrested by a militiaman for handing out pamphlets in Red Square. 'But they are all blank,' he protested. 'Why on earth do you hand out blank pamphlets?' asked the stupified militiaman. 'Because the people already have everything.' Other jokes turned on the gerontocracy in the Central Praesidium, on the Iran–Iraq war, on prohibition, and on historical paradoxes at the end of the second millennium: 'The Jews are soldiers, the Germans want peace and the Russians are sober'.

In Friendship House, a dinky little castle modelled on a palace somewhere in Portugal, we had one of our round-table conversations. The usual topics were gone over, and then one ex-serviceman chimed in; he had recently been visiting Victoria and asked us to convey his warm greetings to Bruce Ruxton and to 'Sir Murray'. Discreetly, we did not pass comment on our lack of sympathy with Ruxton, nor on 'Sir Murray's' recent dislodgement from Government House. The building had a particularly impressive entrance hall. Light stanchions like mailed arms were brandished from the wall. We waited for Beast to come panting in and delicately court his Beauty. 'Hush! The wooden squirrel freezes on his bough. And the stag dreams'.

It was a time of energetically busy days, of colourful dreaming, waking in the night, and writing until I was tired again. I even wrote a dramatic monologue spoken by a girl, one night when I could not get back to sleep. This possession of my self by a female muse was an unprecedented experience. The poem crystallized, and has survived into print.

Sleep was not a serious problem on the overnight train to Leningrad, although it came and went in waves. We were woken in our sleeper by recorded birdsong, which gradually modulated into music. The countryside was snowy and twiggy. The train pulled into Leningrad on time, and we were met by 'Alexander the Second', a short, helpful man from the Writers' Union, who whisked us off through the city's large Pieran perspectives, past rococo facades washed yellow, blue, green white, to our hotel, the comfortable Astoria, where Esenin hanged himself. The city is soaked in literature, saturated with culture; one reads it through books: Pushkin, Dostoevsky, Gogol, Akhmatova, Mandelstam, they have overdetermined all our responses. It was hard to take in on the spot that the longed-for Hermitage was *also* the Winter Palace, that art and history inhabit the same site, that Matisse nudges Eisenstein aside. And is it really true that Kerensky missed out on a job in the Russian Department at Melbourne University?

Years ago Jim Davidson had typecast Sydney and Melbourne as Tinseltown and St Petersburg. While I was in Russia I often felt he had it wrong. Moscow was the place of power, politics and the reality principle; Leningrad stood for aesthetic pleasure by comparison, despite all that the war cemetery recorded. At a party in Moscow, one writer said to me, not without a hint of approval, 'You know, Nabokov is the typical Leningrad writer'. And a Leningrad official of the Writers' Union said that 'Moscow writers are more interested in politics. We are more interested in literature'. However, we did talk a little, dilute, politics with journalists from *Novy Mir*.

Apart from the war cemetery, suitably stark under its cover-
let of new snow, so much was striking or imposing about this
city. Little older than the European settlement of Australia, it
seemed to bear an almost intolerable weight of history. It is
peculiarly moving, even alarming, to think that the Soviet authorities gave such priority after the Patriotic War to rebuilding
the palaces of Peter the Great, Catherine the Great and the
eighteenth-century gentry. Aristocratic and bourgeois greatness underwrites the visible beauty of this peculiarly European
Soviet City. Even the incomparable Matisses and the historically crucial Picassos pay silent tribute to the bourgeois taste of
Shchukin, who bought them for his walls.

On St Isaac's Square I was moved to a grossly-rhymed tercet
about this city of inordinate display:

Snow lashes the Marinsky Palace,
The Admiralty is a golden phallus:
I am lost in wonderland like Alice.

But for all I say about display, there was a modesty, or infor-
mality, of personal style, especially when compared with the
visible elite of Beautiful People in Moscow ('Dangerous, easy,
in furs, in uniform,' as Auden puts it). The people we spoke to
in the northern city struck us as much more matey. There was
even an unbuttoned air about the Astoria, where young, blond,
stonkered Finns could be seen swaying along the corridors,
ready to rage on in a mate's room, vodka bottles clinking.

It was here in Leningrad that we first saw sunshine, the custard-
yellow facades abruptly glowing, the patterns of light and shadow underwriting Peter's honey-classical perspectives. On the
radio in my room I could hear bad rock from Radio Riga,
such blare curiously out of kilter with my serene prospect of
St Isaac's Square, the only public space where I ever saw the
statue of a Czar. It was impossible to feel any truth here in the
accusation I heard later from a Muscovite that the Soviet Union
has become 'one great museum of kitsch'. Not even in Tashkent
would I feel this—despite its unspeakably wretched Museum of
Literature. At the farthest extreme from kitsch, we saw the
Kirov Ballet doing a new piece, a compelling ballet on the life
and death of Pushkin. I had been told that the Kirov was far
more impressive that the Bolshoi, and so it proved.

Neither the Astoria nor any other hotel we stayed at produced what we encountered at the Ukraina: an efflorescence of

mini-clad 'hostesses' hanging around the tables and dance floor after dinner. That had been something completely at odds with the rest of our Soviet experience: an isolated hint of sinfulness.

Things inhere in the memory for very different reasons, in very different modalities. In some cases the mode is spatial, as for example with my clear memory of the glittering Hall of Mirrors in the Catherine Palace at Pushkin, pure sculpture of air and light and glass, or with my recall of the distinctively stuffy, reconstructed rooms of Dostoevsky's house in Leningard. Sometimes they attach to a face, like that of the merry, blond, boyish young man who came along as a photographer from *Novy Mir*. Sometimes an utterance gives focus to the whole gestalt, as when we were having afternoon tea with the Rector of Zagorsk monastery and I began discussing Soviet Islam with Alexander Koriakin ('Alexander the Great'); we moved onto the dangerous territory of Afghanistan and he suddenly remarked, 'The anti-progressive forces recently launched a rocket attack on a mosque that was full of people worshipping'. There was no accessible answer to that. Another patch of recollection turns on Boris Messerer, Bella Akhmadulina's husband, taking me to an upstairs window, from which we looked out over the modernist shopping complex on Kalinin Prospect and remarking that this was the new Moscow; he then led me further upstairs, to the very top of his studio, and opened another window, which gave onto old tiles, decaying chimney-stacks, rooftop grass and a small birch tree growing in its rooftop patch of accumulated dirt, high above the centre of the city. 'And this is the old Moscow,' he said. 'Which do you prefer?'

Some things vanish entirely. I have not a single memory trace of the return train journey from Leningrad. Where do lost memories go? Where are the snows of yesteryear? This sense of lost things keeps turning me back to the lovely beginning of Mandelstam's poem,

We shall meet again in Petersburg
As if the sun was buried there
And proclaim for the first time
The immaculate and meaningless word.

Perhaps our lost things are not in the lunar sphere, but clustered around that primal immaculate word. We struggle towards it, of course, using the old familiar set of shopworn signifiers.

Our party with unofficial writers and artists kept figuring in our imaginations as a symmetrical opposite to our meetings with Writers' Union officials. We kept constructing it as such, sometimes too easily. In each case we gathered around a large table, ate and drank, talked literature and cultural politics: by day more or less solemnly but by night jovially, jokily. At the party (it is striking that the same English word is used for a political organization; are feasts like political structures?) we felt an intimacy of address, what you might call coming to tutoyer our hosts, and they us. Individualism had asserted itself over the meats and salads, over the white wine and Georgian cognac. And the jokes were intellectual, at their best dashing and witty, bouncing from topic to topic. By day we used plural nouns and general truths. By day we talked about the situation of Aboriginal writers: at Bella and Boris's we talked about a film which memorably showed tribal Aborigines eating the brains of a dugong. By day we were all representatives of something; at the party we discussed what it meant to fail your Marxism–Leninism exam, what Budapest means as an exotic capital, novelists from Gogol to Kundera, Islamic architecture in Central Asia, and the extreme, shaky old age of Chernyenko. And we laughed like steam.

The differences were so tempting to categorize absolutely that it was important to jerk at one's own bootstraps and recall the difference between a small party at home and, say, a lunch at University House for visiting writers Blogz and Spass. We had to avoid a naive division of people into bureaucrats and dissidents (indeed, Kundera has warned westerners about their easy habit of labelling all sorts of eastern thinkers 'dissidents'), especially because we struck all manner of intriguing divisions between public and private realms in our conversation with Soviet citizens. Everybody had ways of defining public realms; everybody also cultivated some carnivalesque home paddock, where they would grow their private fancies, often archaizing or religious fancies, but sometimes just a dream of jazz, travel or capitalist consumer goods. Many Russians longed to buy more clothes and books from Western Europe, officials included; almost everybody wanted to travel to the United States, but only for a visit.

In Moscow we now had to sing for our supper, prosaically. Enough of those playful toasts, *Za fantasia*. Meetings and TV interviews filled our days, one of the former including Georgiy Markov, a major power-broker of the Writers' Union. I was cautious, having already chyacked a member of the Central Committee during an embassy lunch. Markov was very well dressed indeed, in an old-fashioned idiom. Twenty-two years earlier Alan Sillitoe wrote of him that he 'had fair thinning hair and gentle Siberian-grey eyes, the patient eyes of a hunter looking across great spaces'. Now he scans diplomatic spaces. Intriguingly, he is everywhere described as a millionaire: the term conveys considerable respect.

I had to learn to sport a tie at these meetings: tie-wearing is *de rigueur*. Over an ample lunch I manoeuvred one of our hosts into admitting that Moscow writing tends to be . . . long pause . . . conservative.

Many hints and signs were hard for us to interpret. As Mary Seton-Watson wrote in *The Listener*, back in those days,

It is almost impossible for a foreigner to make out how much of inter-nal criticism of aspects of Soviet life is actively tolerated or even encouraged by those in authority, and how much of it perhaps managed to slip through the censor's net. Even more difficult is to get any idea of the intellectual climate in which Soviet writers live and work . . .

We built our castles on small bits of evidence. When I asked Natasha where I might be able to photocopy a poem she an-swered that she did not know of anywhere, adding, 'You can't have such machines anywhere. People might want to copy un-suitable material'. But she also yearned after overseas travel, American jazz, Austrian clothes. Poets might express them-selves obliquely in prose; painters might sell their work pri-vately. The thought of living away from their homeland was often troublesome; an artist said to me, 'Joseph Brodsky has had a very difficult life—as difficult as Nabokov'.

Attitudes to religious questions provided an interesting hinge of difference. Many of our hosts were serious about religion, whether from an atheist viewpoint or dipping solemn toes in its waters. We saw numerous icons in private homes, heard much speculation about comparative religion. Around the Writers' Union table in Leningrad we heard an official expound his interest in a mystical pantheism which had a sniff of D.H. Lawrence about it. Amateur iconography blurred with anti-quarianism, and even with a new wave of conservationism. (Why don't they start with the all-pervasive smog?) In a gallery

Natasha admitted, 'I was really interested in Jesus when I was a girl. I can remember my disappointment when I found out he was a Jew'. And the maintained sense of poetry-as-mystery at Bella's apartment was enforced by a gilded crucifix on one wall, a magnificent polar bear skin on another: classic photographs of Mandelstam, Tsvetaeva, Akhmatova and Pasternak also declared this place to be a shrine of poetry. When we were about to leave, Bella handed me a large, volute seashell, saying, 'Take this, dear Chris. When you listen to it you will hear my voice'. Attitudes to literature like attitudes to religion kept catching me on the hop, making me feel too light, too playful, too sceptical. The Australian soul takes wing easily.

Probably I could say a great deal about Tashkent, but pumping up a monotonous city requires a different set of prose habits from toning down two constantly exciting ones. This central Asian city, this vast Wangaratta, we took to calling Mañanastan: it was like Milton Keynes crammed with roses and stuck in a drowsy Deep South. True, it had a small mudbrick casbah, watermelons, shashliks and an excellent modern painter, A. Mirzaev (b. 1948). But incompetent Uzbek officials kept preventing us from getting on to longed-for Samarkand, so that we were finally obliged to give a public roasting to our local guide, high-heeled Marina. Only the day before I had explained to her the phrase, 'Up shit creek in a barbed-wire canoe without a paddle'. If locals thought of Tashkent as the seat of Babur, I thought it a beautifully apposite place to read *Dead Souls*.

Samarkand lived up to every possible expectation, but that's another story, a romantic tale of Central Asia, and we were only allowed to be there by night: long enough for me to visit Tamburlaine's starlit tomb three times. Ural, our local Writers' Union mentor, was a keen young man and I'm afraid we gave him a sleepless night. Soon enough we were off past the dawning Registan to the airport, the front of the queue and Moscow.

Gorki Street, Mayakovsky Square, Vorovsky Street, it all felt like home the third time around. In the remaining twelve hours there were more interviews and discussions on our plate. Tom remained the diplomat, Olga was tired out (she had not recovered from the heavy hardware ordeal of the Revolution Day parade on Red Square five days before) and I was looking forward to a quiet flight home—though fate was preparing a sub-plot to this story. After a good argument with Valentina Jacque and the staff of *Soviet Literature* over tea, chocolates and Schwarzwalder Torte, in which we unravelled the aesthetics of translation, we buzzed off a radio reporter and were driven back to the Hotel Pekin.

Tom and I had two or three hours left to play with. I rang friends and then we stepped out along Gorki Street looking for somewhere to have, or buy, a drink. The peak period crowds were out and moving. We noticed an especial buzz outside the only, how shall I call it?, fashion boutique in that part of town. But new prohibition dogged our steps. After walking for miles, we headed back dry to the Pekin and sat down in the dining room over two small plates of calamari and a bottle of cognac. Relaxation was settling in. At the clean, uncrowded airport I was so relaxed in the long run that I slept through take-off. Pleasantly awake as we turned towards south-east Asia, I got out Pushkin's poems, Cadoux's *Life of Jesus* and Dorothy Farnam's very creepy *Auden in Love*, preparing myself for an easy flight home. I had no inkling that we were going to break down at Delhi and spend twelve frustrating hours in the transit lounge, *not* being given information by our crew.

A little over two weeks had passed. We had scratched the surface. I had begun to get the taste.

*   *   *   *

The self who delighted in his Soviet experience, back in the late autumn of 1985, was very much a tourist self. For the tourist, everything is significant and vivid: signs are taken for wonders. But the tourist self is also ahistorical, like a lyric poem. He or she cannot know long sequences, cannot feel the strong, un-coiling logic of historical change. A visit cuts slices across process, rather as a camera does, and a traveller's memories are like snapshots, curiously portable.

From another, temporal point of view it could be said that I visited the Soviet Union at a significant moment, early in the unleashing of *glasnost* and *perestroika*. In the following year Bella and her aesthetic allies would be readmitted to the Writers' Union; some of them would be elected as office-bearers, Gor-bachev himself attending the election. In January 1987 the long-delayed Plenum sat and his major reforms swung under way. And by October 1989 eastern Europe was transforming itself into something else, with revolutionary speed.

Accordingly, the slice of life recorded in this chapter has changed its character even more rapidly than texts do as a rule. To speak in the colloquial voice, it has become history: a Muscovy of the remembering imagination.

16

Hiccups

The noun, thought, implies a past tense. Thinking succeeds thought, which lies around us like a heap of ruins—or like history.

Reverie is an even better word in French, more even. Reflections is a deeply misleading term. Yet it has considerable appeal. Reflections flicker on the page.

Can one make them as subversive as mirror-images usually are? Lewis Carroll knew the depth of such subversion, its yawning anti-world.

It is wiser not to ask questions about black holes. It is also wiser to take modern astronomy with at least a small pinch of salt. Some of the problems are linguistic. The challenge of an expanding universe is also a verbal one. Wittgenstein says that 'we get to the boundary of language which stops us from asking further questions'. There we are. Looking up, one does not imagine reject hardware lying on the moon, or trundling round us in orbit.

* * * *

All art is spilt magic.

The ocean remains multiply magical: waves always recur. Rhythm is our deep, central reservoir of significances.

For all its faults there is something extremely pleasant about nature; and not only the fact that it does not whinge. The beauty of stars is much enhanced by their cold indifference.

Lightning perfectly combines movement and stasis.

Waves reinforce our sense of rhythm and duration, hence of mortality.

Few things give poets more pleasure than storms do: thunder, lightning and heavy rain on a tin roof: what could be lovelier? The dramatic is inherently pleasurable, even if destructive. Looking on the incredibly luxurious roses at Beechworth, I found myself thinking on why it is that roses became one of the great central symbols. Partly because they are richly multifoliate, because of their thorns, because they grew all the way from Persia and India to the cold, wet North: from Omar Khayyam to the Brothers Grimm. Lampedusa's Prince sniffs one and it reminds him of the thigh of a dancer: this seems a little far-fetched to me.

Such fancies, full of flourishes, are at the other end of the spectrum from the lucent models of atomic theory. Yet it was mesons that first disturbed my world-picture. We do not expect a maximum, but we do look for a minimum.

*   *   *   *

Dance, though speechless, captures the *weight* of feelings. What could be more dionysian than 'I'm going to dance right out of my shoes/when they play those jelly-roll blues.'! And that is only the ghost of a dance, played out in language.

As gestus is to dance, so killing is to tragedy.

The human body is a historical anthology.

Is tragedy usually myopic or presbyopic? The latter. It looks from so far, and so oddly, that libido and the universe become one. Both sociology and epistemology are incompatible with tragedy: or is it that tragedy defines their limits, and their limitations? To generalize is to be a nationalist.

Comedy is a sociological art form—or a psychological one. Tragedy despises character and class. Narcissus had a tin ear; Polyphemus was presbyopic; Odysseus was tone-deaf. There is nobody so blind as he or she who demands an eye for an eye. On grammar as a form of action see Borges in 'The Theologians', where he writes of Aurelian, 'He erected vast and almost inextricable periods encumbered with parentheses, in which negligence and solecism seemed as forms of scorn.'

The indicative mood does us all good.

*   *   *   *

There are many places where the mystical may be glimpsed or intuited in life, if we keep our wits about us: there are very few such places in books.

The mystical is by definition impossible to define. It remains, however, eloquent like the future.

Excessive disparity or fusion between body and soul has a mystical component.

Pain cannot be mystical; for pain distracts, rather than contracting.

Man-made beauty can serve as a tolerable approximation to mystical awareness: say, walking through a formal garden by moonlight. Dreams and the mystical also touch, but not at all consistently.

One most choose between the dramatic panorama offered by polytheism and the ethical landscape demanded by monotheism. Or else reject both and go in for Enlightenment teleology as world-picture: the god-clock or clockmaker-god.

God is also a node of metaphors: a rich lode of concentric tropes.

How many kinds of trope is the name, Jesus, then?

By definition, God can never be used as synecdoche. Nor can his supposed presence, however hard Hopkins tried, generate onomatopoeia.

The boundary which we can discern is thereby not a final boundary. The end of The End is at the final downstroke of the d; but then what lies on the paper beyond it? Only the world, I suppose. We would feel things very differently if we were covered in fur and walked on all fours. Also if our life-span were remarkably different. But we could not know that we were different from a presumed norm.

History locks us into a personal style. It is sometimes called personality. We are like National Trust houses.

Imagine the blow to the very foundations of our thought and belief if it were suddenly proved that animals have a sense of humour and that they are capable of telling jokes.

*   *   *   *

Dreams are more frequently remembered in hay fever season, but one has correspondingly less energy to reconstruct them properly. Physiology determines psychic responses as much as vice versa. My body teases me out of thought.

Sometimes (oh dear!) you can feel time in your face.

Time limps: flies fly. Duration is up to something offstage.

*   *   *   *

What does physiology have to say about the insidiousness of music: magical and stirring as the cold stars? But then so many of the stars are still hot.

Sometimes a piece of music can transcend all music's ordinary properties and ravish you to the depths of your being. So, this morning did Stravinsky's *Pulcinella Suite* exceed its normal effect and crack the summer open to its inmost sweet kernel. On another day it will be something quite different, Bartok's *Concerto for Orchestra*, maybe. Or *Don Giovanni*.

Music, smells, tastes, the modes of wordless eloquence, leap-frogging temporal sequence. It is precisely the incomprehensibility of music that makes it so eloquent, so dangerous. It arouses the passions illicitly. You can't beat it.

One goes on discovering more and more kinds of time. Does the penis have any kind of temporal awareness? If it has, it will not tell.

Time jellies around us, like a thick aspic, impeding our strides. Forgetting is the great muse, the imaginative spur we should all really know about. Certainly Hardy and Proust knew its benevolent features, its powers.

When you can forget, all becomes possible, even imaginative recollection, even metamorphoses. Everybody should be allowed to have five personalities.

Forgetting, you can truly apprehend the thinginess of things. The world at such times becomes as available as mathematics. But mathematics is a remarkably pure joy, with no hangover. Zero was the great Arabic invention. Zeno was also Asiatic. After the letter Z we arrive at the mystical.

Xmas Day. Despite all my long lack of religious feeling, I can never quell the childish loveliness of carols and the Christ-child's birthday.

Sentimental. Carol-singing gets in under my guard. Bethlehem means magic.

Phrase from an old dream: 'We cannot can this gauche nostalgia'. Strong feeling is sometimes dynamic, sometimes sedative.

*   *   *   *

'This is not magic but work' (Brecht). Work, riddles, games, enchantments, all are made out of successions of signs in time. Part of us always goes on clasping immortality; only others are surely wobbly enough to die. What a devious word *surely* is. Death does not seem at all magical. Just crass.

Indeed death is quite as vulgar as sunsets. But far more musical. It may be, however, that death exists to push the chameleon self into contemplating one big thing instead of plurality, multiplicity, division. (Mathematics are everywhere.) It is the ultimate think-tank.

When we grow up we bolt the door on a horseless stable. Does one conceive of onself as a whole, as many things or just one segment of Brahma? The body is our central lexicon: the ark or storehouse of language and syntax. Misery damages the muscle-tone.

As David Malouf has remarked, after puberty the erotic delight of many kinds of literature (few of them merely sexy) presents itself to us.

*   *   *   *

I am what I was yesterday but surely not what I was years ago. (But in some respects . . . .) The mole beside my chin was there when I was as smooth as a peach.

What joins my head and my hand is bodiliness. What enters at the heart comes out through the fingertips.

Are dreams sent to a sleeper by the gods? It still seems one way of looking at them.

Legs cannot dream, but they can think. Can the palate think? Or the penis? Surely not the latter, in any refined or subtle sense. Is a good backhand a way of thinking? A wrong'un mixed in an over of leg-breaks clearly is. One can just imagine reading a text backwards, but it is impossible to contemplate going through the acts of love in reverse order,

*   *   *   *

Freedom is perhaps loveliest as a mere word. Many people would rather be dead than free; a few would rather be free than alive. On the other hand, bullies have an especial interest in advocating pluralism. It gives them an open slather. The greatest political safeguard is the fifty-one percent rule. No social order can change the intrinsic nature of sunsets or death. But the pigeonholes into which we try to put them may be entirely different. Sunsets appear to be entirely exhausted. But then Hardy thought nature was exhausted.

Verse-forms affect the shape of our minds. Metaphors can help us to exist. If you step twice into the same stream it may burn you off at the ankles.

The important thing to ask ourselves is this: what dichotomy runs at right angles to the one I'm deciding about at the moment?

Spatial models hold many short-cuts in store for us; but they can also entrap and bind. They also give pleasure, no mean thing.

Pleasure is the dynamo of all narratology, or should be. All literature aspires to the condition of either nursery rhyme or fairy tale.

We all like poems with three or five stanzas. It is a matter of Pythagorean mysticism.

Maps are of more lasting interest than most pictures: it is hard to wear a map out. And they have all those exotic names in them.

* * * *

G's last letter raises this question: if one chooses to write a letter in French, how far does this determine the forms of one's thinking? That is to say, how far does our tongue choose us? Or at least select our attitudes for us? What to make of the constructions of a tongue in which *heureuse* is the term if a woman wants to be happy!

How can you write a story or poem about your mistrust of language, and not lie? If it comes to that there's something odd about *publishing* a tragedy.

Metre creates realities, adding to the number of real things in the world. Things which are not in the world cause us the most trouble.

Why do the mad and near-mad ask questions to which there are no effective answers? To defend themselves on all fronts, I presume.

How can you judge the reality of someone's fears? By whether they fall sick and prove themselves correct.

Does one remember fears or only remember triggers to set off renewed fears? This one goes round and round, I fear.

What spells can one pronounce on falling into that mood Freud was in when he lamented that unfortunately his dear fellow men were mostly worthless?

We always lack adequate images of the future. This is why the future is so boring, in the short run. Likewise science fiction.

But the future waits there, a gorgeous drug. Like poetry, it goes hand in hand with magic, or what remains of magic.

What does one aim to do with the rest of one's life, apart from more of the same? Learn something, one hopes. From one point of view, personality is no more than a slow event. Or, personality is what others have, poor souls.

Man's silliness reveals the depths of his pain.

Nowhere are men and women more original than in their kinds of silliness.

To be silly is to be human, not to be silly is to be asleep, or dead.

All work like puritan craftsmen at the business of being silly.

The fool grows richer and more grotesque with age.

'How could fools get tired?' (Kafka) Yet fatigue does not guarantee wisdom.

Fools are needed to provide characters for books.

One cannot, however, imagine a painting entitled 'Landscape with Fools'—except perhaps for one work by Balthus . . . . and even his figures are more likely to be psychotics. Folly is not truly picturesque. Jesters are, though.

There is a tendency for fools to have small ailments all the time: it provides them with their only materials for conversation. In their own judgment it keeps them always fresh and interesting. It is also like continuous television, many small familiar plots.

For a similar reason, fools are keenly interested in talking about prices and bargains.

Photographs are a great resort of the foolish, providing them with substitutes for living.

A highly-developed fool can sometimes prove quite witty: but don't share a desert island with him.

Female fools are not called foolesses.

Query: are there any fools in Heaven? If not, why not?

Fools are always trying to keep in step.

There's no fool like a strong fool.

Nothing on earth so much embarrasses folly as genuine eccentricity. Hooray for *frollification*!

Folly and faddishness are first cousins: their common grandparents were Property and Propriety.

Do you know how to make fool marmalade? Use only the best strawberries.

'As thick as a cathedral door' (Causley), is a nice figure for the stability of a fool's personality, his steady, oaken ego, creaking iron hinges.

*   *   *   *

Rebellion is coiled around the roots of human behaviour. Even small children become most themselves when revolting: no, *especially* small children.

Perhaps God needed Satan.

Atheism appears pretty limp because it leaves the rebel with no worthy antagonist: the mind simply whirs away in a vacuum. Manichees are far too symmetrical.

A house is defined by the surrounding wilderness.

The act of rebellion is morally neutral but its results fall within the territory of the ethical.

Camus observes of the metaphysical rebel that 'he attacks a shattered world to make it whole'. Wholeness equals instantaneity.

Art is the high rebellion against Things As They Are. It sweeps them away and replaces them, yet its impulse is, in the same knot, conservative. The knot of art is a complicated not. The artist dies a little in every affirmation.

Rebellion placards onself on the universe. The highest pleasure lies—or stands—in saying no, and then again no. A rebel eats badly. Appetite belongs to that other world he or she wants to erase. On the other hand rebellion is intrinsically erotic. A rebel stands up like an erection. The rebellious posture can't last long.

Some god throws down the gauntlet.

Is it possible for a Neoplatonist to be also a rebel?

*   *   *   *

Can sense perceptions help in the formation of the just society? On the other hand, the just society may be no more than a cluster of sense perceptions.

Politics provides all the pleasure of spectator sport, plus real anguish. Yes, those are tears that we see.

One votes Labor (or Liberal) for pre-rational reasons, attaching new affects to habit. It is the indeterminacy of swining voters that gives them their disproportionate social power.

Politics thrusts the *timor mortis* aside.

A federal election is as erotically charged as a great poem. What personal drama can match election night in front of the TV? Politics is full of courtship and foreplay.

Image loves power, power image. Metaphors have voltage.

The brain is still in love with the archaic cortex.

Political structures acquire their expressiveness from their elaborate forms and conventions. They are as weird as sonnets and villanelles, as archaic as drott-kvaett.

The libido abhors system: it is much easier to be an anarchist in practice than in theory. On the other hand, as Barthes has observed, 'for everybody revolution is a pleasant image, and yet it is certainly an unpleasant reality'. Hence anarchism and revolution must part company: this was demonstrated in Barcelona during the Civil War.

The essence of anarchism is to be momentary, like colour-perceptions.

Pater stands alongside Nietzsche as the tutelary saint of our century. No wonder he was called Pater.

One cannot easily decide how far people are chosen by their names. But some demonstrably have been.

We invent appropriate childhoods for the ourselves. Libido is the stern god of the past. Janus yields.

We think on the seat of a bicycle.

I could die laughing.

*   *   *   *

The tyranny of narrative blurs the images. As the story grows stronger its local affects tend to become weaker, all having been conscripted for the greater good.

Narratives are so disciplined. They at least are able to say 'The End'.

Dreams lead only to waking. Yet dreams are pure narrative pith. Unlike ourselves, narrative has access to the past tense. Well, we do too if we tell ourselves as a story. And then, we have thought to fall back on.

Dreams are far more tolerant than we ourselves. They also lack punctuation.

The writer collects the archives of a world quite other than his or her daily one.

Sunlight is tacitly meaningful. Nature has to co-operate. The present tense is surely the most mindless. But powerful expressionism makes the heart leap with red blood.

Where, in fact, have the past years gone? As Virginia Woolf once said, 'Life escapes'.

Much as autumn and spring overlap in Australia, the time-schemes of the skin and of the cerebral cortex keep overlapping. Texts lust after bodiliness: bodies long for textual definition. It is even harder for paintings to represent time than for music to represent space. It was not so hard for Mediaeval pictures to do so, but the invention of point-of-view destroyed painted time.

We do not think sufficiently about antonyms. 'For every

action there is an equal and opposite reaction', said Newton; in saying so he was merely being positivistic, not, I think, metaphysical.

Opposites are tied together by bonds stronger than life itself. In the interests of psychic health we need that which is the opposite. In dreams we actively welcome it.

There exists a snobbish prejudice against adverbs, sadly. Every sentence should at some stage be tried out reversed. It is only the night that makes the day so valuable. As A. F. Davies has said, try it again with a not in it.

Is amnesia a specialized kind of remembering? Forgotten material resembles those white margins which make a page readable; or else a gallery wall.

The future tense is a cop-out.

Alcohol purports to heal chaos, to be the Word. Its words are huff and bubble.

We do not have the words to describe a garden of diversified foliage: nor, even, did Monet's brush. I will not make much headway with *lanceolate*; nor even with *scruffy sclerophyll scrub* or *glaucous venation*.

It's very hard to think of what night means to trees. Or of what life means to them. More than that, it's hard to contemplate trees as living beings (or 'creatures') at all. Is this because our view of everything is so hopelessly anthropocentric? Of time, for instance, as Collingwood pointed out. What would it be like to remember like a mountain, or a virus? Dogs, poor lambs, are marooned between there and here. We have dragged them out of nature's realm.

Having fallen out of it ourselves.

Telling the time is quite different from making sense. What would it mean for our lives to 'make sense'? Just to produce a moment's clarity on our death-beds? Or to keep giving us a sense of the One?

What answers you get depend entirely on what questions you ask: the more the muddleder. But what imposed model is it that even leads us to expect such a thing as *answers*? Perhaps Joyce was right and catechism is one of the deep structures at our life's core. Why? Because. Where? Here. How? That would be telling. The starfish thinks he is the greatest wit in the pool, the verb in the sentence.

It would be interesting to know what in our personal economy corresponds to English punctuation: the stop, comma, semi-colon and let us not speak of the colon. Quotes are also very funny.

Conventional signs promote camaraderie. But the vulgar dash is like a hiccup.

An oxymoron resembles the first act of a play. A pleonasm resembles traffic.

The sonnet is a peculiar psychic irritant, the sestina merely hateful (except for Dante's 'stony sestina').

It is curious, but appropriate, that while we are externally symmetrical, internally we are quite asymmetrical. The building contains strange furniture. Bowels can never become objects of beauty or admiration.

'What lovely bowels you have' will not do.

*   *   *   *

Having small children does not encourage reflection. But then, does not reflection encourage you to think about narrowly reflective topics? In the long run our intellects need the cutting-edge of the practical; lacking this, we drift into the endless libraries of Borges.

All reflection is in truth refraction.

'Revolution, like the religious act, has need of love.' (Jouve) Ideas are sexy. So is the energetic play of syntax. The erotics of writing consist in making the text bounce back to one's personal touch.

Radicalism may be pursued as a source of personal glamour. And it often is.

On the other hand, conservatism keeps reasserting father's phallic power. That, and mother's patient materialism.

Is humour more democratic than other modes? Also more aristocratic?

Jokes may be considered as a miniature, and highly structured art form.

A joke is a plotty haiku.

Literature has nothing to say about the pleasures of farting. Which is to say that this is a very low pleasure.

Literature is at root about fibs, puns and metaphors.

A good pun is your perfect poem. *La mort*: *l'amour*. We make love upon our gravestones.

Related rogue-terms: manic, panic, mayhem, berserk, amok.

Rogue sentiment is always good for a frisson. Baddies provide the most fun.

And, as Larkin has written, we all enjoy 'Take that, you bastard!' What happens when, as Gary Catalano says, 'the mind divests itself of any belief in the mental'? First and foremost, I should substitute 'intellectual continuity and coherence' for 'the mental'. The question makes good sense (= non-sense, in fact).

* * * *

What are the sources of equanimity, is the kind of question which may be answered in many ways depending on which discipline we are paying court to today. One might as well ask Malcolm Fraser why he is not a radical.

Moral bludgeoning is the Higher Boredom. Today's flail is yesterday's willow tree.

The circuits go on transmitting their messages. They serve the *Primum Mobile*.

Reading, especially late at night, I am always seeking the gnostic word, the magic formula which gets it all encapsulated. We are all after the great key—which, of course, does not even exist.

The best we can probably hope for are instantaneous gods.

All critics bend the texts they are let loose on. Otherwise, why bother? No-one, not even a critic, wants to play second fiddle all the time.

The great key is more like a lever or wrench. But it needs a fulcrum and a wrist.

Reality, when considered, proves tractable. But this is only a point about the nature of considering.

* * * *

Effects of very hot weather on the mind: relaxing but fatiguing; thoughts have a short span.

In summer one knows how little is compulsory.

Camus wrote tellingly about the *ambiance* of heat. Isn't *chaleur* a marvellous word? Heat loves to caress the body.

The life of the scents: a theme. They are all quite other in warm weather, different again on those rare tropical-sticky days. And they can tap the *mémoire involontaire* unimpeded by our taxonomies of knowledge.

What rules do I propose to myself, according to which I sternly try not to distort anything which I write down in this book, nor even to neglect entering my dreams here? Is it a

general regard for truth, or perhaps the historian's heresy—
that collecting it all in archival form may eventually prove
something?

One of the great myths of our time is that there are Celts.
The concept of race proves magical.

Colours are the most subliminal form of knowledge.

You cannot argue against yellow or indigo. But you can place
them side by side.

There are no names
for the colours that really matter,
our bluish tans of pity,
dark white
and the future's matt blocks
of sandy deep-green.

*   *   *   *

Mathematics is solitary. It is summed up in the decimal point.
We do not live to experience minus.

Fiction is like particle physics. The component parts dissolve
on inspection or else come up with exactly what you intend
them to. The subjective runs riot. Is there a distinct grammar of
mysticism? Is there a grammar of joy? 'Is pleasure only a minor
bliss? Is bliss nothing but extreme pleasure?' (Barthes)
Thoughts fly away fast on holidays. They shoot through unimpeded. Is there any kind of art that can have the same effect
as skinny-dipping?

The range of effects in a clouded sky or a rocky beach
exceeds the whole range of language in just the same measure
as the language-field exceeds any human mind.

On this vast coast we are all diminished. It is quite pleasant
to be tiny.

Poems written amid the joys of summer vacations are nearly
always bad.

Surf is no muse, sand no easel. Ideas are soluble in salt water.
It is strictly nonsensical to ask what lies beyond the universe.
Language belongs inside the universe. Canute-like, we go on
asking.

Controlled paranoia generates all intellectual life: anxiety
alone produces ideas.

Frank Knopfelmacher has remarked that music only goes
from Mozart to Mahler.

Why is it that so many people can read overwhelmingly

modern books, look at modern paintings, but never enjoy any music composed after 1920? It's a common weakness, and what does it say about music, its essential difference? Are we all (or almost all) musically conservative?

* * * *

Everybody wants something from grandma's house.

* * * *

The *Candide*-like error into which we fall is our assumption that the best art will be produced by the most virtuous men and women, Auden in *New Year Letter* chastised this fallacy. As one of Molière's characters pointed out, a man may be perfectly honourable and yet write bad prose.

We do not expect great engineers or great mathematicians to be notable for virtue. Skill is abrasive.

A certain amount of hatred does wonders for comedy.

What in the individual psyche corresponds to a quantum jump?

The book destroys or replaces its author, who accepts the fact, none the less.

The writer inventing the writer who writes him down. 'I cannot know things', I say, but still put the utterance into words. 'Don't bother to read me', say the writer, lying. But then his enchantment for us may consist in our knowing that he is a liar. He or she is another prestidigitator.

The words are getting away. The commas are falling out. Sentences shrink if you don't wash them carefully.

* * * *

Life is a terminal illness, that much is sure. It seeps away. Consciousness dangles death before our eyes like a black carrot. How should one's coffin be equipped? And what music played at one's obsequies?

Surely *The Rite of Spring* will be necessary.

The swerve away from death, that is the act of gesture in which we get something done. But the swerve towards death has its own libidinous power. Think about the word, *brink*. And then perhaps drink.

Personal style is a form of work, unpaid.

Charm can be as deliberate as disease. But charm suggests ease. *La vida es sueño*: what difference would it make, anyway?

We have no personality at all in our dreams, yet we are perfectly aware of ourselves as ourselves.

Autobiography is a war against time. The writer goes out like a chevalier seeking to rescue or redeem privileged moments from the indifferent, inexorable process of time. He constructs a cunning web, by means which those moments can be recovered and given an unshakable place, a new location in his still pattern of meanings, his construct out of the flux, against time, giving new names to time, since it—although his enemy—lends dignity to his campaign and illuminates all his trophies. However he, or she, may claim to resent time's revolting depredations, he knows it is just those cruel wheels or satanic mills that give life to his art, burnishing each prominent facet of the final artefact to a steady platinum glow which seems to say, Look here, I have outwitted time. There stands the masterwork on his study table. Knuckles rap on the door. He would like not to answer.

All those neglected moods and emotions: how few poems take as their theme understandable ignorance, lack of appropriate feeling, forgetfulness, physical clumsiness, being lazy, indecisiveness, indigestion, hiccups, handwriting, a tendency to sweat, even toothache or one's own gluttony. In our writing we are inclined to portray ourselves too grandly (which includes elegiacally). We want to glow.

Because our authors are so proud of their memories and notebooks they seldom portray forgetting convincingly. Hardy does, though, killingly.

Can the parts of a work also represent the *principles* upon which the whole is constructed?

Can a work convincingly dismantle form as it goes alone and in the same breath build up a radiant new form? Surely, yes. Works of literature are never really about dying: at most, it is a trick to catch the reader's deepest attention. But it is still the writer's profoundest trick; it brings the house down. I often wonder where forgotten material goes to.

*   *   *   *

As the years go on, the pain of forcing oneself to read what one should read for improvement instead of what one plainly *wants* to read (Proust, Jarrell, Stendhal, Auden, Woolf, Keats, Hardy, Bishop, Furphy, Yeats, Benjamin . . .) grows harder and harder, like a tearing up from the roots.

The wish to change resembles the habit of taking cold showers. It is hard to explain to unbookish people that we *expect* literary works to be muddled. A nice contrast is with politics in which we expect the theory to be lucid and only the practice muddled.

That political practice can never be perfected is a truth by definition; just as psychology can never arrive at a wholly convincing praxis. It is inconceivable that the knowing agent could wholly know itself (unless it be God, whatever that may be).

Political theories exist either for sheer intellectual interest-value or to provide politicians with a source of energy. Or to provide a new style of corruption.

There is an odd, perhaps an unnatural, relationship between war and history.

Violence makes for strong narrative.

Approaching the Greek oracles, one would drink first the waters of forgetfulness and then the waters of remembering. It sounds like a perfect regimen for a writer.

What general analogies are there between the life of art and the art of life? Few and complicated ones, I suspect: all misunderstood. One is said to be long and the other short. It seems that language is to blame.

Those who make a living teaching words to dance are always whingeing about the faults of language: a bad workman should get his hands out of his pockets.

Language may well be to blame but good wine is capable of granting it absolution. Indeed, the subtly differentiated innocence of wine is a continuing marvel.

In the beginning was the word; but was there chaos before that? If so, utterance must always have to struggle against the priority of chaos.

Dreams are our way of turning the cognitive flank of language; even the linguistic elements in dream have already been perverted: they try to get straight through to Logos by dialling collect and then speaking a primitive Modernist babble. When you try to harvest dreams you commonly winnow weevils. They are full of tacit mockery.

Because dreaming contains so many good jokes, it must be wise. Dreams hatch counterfeit proverbs, like 'Being asleep with glasses on you might bite your tongue'.

Every joke is a little triumph over death.

*   *   *   *

What was the Logos made of? Was it, proleptically, the body of Christ? It does not seem conceivable that the Logos was subject to grammar. Maybe, as in *Finnegan's Wake*, it was nothing more than a primitive, knowledgeable cry. The scriptures would be very different indeed if John had written, 'In the beginning was Aaargh!'

Protestantism disenfranchised the Father, replacing Him with the inexhaustible narrative self. It also disenfranchised the Virgin Mary and replaced her with the pleasures of adultery.

Does the Life Spirit despise us at all as it uses us?

Joy is our moral duty, but it is not always easy to manage. Perhaps we need to call on a hybrid cupid, a creature halfway between Eros and Agape.

*   *   *   *

A text is a book with somebody's finger up its nose. It begins to be a text when it starts being defaced by a critic. On the other hand, a work of great literature slips its tongue into *your* ear. Seduction is what it's up to.

The real power of literature is found in its feigning displays of weakness.

Help me out, it says, the world doesn't understand me.

Yet in the very same gestures with which it seduces its readers the book goes about the business of healing the soiled life of its author.

It is not merely that authors play god: they even muscle in on accidents. But then, they have themselves been subject to accidents. I reckon they have to get their own back.

Ancient libido is always there in the shadows, reading over ego's shoulder.

Ever since the Fall children have behaved abominably at table; hence, no doubt, mess parade.

Stiff cheese, Democritus, almost every kind of subatomic particle is highly unstable. Indeed some particles might be said to be products of linguistic philosophy.

The more we know about particles the less we come to know.

*   *   *   *

Je est un autre.
Je est un auteur.
Je est un hauteur.
The suasive plausibility of print. A comparison: *print, prince*.

Authority is what's at issue. Compare the stamping of coins, which in fact wear a prince's or a president's face. You think that if you really put your mind to it you might get everything written, then one glance around you shows that you can never write down more than a few salient epiphanies, however hard you try. The world is many, but words are few. Again, isn't it vain to want to turn all those phenomena into *your* words. How we all like to cover paper with black marks. No, some people deeply fear blank sheets of paper.

Books are cemeteries where a host of old feelings are put to sleep. We visit them, without flowers.

Well-printed prose is peculiarly soothing, peculiarly still. Texts aspire either to the excitements of narrative speed or to that density which produces 'sweet reluctant amorous delay'. Pronouns in narrative are apt to be like those crossed swords on maps of Europe, marking the places where the battlefields have been.

It takes great gumption, or innocence, to say 'we'. Except, of course, in so far as we stand against 'them'. They are the end.

Verbs come easy: anyone can lay claim to action. Adverbs are languidly sly. Crime is very seldom treated in verse. Why? (cf. Benjamin on the decline of the story.)

Comfort isolates. Wealth immures.

A morning shave is as good as the confessional. Likewise a morning bog.

Violence is a short-cut through to attention. There is no imperative like 'bang-bang'. Aesthetics come loudly out of the barrel of a gun. Comedy loves gunpowder.

But, waywardly, here and there, we find odd cores or nodes of meaning: there is that mysterious, sacred, sordid river, the Maribyrnong: there are those germinal points of seasonal change which encapsulate all the past; there is a sign at Flemington saying PROTEAN ENTERPRISES; there is that marvellous line from Wordsworth, 'We wonder at ourselves like men betrayed'; and there are streets or parks where time once briefly stood still.

Since we were all betrayed into life first up, it's up to us to make the most of it. And the most is what we should be able to make best.

Faith tends to be manifested through vivacity.

I write, therefore I believe. Believe in what? At least that there is something going on. Perhaps we write in order to keep the gods alive.

Poetry keeps on tilting at the divine.

And then there remains the Neoplatonic interpretation of our experience. Under this rubric, the world is one vast hieroglyphic text and all our works of art are either (a) acts of interpretation, being parts of a hermeneutic enterprise in which we try to crack the code, or (b) acts of magic by which we seek to break our way into the mysteries. All of us catch a glimpse of such a world-order from time to time, and are variously tempted by it.

The universe teases us with glimpsed harmonies.

Inspiration and love feed upon correspondences. For a lover, 'the world is a universal trope of the spirit', and everything rhymes with something else. Even the loved body is a text of the divine.

*   *   *   *

Intellectuals like to pretend they believe less than they do: there is something macho about scepticism.

The perceived world is a product of our desires.

We are all *bricoleurs* of Brahma.

*   *   *   *

Language is limited and inexhaustible.

I simultaneously want to break the moulds and to be saved by the forms: to have my cake and eat it too.

How can one draw a picture of hope?

There is major division between those who have hope and no joy, and those who have joy but not hope.

*   *   *   *

All making countermands natural chaos. But all good writing perves on the chaotic.

Nothing is hardest of all: amazing word, nothing. And what about that bizarre phrase, 'nothing at all'? So that is where nothing resides. But then, I have frequently wondered where *all* is.

Sometimes I imagine a battle on the plains of Heaven between those whose language is all nouns and those whose language is all verbs. From time to time casualties fall out and tumble like Lucifer to earth, into diction, into the divided syntax of humanity. Grammar receives them joyfully.

17

Self-consciousness

In moving from express examples of the autobiographical genre to poetic manifestations of self and then to disclosures or representations of the critic's own self in various aspects, various genres, I have engaged in slides of association which will hardly be surprising to late-twentieth-century readers. We are all caught up in an age which, despite its post-Modernist claims to irony and impersonality, simultaneously believes that the arts treat of what John Bayley has called 'the self as available reality'. Closure goes along with disclosure; the artist who enjoys dismantling reality also wants to be recognized in his or her artistic mantle; the anarchist, however extreme or subversive, is happy to be interviewed for a little magazine. And what does this interview contain? Why, the representation of a self, however ironized by the interview genre, that big cog in the publicity machine. The self keeps coming back.

Nietzsche saw such manifestations of doubleness as inevitable, and comic, writing that 'He who truly despises himself also esteems himself as a self-despiser'. This is harsh, but it points to one essential feature of modern consciousness: we have abolished Albertian perspective and write ourselves into the picture from different points of view, retaining the voices of a self but discomposing those who hanker after the security of a stable viewpoint. Bayley, aesthetically optimistic, claims with reference to one of Berryman's *Dream Songs* that 'What is funny and moving . . . is also what has also been true: that the disintegrating poet cannot help but produce undisintegrating verbal patterns', but this assurance will not always be shared by readers.

Certainly modern writers have known that there is considerable charm to be wrung from the simultaneous mantling and dismantlement of self, from texts in which the readerly contract is twitched to and fro for titillation. Such pleasure can be derived from 'The Man with the Blue Guitar':

I know that timid breathing. Where
Do I begin and end? And where,

As I strum the thing, do I pick up
That which momentously declares

Itself not to be I and yet
Must be. It could be nothing else.

Or from another poem which takes a stand amid the visual arts,
John Forbes's 'Four Conceptual Heads', which includes this
gracious glide: 'The head, at/ last one with the world, dissolves.
The artist changes genre.' And again, there are Ania Walwicz's
remarkable stories—or prose poems, or language poems, or
performance pieces, or whatever we dare to call them—which
dismantle and reconstruct syntax in such a way that it will feel
utterly different on the page from when it is read aloud. In each
case, an important part of the reader's satisfaction comes from
glimpsing what appears to be the authorial self through shifting
cubes or veils of language.

All of these texts, and the hosts of others which variously
resemble them, can be characterized as self-conscious. Indeed,
the whole era of autobiography, stretching down from Rousseau
and Wordsworth to the present day can be seen as privileging
self-consciousness in literature; it is plain that the self has increasingly fallen to pieces. But 'self-conscious' is a particularly
interesting word, since it can range all the way from approba-
tion to censure. At one end of the field, it can be used to denote
self-awareness, percipience, a particular quality of intelligence;
at the other, the awkwardness which comes from not knowing
how to present oneself in public.

By the same token, writers may lament the loss of some old,
unitary ego. But they may, just as easily, be disposed to welcome the new metropolitan diversity of available selves, much
as Baudelaire's *flâneur* welcomed the array of possible roles,
gestures and anonymities which the busy streets of modern
Paris had to offer. They too can play the sparrow on the gravel
path.

If you present your self (or your available repertoire of
selves) as manifold, transitory, faceted, metamorphic, you have
escaped from any single judgement of your personality. You
have slipped off a certain moral hook. The selves which you can
set down in written, typed or printed *characters* will not, from
their thronging plurality, admit of anything so unitary or

plonking as character. You have lots of new tricks, for the self is variously empowered by its dispersal. It was just such a Modernist instability as this which Matthew Arnold was lamenting in the winter of 1848–49 when he wrote grumpily to his old friend, Clough:

My dearest Clough
    What a brute you were to tell me to read Keats' Letters. However it is over now: and reflexion resumes her power over agitation.
    What harm he has done in English Poetry. As Browning is a man with a moderate gift passionately desiring movement and fulness, and obtaining but a confused multitudinousness, so Keats with a very high gift, is yet also consumed by this desire: and cannot produce the truly living and moving, as his conscience keeps telling him. They will not be patient, neither understand that they must begin with an Idea of the world in order not to be prevailed over by the world's multitudinousness: or if they cannot get that, at least with isolated ideas: and all other things shall (perhaps) be added unto them.

Arnold is right about both the restlessness and the multitudinousness at the heart of what Keats has to offer; where he parts company from my own sympathies, and surely from many modern responses, is in regretting these traits. That he can, in the middle of the nineteenth century ask a poet to begin with an 'Idea of the world' seems remarkably *retardataire*, or should I say, Canute-like. But it may be acutely to the point that this letter was addressed to Clough, whose lethargically comic irony was one of those forces which were combining to dismantle any such controlling Idea.

It hardly needs emphasizing that the line of multitudinousness has close affinities with the line of perceptionism, that powerful mimetic tradition which runs down through Keats, Browning, Pater, Hopkins, Eliot, Slessor and Elizabeth Bishop, not to mention its many paths into fiction. According to this tradition the vividly recorded perception is a guarantee of genuineness; Ruskin put the moral value of true seeing and true telling even higher, but then he had a remarkably confident view that prose could work with all the visual immediacy of a painter's sketchbook, a view which he bodied forth in such performances as his 1872 comparison of a princess by Carpaccio with two young American girls on the train from Venice to Verona. And in this tradition abstraction is a sign of artistic weakness, of failure, perhaps of egotism uncontrolled.

For the writer, self-consciousness is akin to Bloomian belatedness: it can weaken writing, or positively empower it. As Hope has written in his 'Pseudodoxia Epidemica', 'Taken full strength, truth is a drug that kills', itself an oracular rather than a self-conscious remark. And the truth about one's own modern dividedness may provide a wonderful kit of tools for modern writing. Even Eliot, one of the poets who most passionately regretted the fragmentation of twentieth century culture and the damage to the self, derived the astonishing power of 'Gerontion' and *The Waste Land* from just such regretful awareness.

Another tactical development is that of Robert Lowell's *Life Studies*, in which family materials, the disclosure of which we might regard as a betrayal of privacy or of insignificance, are organized into a little chain of ironical narratives, the narrator securely in control of his effects. In lines like 'Cured, I am frizzled, stale and small' and 'I was a stuffed toucan/ with a bibulous, multicoloured beak', Lowell the narrator knows exactly what he is doing with Lowell the protagonist: and with us. Authorial power is acquired at the expense of another, ridiculous self, much as in Sartre's *Les Mots*.

We are moving down the line to a point where the poets have learned many comic games from their subjectivity. We live in the Age of Inverted Commas. We can slide easily from the question, is this a joke about literature itself?, to, is this a joke about 'literature'?, and thence rapidly to, is this a 'joke' about 'literature'?, and so there we are, or are not. Is John Forbes's 'Malta', which is crammed with funny quotations, artfully scattered around in imitation of somebody being self-conscious about the comic genre, merely funny? Perhaps it is merely cool. We are sharing the difficulty of Frank Kermode, who writes in his essay on 'The Modern' that 'I myself believe that there is a difference between art and joke, while admitting that it has sometimes been a difficult one to establish'. What we need is a term for readerly self-consciousness.

For literary and cultural critics, this devolution of self has made available many new postures and strategies, some of them marked by that play of false ingenuousness which we call Martian; recent decades have afforded critics a great deal more power, manifested in new postures and scepticisms, more ways of writing criticism's secondary or tertiary narratives. The analytical commentator ceases to represent the idea of a community and increasingly becomes what K. K. Ruthven has ruefully dubbed The Critic without Qualities: a sort of nippy but unrealiable rover around the packs. And, conscious of his or her wardrobe full of tactically possible selves, there no longer seems any reason for the employment of the one methodology from beginning to end of a book. The critic can devolve into a little team of approaches.

One recent example of this critical instability can be found in Andrew Taylor's *Reading Australian Poetry*, a book in which the scholarly tone is consistent enough, but where a different theoretical armoury is brought to bear in each chapter, or on each poetic subject. Tactically very different is Peter Steele's *Expatriates*, which is a book 'on' modern poems, but in which Steele allows himself the ludic freedom to write Essays in an almost old-fashioned sense: essays which can wittily turn to and fro, throwing off aphorisms about poetry, life, death, God or eternity, in obedience to no recognizable current discipline. A third case, different, again, is that of Brian Matthews' *Louisa*. Ostensibly, and deeply, a biography of Louisa Lawson, this study fragments the critic himself into two people and his/their text into an ironically zigzag series of chronotopes, all enlisted in search of that culturally shrouded figure, the mother of Henry Lawson.

Some cultural analysts, even relentlessly deconstructive ones, can still display a sad, romantic sense of loss. Thus, at the very core of Lacan's *Ecrits* there remains a naively Neoplatonic yearning for the condition of innocence and wholeness which, on Lacan's reading, we all lose in our early infancy. Emotionally if not dialectically, Lacan is at one with Arnold. Rhetorically, however, he went about smashing up the nursery.

Difficult and wilful though Lacan's writing is, then, it is hard to feel that he felt any joy in dismantling the concept of articulate subjective identity. The infantile excesses of his writing kept bearing witness to the natural, dispossessed infant (his own term was *infans*), somewhere back there, terribly previous, antecedent to language, yearning to be released. By whom? Why, by a critic-analyst deploying his powers of language: by a critic who delighted in employing the rhetorically flashy excesses of literary French.

The more one reads Lacan the more it becomes plain that he was not one of those who could delight freely in what Kermode has called the aleatory openness of Modernism. His disorderly, magisterial prose wanted to put the world together again. For all his surface playfulness, he remained hostile to 'the shoddy Nietzschean notion of the lie of life'.

Self-consciousness as fragmentation may be servitude and it may be freedom. It is possible to feel one's roles as elective and polymorphous, while yet seeing one's life as a site—in the words of the new materialists—on which an array of discursive forces have fought for the upper ground. The term, site, is ultimately wrong in its passivity, however textual or intertextual our lived selves may be, since they are full of such mobility, such cunning, or at worst such neurotic intensity, as they seek power and persuasiveness.

From among post-ego theorists, the account of the polymorphous self which I find most convincing and cheering is that of Hélène Cixous. In her 1974 article, 'The Character of "Character"', Cixous writes that

'I' must become a 'fabulous opera' and not the arena of the known. Understand it the way it is: always more than one, diverse, capable of being all those it will at one time be, a group acting together, a collection of singular beings that produce the enunciation. Being several and insubordinable, the subject can resist subjugation. In texts that evade the standard codes, the 'personage' is, in fact, Nobody—*personne*—he is that which escapes and leads me somewhere else. How could he carry me away otherwise?

Selves, however defined, are only of interest if they are mobile and dynamic.

It is the divided self mobilized into facets or fictions, masks or episodes, that we respond to in much contemporary writing, from Elizabeth Jolley's dangerous archipelago of novels to Dorothy Hewett's *Alice in Wormland*, from Hal Porter to Peter Porter. The manifestation of division makes for a desirable narrative. The authorial self may give more readerly pleasure if, like Les Murray's, it dissolves into a torrent of swirled kennings or if, like Jack Hibberd's, it subordinates its created characters to the to-fro play of wilfully mixed diction.

But, as I have suggested, the dividual is a rewarding model for the consideration of serious readers only if such plurality entails flexibility. Against traditional Christian and psychiatric desiderata we must set the successful protean strategies of many a creative artist: Swift's parade of self-consuming stooges, Browning's men and women, Yeats's doctrine of masks, Borges's vision of Shakespeare as 'everything and nothing', Gwen Harwood's subdivision into her nominal self and those four personae-poets, Geyer, Lehmann, Stone and Kline. The very practice of lyric poetry tends to be dividual in this way: every poem contains a new imp of self. What can be said of Ania Walwicz's coruscating prose poems could be said of any poet's works, that each is a new self-text, a fresh tale incorporating a newly told self. What holds them together is a strong poet's style, a ringmaster's assertion, self-consciousness insisting once again that after all it was free to choose, free to subvert, free to create in the heavy medium of language.

It is true that we all seek ways to characterize different personal styles, generic preferences, dispositions. Such taxonomies range all the way up to Robert Bales's immensely complicated global model which incorporates three sets of twenty-six positions each, graphing personal styles against world views against interpersonal styles. Far more simply, I have had pleasure (in *Toil and Spin*) in employing a small figuration of available poetic dispositions which graphs wisdom against mimesis, expression against construction, and high diction against low. What stays unfixed about such models is how far the self is free to choose and change, how far the agent overcomes the patient. For an answer of some human consolation, I would turn to Alan Davies's remark that environment and conditioning provide us with a elaborate set of pigeonholes, but that we still have to decide how to make use of them. The pigeonholes are, it goes without saying, innumerable. Making sense of our lives has its laws, but is unbounded and unpredictable, like the interpretation of dreams. Just as dreams are, the life process is insufferably witty.

Take scepticism far enough, take late deconstruction far enough, and the dividual collapses into a succession of sentences. Over them all, however, there still reigns a life sentence which manifests itself in two important ways: through intentions carried out and through style. No critical method, among all those which have thronged the media and the academies in our century, has yet found an adequate way of talking about style. Yet it is style which finally discloses the characters of self-consciousness. It is also the root source of readerly joy.

18

Gothic Charms and
the Big Picture

*As compared with all these rationalizing pictures, the pluralistic
empiricism which I profess offers but a sorry appearance. It is a
turbid, muddled, gothic sort of affair, without a sweeping outline
and with little pictorial nobility.*

William James

At sceptical moments, I am inclined to think that we poet–
academics are in the universities under false pretences. This
is not because our teaching flair or our critical insights are
necessarily inferior to those of our 'straight' colleagues; it is
because there is a sense in which our primary allegiance is
elsewhere. The scholar–critic who is not also a practitioner of
imaginative literature may be presumed to be constructing, at
least intermittently, an intellectually coherent work, a great
house of the mind, in the course of her or his adult life. In my
experience, the poet–critic feels a certain freedom to claim that
his/her cardinal matrix is to be found in the poetry, and that the
criticism consists of a series of privileged raids on interesting
parts of the literary terrain.

To be interested in ideas, to be avid of the kind of enquiry
that universities foster, is of course to be interested in theory.
And the rapidly expanded interest in openly-declared system
building, the now-contagious sketching of large ideological
panoramas with onself shown small and pink in one corner,
these are very genial developments of emphasis indeed. Like
everybody else, I practise nostalgia compulsively, but when
I look back to the kind of English department I worked in
twenty-five years ago, I am aware of how grudging the interest
in abstract ideas was, how suspicious we were of philosophy,
and how bizarrely indifferent we were to examining the culture
of our own country. It would seem certain that the post-
structuralist pluralism of abstract enquiry which has made its

way into the English departments has been responsible for changing, not only the first two aridities, but even in part the academic disinterest in Australian writing. For all of these I find myself extremely grateful.

Particularly important, though, has been the insistence within these newer forms of intellectual discourse that they should put their own cards on the table: that the enquirer should not remain unenquired. To be sure, this intellectual reflexiveness can seem irritating, with three-quarters of a typical article being devoted to the question of how it should be going about its business, rather than getting in there close to the text, a neighbourliness which used to display the stamp of the genuine, back in the heyday of slow reading. But as one who so often felt excluded by the powerful show of consensus which a supposedly 'common pursuit' enforced, I chiefly welcome the present kinds of disarmament. One can even feel free under this new dispensation to make a virtue of inconsistency, if one declares the motivations and styles of that inconsistency. This has already been discussed under the heading of 'The Textual Self'.

Grouches and grumbles against the role of post-structuralist theory in the literary critical discipline are commonly based on two things: that it generates repellently abstract jargon and that it yields too much ground to the arrogant desire of critics to exert power over the texts they purport to examine. But even these complaints are soon qualified if one turns back to the admired practising critic of a quarter of a century ago. Memory plays strange, rosecoloured tricks on such phenomena; over the last couple of years I have returned a number of times to English and American critics of an earlier dispensation, thinking to find the kind of close, suasive readings which might be instructive for some of my first-year students, and finding instead a surprising incident of jargon and self-assertion. And thin gruel.

So far I have been speaking geographically, locating myself at a point in the scrub between large areas of discourse. But it is also plain that any talk of poetry and theory might invite us to talk about the relation between our own poetic theories (not necessarily our *poetics*, which is probably grander and more overarching, if we have it at all) and our poetic practice. This puts another aspect on things. Perhaps one can make the transition best by way of the road marked Mimesis.

Yes, as readers we commonly find that the hinge or cusp

which tips us from conceptual geography into particular
psychology, from the mezzosocial arena into the microsocial,
is mimesis. Any young poet, at setting out, believes that the
medium is potentially transparent, that mimetic truth to
emotionally charged vignettes is what's at issue. The poems give
onto life. If they work, they depict external life with concentrated accuracy, focusing perhaps on some telling *gestus* or
epiphany, and their language is orchestrated so as to add a
music to the delineation—as in a film.

Soon enough, though, one arrives at outcrops of the mimetic
paradox, and must be cast into doubt. Basically, the mimetic
paradox goes like this: certain poets behave as though they
are driven by the belief that language can depict experience
clearly, vividly, tangibly even. Why, then, do these poets
(Keats, Browning, Hopkins, Marianne Moore, Heaney) need
to craft, warp and complicate the language so much to achieve
their end? Why make play with the convergent tropes of synaesthesia? Why is rhythmical variation asked to carry so much
weight, as though it were a comprehensible discourse system? If
the English language is transparent, it doesn't need all this
artful crafting; if it is not a mimetic medium, why does all this
carft and manipulation metamorphose its essential nature,
enabling it suddenly to render or 'enact' the phenomenal
world? How can sheer craft harvest the things of life?

As the poet matures, another troubling paradox becomes
evident. The poetry crushes non-textual life. It can be said to
devour experience, as in A. D. Hope's early wish, 'To be the
Eater of Time, a poet, and not that sly/Anus of mind the
historian' (though I do not know why he was so scatological
about historians). To put the case personally, I can recall
certain scenes or situations with especial force and vividness.
Then, scanning a manuscript, I realize that the *éclat* of the scene
derives from the fact that I have already made it over into a
poem: what I am remembering is not the raw scene, but the
morphology which my own making has already imposed on it.
The situation begins to resemble that of dream recall, where
what we hold in mind is usually the secondary elaboration of
that faded first experience. In dreams begin retellings.

As a poet, then, I simultaneously have a sensuous hunger to
capture the world through depiction and a sceptical awareness
that such depiction depends on conventions of discourse which
are historically bounded; or, worse, linguistically doomed from

the start. How do you write down the leaves on one small tree in your backyard? To this doubleness I tend to respond manically: over-reacting, I signal my awareness of a disabling gap by upping the ante, mixing the dictions, breaking decorum, doing all that I can to syncopate readerly expectations. To exemplify this anxiety in action, let me cite a poem of mine which is precisely about the desire for *das Ding an sich*, the mimetic hunger to entrap substances, facts, textures and gists in a web of language:

THE THING ITSELF

The important thing is to build new sentences,
to give them a smart shape,
to get acquainted with grammar like a new friend.

One rubs down syntax
into a coarse familiarity,
such foreplay as closes down all thought.

Were it not
that the undertaking is too mannered
(as gnostic as a shower of rabbits),

I would like to go right back,
devising a sentence
unlike any such creature in creation;

like nothing on this planet:
a structure full of brackets and cornices,
twigs, pediments, dadoes and haloes and nimbs,

full of nuts, butter and flowers!
sinewy, nerved,
capable of blotches or of waving hair.

That would be a sentence to really show the buggers,
like a cute
new thing

or like a tree
recently invented
by some utterly brilliant committee;

it would glitter, articulate,
strum and diversify.
It would be the thing itself.

So het up is this poem about the disconcerting question that it does not even direct itself to any particular scene or configuration. It makes a general case about particularity; and that sentence may turn out to be a very fair definition of the thrust of lyric poetry. It should be just as particular as it is general. It should have shoulders and elbows to guarantee articulation.

A different point: the poem just quoted should make it clear how far I have been shoved, cajoled and seduced by current theories about the limited capacity of language to signify anything external to it. Yet I would suppose that I resemble most other poets in my sense—my faith, if you like, but we don't talk about *faith* in the academy—that, however boxed into resignation, poetry or fiction retains a peculiar primacy over commentary. As Philip Mead has written recently, 'Like all works of art, poems can't be fully represented, except by themselves'. It was only on reading this that I could fully admit to myself the dream which every imaginative writer must surely nurture somewhere in the brainpan: of a critical commentary which will exactly reproduce the full thrust of one's poem, or story, or novel. The only such critique would resemble the *Don Quixote* of Pierre Menard, and even this, Borges admits . . . but enough of that. The critic cannot inhabit the examined text meticulously, entirely; she or he has other fish to fry, including the big fish of theory. As poets we want self-abnegation from our critics. But I think we are also teased by the fact that continental speculators (Benjamin, Barthes, Foucault, Lacan) employ the gorgeous figures of literary rhetoric themselves.

To be a little more respectful, there are other things that poets look for, hope for, from critics, and not mere replication. The poet wants to be told things about her or his creative process, posture and place during the writing of the lyric in question: insights that were not apparent during the creative process because the writing nexus kept the poet at full stretch. As this last remark admits or pleads, we are often too busy writing the stuff to know what our own poetic theories are. Can the water in the stream erode itself? And if we look up from the typewriter to see further we are less apt to be exercising theoretical muscle than to be asking the mainline questions of our profession: how does this poem go about the business of conducting its argument with the rest of my *oeuvre*? in what ways is this poem enabling for the next one I shall need to write? will this be understood? does this utterance narrow down into self-parody? and, how many years do I have before the onset of Alzheimer's disease?

The academy and its disciplines, above all current critical

theories, these make up an overlapping set of scepticisms, and inasmuch as they do will always be viewed as oppositional to that aspect of the poet's art which is concerned with making an icon: constructing something which will seem sacred, or erotically charged.

But these scepticisms are themselves an intriguing phenomenon. This is so, firstly because the scepticism itself can drive an imaginative bargain which we feel as stimulating because hard-edged and punchy: think of some of those breathtaking moves in Hume, in Nietzsche, in Freud. Think of Wittgenstein's remark, 'The question, what is the nature of a joke, is like the question, what is the nature of a lyric poem'.

From a second angle, though, I've always been fascinated by the ways in which we can observe a hierarchy of partial scepticisms. For example, some of those whose deconstructive allegiances might seem most sceptical turn out to be fussily right-minded about their constitutional rights at meetings; whole-hog Nietzscheans of the mind perform simultaneously as good administrators; principled anarchists worry about the status of underdogs or junior employees; hardline textual subversionists are still willing (I don't know why) to expect logical coherence or correct spelling: shouldn't they take more note of Randolph Stow's objection that 'There is nothing romantic about good spelling'? One of my dreams is of the completely misspelt text. But I, too, like to communicate, I'm sorry to say. We are all in this boat.

In my own unsystematic case, one of the things which has appealed most about the deconstructive liberties has been the way in which they have allowed critics to move in fast, almost randomly, onto some symptomatic detail, to show up something ironically warped in the sub-text, or in the societal context, of a book. I like the speed and dash which are now permitted in a more sceptically open zoo of methodologies. And it is probably for his speed and dash that, stepping backward for a moment, I share Fay Zwicky's high valuation of Keats' poetics.

It is pleasing for a poet sometimes to view language instrumentally; and in such a mood to assert that the aim of poems is to reconstruct cliches and reassemble them as dynamic entities, whether with a tilt towards the natural, or the psychological, or the linguistic. Yet I also want to maintain the aura of high literature: the aura which for me manifestly surrounds 'To Autumn' or 'The Steeple-Jack' or 'Five Bells'—or *The Tempest*, to change genres in mid-ocean. My passion for art is unregenerate.

By now it will be quite plain that I speak as a *handyman* rather than as a pharaoh. For all that I have devised a few stringybark taxonomies, I have no big picture to offer. Perhaps this is because at heart I adhere to that modestly empirical conception of the thinking process which is depicted in the first five lines of 'Introspections':

Have you ever seen a mind
thinking?
It is like an old cow
trying to get through the pub door
carrying a guitar in its mouth.

And perhaps it is because I regard the poems themselves as tesserae which, taken together at the end, will make up a big picture which more or less corresponds to the life itself: an epistemological life-story done in fragments. Like Keats in this, I do not believe that CWC's identity is to be found expressed in these separate poems; but I do hope that they will add up in the end to something which may be *me*. The self may well be problematical but I am still perfectly able to tell when I have finished something:

Whatever has been writing this down gets out
from behind the wheel and
walks away.

The closure here is one of the punctuation marks in a process which can reasonably be called my life.

But this ending of a poem, like most textual endings, does not really wind up the whole box and dice. The reader goes on, reads on as it were into the white space at the bottom of the page or the white pages at the end of the book; also continues to make assumptions about the authorial self which inhabits the book but is not really bound by it. This is as true of my relatively sceptical presence as it would be of the strong, rhetorical, activist presence of Lionel Fogarty. The driver may have walked away, but you have got his number—my number.

This book has looked at the many procedures by which an author writes a version of the self, or falls into language. Left with the traces of that language, readers have been given a licence (it is part of their contract) to reconstruct the anatomy of a self from it: that is to say, to read.

What we find in a text is something both personal and anthropomorphic. After all the scepticisms we may bring to bear on the literary work, we still except it to depict a congeries of individual affects. Let Keats, who means so much to me, have the penultimate word:

I will call the world a School instituted for the purpose of teaching little children to read—I will call the human heart the horn Book used in that School—and I will call the child able to read, the Soul made from that school and its hornbook.

Eloquent and appealing surely, not least because its tripartite circularity savours both of syllogism and of charm or proverb, but how are we to read this, in fact? It points to a world where discourse generates the responsive self; but also a world which can only do so because it is permeated with self (Brennan's dream, and Brennan was a sort of failed, or theoretical, Keats). We can glimpse the runnel where Neoplatonism spills over into Romanticism here, the world offered to us as a significant palimpsest. Keats's trope of 'the human heart' might be translated as 'charged with affect' or as referring to nature when it is so charged. We are here, then, located in that Romantic contract which recognizes the active cusp of 'both what they half create/And what perceive', but which does not go all the way into the subjective swamps of 'we receive but what we give/And in ourselves alone does nature live'.

The most lively imaginative enterprise surely recognizes a model in which self and nature, self and language, function symbiotically, giving and receiving, making and being made. That the self should be merely a crystallization out of given discourse systems is both abhorrent to me and, blessedly, unknowable by anyone. That it could be a free agent is a primitive dream.

Why, lastly, does Keats preside over this largely Australian book like a tutelary spirit? Partly, it seems to me, because he offers a poetic and epistolary self which remains irreducible in the end, being so democratic, aesthetic, secular, witty, robust, mysterious, urban, cheeky and civilized. But to say this about him presumes a distance, an elbow room, which I cannot really boast. As was revealed in 'The Textual Self', Keats, and through him Palgrave, and in Palgrave Keats again, was a major influence on my adolescence. In looming as such an influence he was superscribed on a childhood, an environment, that was already post-Romantic. There was no likelihood that he would ever lose out. And, impersonal personality of tactile sensations, he could inscribe himself on my reading life as the precursor of Slessor and Hopkins, *The Moving Image* and *The Wandering Islands*, Marianne Moore and Seamus Heaney. From his example, as from some kinship with the visual arts, comes my sense that literary creation has the character which Kipling described when he wrote,

I worked the material in three or four overlaid tints or textures, which might or might not reveal themselves according to the shifting light of sex, youth or experience.

This points to precisely what I most value in literary texts: resistance, or that density of medium which keeps on calling for rereadings.

In the end, then, historical selves are eclipsed by the texts which they make out of themselves under the profound influence of previous texts. We lack the signified life when we read, we yearn for it and we tacitly write it in. The mystery of the self within (above? behind?) the writing which bears its name is not so very different from the mystery of the self as a passionate organism flaunting its cussedness among the social systems, burdened by pain and delighted by art. A rich residue of psychological mystery is not only a source of value but the very ground of realism. We shall never be completely known.

So, if authorial responsibility is still in order (writers will certainly go on believing that it is), this book has been about responsibility and abdication in books and poems: even in epigrams. It has asked what really happens in that contract through which readers grant the presence of an authorial life in the printed pages they are reading. Moreover, it presumes the presence of an authorial subject who is Australian, poetic, liberal, by and large a sceptical aesthete, and located in the late twentieth century. In token of his plain dealing with you he has deliberately added his own scrutable stamp to the tracks of other writers whose autobiographical traces he has been following. In the end I rejoice in what the incorrigibly romantic Lacan has lamented: that we have fallen from infantile innocence into language. So here we are, doing what we can to bend that language to our specific purposes. Believing that we have free will is finally the same as having free will.

Along with my poems, these chapters are also protests against death, against the ultimate stupidity of fate. Every writer goes about setting up fences against death, our annihilation after a desperately short innings on this greenish-blue planet. With Hope's unseen guide, we ask, 'Who are we, stranger? What are we doing here?' Our writings dramatize the life which is constantly slipping away from us: they replace it with marks on paper.

Bibliography

Ethel Anderson, *Squatter's Luck: With Other Bucolic Eclogues* (Melbourne University Press, 2nd edition, 1954)

W. H. Auden, *Collected Shorter Poems: 1930–1944* (London: Faber, 1950)

——, *The Dyer's Hand, and Other Essays* (New York: Vintage, 1968)

——, *The English Auden* (London: Faber, 1978)

——, *Poems* (London: Faber, 1930)

Bachelard, Gaston, *The Poetics of Space*, trans. Maria Jolas (Boston: Beacon, 1969)

Roland Barthes, *Roland Barthes*, trans. Richard Howard (New York: Hill & Wang, 1977)

Walter Jackson Bate, *The Burden of the Past and the English Poet* (London: Chatto & Windus, 1971)

——, *John Keats* (Cambridge: Belknap, 1963)

John Bayley, *The Uses of Division: Unity and Disharmony in Literature* (London: Chatto & Windus, 1976)

Samuel Beckett, *Proust* (New York: Grove Press, 1931)

Randolph Bedford, *Naught to Thirty-Three* (Melbourne University Press, 1933)

Walter Benjamin, *Illuminations*, ed. and trans. Hannah Arendt (London: Collins, 1970)

——, *Reflections: Essays, Aphorisms and Philosophical Writings*, trans. Edmund Jephcott, ed. Peter Demetz (New York: Harcourt Brace Jovanovich, 1978)

R. P. Blackmur, *Form and Value in Modern Poetry* (New York: Doubleday, 1957)

Harold Bloom, *Agon: Towards a Theory of Revisionism* (New Yrok: Oxford University Press, 1983)

——, *Figures of Capable Imagination* (New York: Seabury Press, 1976)

——, *Ruin the Sacred Truths: Poetry and Belief from the Bible to the Present* (Cambridge: Harvard University Press, 1989)

Louise Bogan, *Collected Poems: 1923–1953* (London: Peter Owen, 1956)

Martin Boyd, *Day of My Delight* (Sydney: Lansdowne, 1965)

——, *A Single Flame* (London: Dent, 1939)

Christopher Brennan, *The Prose of Christopher Brennan*, ed. A.R. Chisholm and J.J. Quinn (Sydney: Angus and Robertson, 1962).
——, *The Verse of Christopher Brennan*, ed. A.R. Chisholm and J.J. Quinn (Sydney: Angus & Robertson, 1960)
Anne Brewster, 'The Freedom to Decompose: The Poetry of Kamala Das', *Journal of Indian Writing in English*, 8.1–2 (1980)
Joseph Brodsky, *Less than One: Selected Essays* (New York: Farrar, Straus & Giroux, 1986)
Elizabeth Bruss, *Autobiographical Acts: The Changing Situation of a Literary Genre* (Baltimore: Johns Hopkins University Press, 1976)
Vincent Buckley, *Essays in Poetry, Mainly Australian* (Melbourne University Press, 1957)
——, *The Pattern* (Melbourne: Oxford University Press, 1979)
——, *Poetry and the Sacred* (London: Chatto & Windus, 1968)
——, *Selected Poems* (Sydney: Angus & Robertson, 1981)
David Campbell, *Deaths and Pretty Cousins* (Canberra: Australian National University Press, 1975)
——, *Evening Under Lamplight: Selected Stories of David Campbell* (St Lucia: University of Queensland Press, 2nd edition, 1987)
——, *Flame and Shadow: Selected Stories of David Campbell* (St Lucia: University of Queensland Press, 1976)
——, *Selected Poems* (Sydney: Angus & Robertson, enlarged 2nd edition, 1973)
Wendy Capper, 'Facey's *A Fortunate Life* and Traditional Oral Narratives', *Australian Literary Studies*, 13, 3 (1988)
Maie Casey, *An Australian Story: 1837–1907* (London: Michael Joseph, 1962)
Helene Cixous, 'The Character of "Character"', *New Literary History*, 5, 2 (Winter 1974)
Joan Colebrook, *A House of Trees* (London: Chatto & Windus, 2nd edition, 1988)
Richard Coe, 'Portrait of the Artist as a Young Australian', *Southerly*, 41, 2 (1981)
——, *When the Grass Was Taller: Autobiography and the Experience of Childhood* (New Haven: Yale University Press, 1984)
'Tom Collins' (Joseph Furphy), *Such Is Life* (Sydney: Angus & Robertson, 1962)
Peter Conrad, 'Footholds in the Sunburnt Country', *Times Literary Supplement* (19 December 1986)
Allen Curnow, 'New Zealand Literature', *Essays on New Zealand Literature*, ed. Wystan Curnow (Auckland: Heinemann, 1973)
——, *Selected Poems* (Auckland: Penguin, 1982)
——, *You Will Know When You Get There* (Auckland: Oxford University Press, 1982)
Kamala Das, *The Descendants* (Calcutta: Writers Workshop, 1967)
——, *My Story* (New Delhi: Sterling, 1977)

——, *The Old Playhouse and Other Poems* (New Delhi: Orient Longman, 1973)

Alan Davies, *Private Politics* (Melbourne University Press, 1970)

——, 'Small Country Blues', *Meanjin* XXXXIV 2 (1985)

Bruce Dawe, *Condolences of the Season: Selected Poems* (Melbourne: Cheshire, 1971)

Antony Easthope, *Poetry as Discourse* (London: Methuen, 1983)

William Empson, *Some Versions of Pastoral* (Norfolk: New Directions, 1960)

John Evelyn, *The Diary of John Evelyn*, sel. and ed. John Bowle (Oxford University Press, 1983)

F. Scott Fitzgerald, *The Great Gatsby* (Harmondsworth: Penguin, 1950)

John Forbes, *The Stunned Mullet and Other Poems* (Sydney: Hale & Iremonger, 1988)

——, *Tropical Skiing* (Sydney: Angus & Robertson, 1976)

Miles Franklin, *Childhood at Brindabella* (Sydney: Angus & Robertson, 1979)

——, *My Brilliant Career* (Edinburgh: Blackwood, 1903).

Sigmund Freud, *The Major Works of Sigmund Freud* (Chicago: Encyclopaedia, 1952)

Rodney Hall, *J. S. Manifold: An Introduction to the Man and His Work* (St Lucia: University of Queensland Press, 1978)

Ian Hamilton, *Robert Lowell: a Biography* (New York: Random House, 1982)

W. K. Hancock, *Country and Calling* (London: Faber, 1954)

Thomas Hardy, *Selected Poems*, ed. Walford Davies (London: Everyman, 1982)

Charles Harpur, *Selected Poetry and Prose*, ed. Michael Ackland (Ringwood: Penguin, 1986)

Gwen Harwood, *Selected Poems* (Sydney: Angus & Robertson, 1975)

Paul Hasluck, *Mucking About: An Autobiography* (Melbourne University Press, 1977)

Seamus Heaney, *Preoccupations: Selected Prose 1968–1978* (London: Faber, 1980)

Zbigniew Herbert, *Selected Poems*, trans. John and Bogdana Carpenter (London: Oxford University Press, 1977)

H. P. Heseltine, ed. *A Tribute to David Campbell: A Collection of Essays* (Kensington: New South Wales University Press, 1987)

A. D. Hope, *The Cave and the Spring: Essays on Poetry* (Sydney University Press, 2nd edition, 1974)

——, *Collected Poems: 1930–1965* (Sydney: Angus & Robertson, 1966)

——, *The New Cratylus: Notes on the Craft of Poetry* (Melbourne: Oxford University Press, 1979)

Gerard Manley Hopkins, *Gerard Manley Hopkins*, ed. Catherine Phillips (Oxford University Press, 1986)

Donald Horne, *The Education of Young Donald* (Harmondsworth: Penguin, revised edition, 1988)

Alice James, *The Diary of Alice James*, ed. Leon Edel (New York: Dodd, Mead, 1934)

John Keats, *The Complete Poems* (Harmondsworth: Penguin, 1973)

——, *The Letters of John Keats*, ed. H. Buxton Forman (Oxford University Press, 3rd edition, 1947)

Rudyard Kipling, *Something of Myself for My Friends Known and Unknown* (New Jersey: Doubleday, Doran, 1937)

Jacques Lacan, *Ecrits: A Selection*, trans. Alan Sheridan (London: Tavistock, 1980)

P. Lal, 'Contemporary Indian Women Poets in English', *Review of National Literatures* 10 (1979).

Clara Elizabeth Lawson, 'The Slanted View; Some Perspectives of Alienation in Modern Poetry: Emily Dickinson, Stevie Smith, Elizabeth Bishop, Rosemary Dobson, Gwen Harwood', PhD Thesis presented in the English Department, University of Western Australia, 1982.

Geoffrey Lehmann and Les A. Murray, *The Ilex Tree* (Canberra: A.N.U. Press, 1965)

Philippe Lejeune, *Le Pacte Autobiographique* (Paris: Editions du Seuil, 1975)

Robert Lowell, *Life Studies* (London: Faber, 1959)

James McAuley, *Collected Poems: 1936–1970* (Sydney: Angus & Robertson, 1971)

——, *The Personal Element in Australian Poetry*, Foundation for Australian Literary Studies 3 (Sydney: Angus & Robertson, 1970)

David Malouf, *Bicycle, and Other Poems* (St Lucia: University of Queensland Press, 1970)

——, *First Things Last* (St Lucia: University of Queensland Press, 1980)

——, *An Imaginary Life* (New York: G. Braziller, 1978)

——, *Selected Poems* (Sydney: Angus & Robertson, 1981)

——, 'The English Auden', *Quadrant*, XXII, 6 (1978)

Roger Milliss, *Serpent's Tooth: An Autobiographical Novel* (Ringwood: Penguin, 1984)

Geoffrey Moore, ed., *The Penguin Book of Modern American Verse* (Harmondsworth: Penguin, 1954)

Marianne Moore, *The Complete Poems* (London: Faber, 1968)

Edwin Muir, *An Autobiography* (London: Hogarth, 1954)

Les A. Murray, *Ethnic Radio: Poems* (Sydney: Angus & Robertson, 1977)

John Shaw Neilson, *The Poems of Shaw Neilson*, ed. A.R. Chisholm

(Sydney: Angus & Robertson, revised and enlarged edition, 1973)

James Olney, ed., *Autobiography: Essays Theoretical and Critical* (Princeton University Press, 1980)

R. Parthasarathy, ed., *Ten Twentieth-Century Indian Poets* (Delhi: Oxford University Press, 1976)

Roy Pascal, *Design and Truth in Autobiography* (Cambridge: Harvard University Press, 1960)

Marjorie Perloff, *The Dance of the Intellect: Studies in the Poetry of the Pound Tradition* (Cambridge University Press, 1985)

Hal Porter, *The Watcher on the Cast-Iron Balcony* (London: Faber, 1963)

Peter Porter, *A Selected Porter* (Oxford University Press, 1989)

Georges Poulet, *Studies in Human Time*, trans. Elliott Coleman (Baltimore: Johns Hopkins University Press, 1956)

——, *Proustian Space*, trans. Elliott Coleman (Baltimore: Johns Hopkins University Press, 1977)

David Rapaport, *Emotions and Memory*, Menninger Clinic Monograph Series 2 (New York: International University Press, 2nd edition, 1950)

Henry Handel Richardson, *The Getting of Wisdom* (Melbourne: Heinemann, 1977)

——, *Myself When Young* (London: Heinemann, 1948)

Christopher Ricks, *Keats and Embarrassment* (Oxford: Clarendon, 1974)

John Ruskin, *Praeterita* (London: Hart-Davis, 1949)

K. K. Ruthven, *Feminist Literary Studies: An Introduction* (Cambridge University Press, 1984)

Edward Said, *Beginnings* (New York: Columbia University Press, 1975)

Jean-Paul Sartre, *Words*, trans. Irene Clephane (London: Hamish Hamilton, 1964)

Elaine Simpson, *Poets in Their Youth: A Memoir* (London: Faber, 1982)

Kenneth Slessor, *Poems* (Sydney: Angus & Robertson, 1972)

Bernard Smith, *Documents on Art and Taste in Australia: The Colonial Period, 1770–1914* (Melbourne: Oxford University Press, 1975)

Daniel Spoerri (with Robert Filliou), *An Anecdoted Topography of Chance* (New York: Something Else Press, 1966)

Peter Steele, *The Autobiographical Passion* (Melbourne University Press, 1989)

——, *Expatriates: Reflections on Modern Poetry* (Melbourne University Press, 1985)

George Steiner, *Real Presences* (London: Faber, 1989)

May Swenson, *In Other Words: New Poems* (New York: Knopf, 1987)

M. J. Tanbimuttu, ed., *Poetry in Wartime* (London: Faber, 1942)

John Tranter, ed., *The New Australian Poetry* (St Lucia: University of Queensland Press, 1979)

J. H. van den Berg, *The Changing Nature of Man: Introduction to a Historical Psychology*, trans. H.F. Croes (New York: Delta, 1975)

Helen Vendler, *The Odes of John Keats* (Cambridge: Belknap, 1983)

Chris Wallace-Crabbe, *Melbourne or the Bush: Essays on Australian Literature and Society* (Sydney: Angus & Robertson, 1974)

——, *Toil and Spin: Two Directions in Modern Poetry* (Melbourne: Hutchinson, 1979)

Patrick White, *Flaws in the Glass: A Self Portrait* (London: Jonathan Cape, 1981)

Brian Wicker, *The Story-Shaped World: Fiction and Metaphysics: Some Variations on a Theme* (London: Athlone Press; Notre Dame, Indiana: Notre Dame University Press, 1975)

John Wisdom, *Other Minds* (Oxford: Basil Blackwell, 1965)

Ludwig Wittgenstein, *The Blue and Brown Books* (Oxford: Basil Blackwell, 1958)

——, *Tractatus Logico-Philosophicus* (London: Routledge, 1922)

William Wordsworth, *The Poetical Works of William Wordsworth*, ed. Thomas Hutchinson, rev. Ernest de Selincourt (London: Oxford University Press, 1936)

Fay Zwicky, *The Lyre in the Pawnshop: Essays on Literature and Survival 1974–1984* (Nedlands: University of Western Australia Press, 1986)

Poetry Acknowledgements

COLLINS/ANGUS & ROBERTSON: David Campbell, 'Summer Comes with Colour', 'Song for the Cattle' and 'The Picnic', *Collected Poems*, © Judith Campbell, 1989; 'I Want Shilling Too', *Evening Under Lamplight* © Judith Campbell; 'Hairbell', *Death and Pretty Cousins* © Judith Campbell.

Vincent Buckley, 'Borrowing of Trees', *Selected Poems*, © The Estate of Vincent Buckley, 1981.

FARRER, STRAUS & GIROUX INC.: Louise Bogan, 'To Be Sung on the Water', *The Blue Estuaries*, © 1937 and renewal copyright © 1964 by Louise Bogan.

LONGMAN CHESHIRE: Bruce Dawe, 'Drifters', *An Eye for a Tooth*, 1968.

LOTHIAN BOOKS: John Shaw Neilson, 'The Petticoat Plays', and 'May', *The Poems of John Shaw Neilson*, 1965.

MELBOURNE UNIVERSITY PRESS: Ethel Anderson, 'Blonde Wheat . . .', *Squatter's Luck*, 1942 & 1954.

WRITERS WORKSHOP: Kamala Das, 'A Request', *The Descendants*, 1967.

Index